2004

SOUTH DAKOTA'S BEST STORIES

Bernie Hunhoff, Publisher

Editing & Writing by
Bernie Hunhoff, Roger Holtzmann, Jerry Wilson
and dozens of magazine contributors

Creative Director
Ben Hanten

Produced by
Katie Hunhoff, Donna Bollich,
Mary Johnson, Myrna Hunhoff
Barb Hanson, Alma Korslund, Jennifer Nielson

Cover Art
Courtesy of South Dakota artists
John Green, Mary Groth, Kristine Gellerman, Charles Greener

Library of Congress Catalogue Number
2003110979
Printed in Korea

ISBN 0-9744044-0-3

Published by
Middle Border Books
PO Box 175, Yankton, SD 57078
Phone (605) 665-6655

SOUTH DAKOTA'S BEST STORIES

MODESTLY GLEANED FROM THE BEST STORIES OF
SOUTH DAKOTA MAGAZINE

We dedicate this collection
of South Dakota stories
to all of our magazine readers.

Your support and encouragement
make it possible for us
to explore South Dakota.

— South Dakota Magazine

Table of Contents

Stories of You and Me

By Bernie Hunhoff

"What is *South Dakota Magazine* going to be about?" People constantly asked that when I started to write stories and sell ads in 1984, in preparation for the first issue. Eventually I grew tired of the question and I would answer, "Nebraska."

I thought the idea of *South Dakota Magazine* was simple. We would hunt for colorful stories to write, then we'd convince thousands of readers to send us a small renewal check once a year so we could afford to print the stories, pay the postage and have something left for office pizza. What a life! I still like it 20 years later and the business plan has remained the same: Write, sell, print, pay postage, pizza.

Don't misunderstand me. It can be hard work. We've probably traveled a million miles. We've explored every town in South Dakota, every highway and many back roads. Personally, I've been stuck in Lyman County gumbo, survived a New Year's Eve celebration in Clark's main street bakery, milked a wild cow at the Irene rodeo, socialized with an old hermit by the Bad River, and nearly stepped on a hissing rattlesnake atop a hill on the Pine Ridge.

I started *South Dakota Magazine* because I wanted an interesting way of making a living in my home state. I confess that I had no noble goal, at the outset. Along the way, however, I realized our stories have worth beyond entertainment. The stories tell us who we are as South Dakotans. Reading the magazine should be like seeing your reflection in the lake. The man in the water grins and you grin. He squirms and so do you. He grows sad and you know why.

It took me nearly 20 years to understand this (not because I'm an idiot, but because I was focused on stories, ads, and renewal checks so I wouldn't have to find other work). But now I know how we are all connected — a child in Wasta, a hermit by the river, a businessman in Watertown and the sweet old lady who scolded that Pine Ridge rattler for scaring me. We share a past and present, whether we recognize it or not. We share mountain-size sculptures, grandiose purple sunsets, the East River/West River divide, ethnic foods and rhubarb, our own pronunciation of Pierre, pheasants and deer, Interstates 90 and 29, and four sharp seasons of weather.

And much more: Canada geese in Capitol Lake, the Missouri River bluffs, our very own Black Hills, the Corn Palace, a devotion to small town life, six public universities, nine Indian reservations and 66 counties (and I dare anyone to try to "consolidate" any of them).

We also share some dark sides — Wounded Knee and a racial divide, the Dirty Thirties, government dependency, killer storms, rural poverty and an exodus of our young people. Whether you've lived in South Dakota for 30 days or 30 years, those commonalities (the good and bad) affect your thinking and actions. Yes, lutefisk and livestock can truly do that.

One of my all-time favorite South Dakotans is Archie Gilfillan. Archie was raised on the East Coast, the son of a minister, and he had only two vices — 1) he liked to drink and 2) he thought being a South Dakota sheep rancher would be the best thing ever. Archie got an Ivy League education; then he talked his parents out of some money and moved to Harding County, where he took up drinking and sheep ranching. Of course, he soon went broke. But he loved South Dakota so he stayed, and was hired by neighboring ranchers as a herder. For eight years, he made daily notes on the goings-on in Harding County as he tended sheep. His sheepherder's wagon is parked in the Friends of the Middle Border Museum at Mitchell. As for his 9,000-page diary, some old-time Harding County families are still concerned about where it might show up.

After his herding days, Archie found time to write the stories he'd seen or heard. He wrote a book called *Sheep* that's really about people. He also wrote columns for the local papers. It's too bad *South Dakota Magazine* wasn't being published then because he would have loved interaction with our readers. The same goes for Badger Clark, Doane Robinson and some other South Dakota notables who were pretty good with pen and paper.

South Dakotans have always been good at verbal story telling. Fortunately, we've also had a few people like Archie Gilfillan with the time, talent and inclination to write down some stories. For many of our citizens, there was always more important work — roads and churches and schools to build, businesses to start, fields to plant.

That's even true of us here at *South Dakota Magazine*. For many years, we were just happy to keep the bills paid. Finally it dawned on us that, cumulatively, those stories represent a mirror to the soul and spirit of every South Dakotan: all our rugged rural spunk and independence, our attachment to nature, the weirdness of living where cattle outnumber people, the work hard/play hard ethic, our skepticism of bigness and the related challenge of making a living in a place without many big institutions.

That's what's in the book you hold. We pored through well over 100 issues of the magazine (two decades worth), searching for our best stories. Then we condensed, consolidated and crammed them into this collection. So what's it all about? You and me and the fellow down the street. We hope you like the reflection.

To the Editor

Thank you for saving my life. I was out of town and had forgotten my wife's birthday. I got home and she said thanks for the wonderful birthday gift.

I didn't say anything for a second and then said, "What?"

"The magazine, hon."

Well, luck was on my side for once. The magazine came on her birthday to save the day. Thanks again.

Andy Duda
Rapid City

Adventure

WHO COULDN'T PUBLISH a successful magazine in a state whose regular citizens have hunted elephants, lions and rattlesnakes, confiscated a cargo plane full of marijuana, discovered a cave used by bandits, "raised" wild horses and fought river monsters? (Yes, those all occurred in South Dakota — those and more!)

Adventure stories are a fun part of our magazine. But they provide more than amusement. They also teach us about ourselves. When ice fishermen from Akaska foiled a team of drug smugglers and corralled their DC-10 cargo plane in the Potter County hills, I always thought it was a great example of how our people face life. Nobody expects to see a DC-10 land just over your head when you're fishing along the Missouri, but if it happens most South Dakotans would go to lend a hand, or pull the gun from beneath their pickup seat: Whatever the situation demands.

Adventure is good for the soul. We learn more about ourselves and our neighbors from how we act than from what we write and say. That's especially true of South Dakotans, an admittedly non-verbal people who often convey more in a friendly finger wave at 65 mph than in an hour of conversation.

Other chapters in this book are more focused on thoughts and feelings. This chapter is about weapons and beasts and bad guys and heroes. It will be the favorite of most South Dakotans.

— Bernie Hunhoff

The Barnstormer and the Baby

Bernie Hunhoff

Clyde Ice, South Dakota's best known pilot, was an aviation pioneer. He went on many mercy missions, none more perilous than the time he flew into a blizzard to save a Harding County baby.

MARCH 20, 1947, dawned blustery and cold in Spearfish. A spring blizzard was whipping the region. Most people were content to stay indoors. Clyde Ice, then 57 years old, watched the storm from the airport and wondered if it would clear before the funeral for his son, Randall, who had died just days earlier in a plane crash near Rapid City.

The telephone rang. Dr. Gordon Betts, a Spearfish physician, asked if Clyde could fly him 80 miles north to a Harding County ranch where a woman was about to give birth three months prematurely. It would have been a routine request, except for the approaching funeral and the blizzard. The doctor knew Clyde had just lost a son, and he had called other pilots first. The others said the weather wouldn't permit such a flight. Dr. Betts told Clyde the young woman was in trouble. Clyde told him to get to the airport. When the doctor arrived, he found a little Cub on the runway, bucking in the wind as a half dozen men struggled to hold it down. Wasting no time, he climbed into the two-seater alongside Clyde and soon they were airborne over a sea of white.

Clyde Ice, many years later at age 96, recalled the scene: "It was a white-out, just like they pulled a pillowcase over your head. We found a telephone line that ran to Camp Crook, and sometimes we ran 10 feet above the wire. We followed that to the Little Missouri River, and followed the timber along the river. I flew just above the trees and we found the ranch."

The pilot and the doctor circled and saw several men waiting on the ground to hold onto the wings when the plane landed. Among them were the woman's husband, Orvin Peterson, and his brother-in-law, Joseph Heggem. Addie Turbivilly, a neighbor woman with some experience as a midwife, was in the house assisting the mother, Eleanor Peterson.

The plane landed on the riverbank and the men quickly grabbed it. At first, gusts of wind made it impossible for the doctor and pilot to exit the craft for fear of it sailing away to one side. Finally the young doctor crawled out and rushed to the house. There he found a weak Mrs. Peterson and a tiny baby they'd already named Marie. He put the baby on the oven door to keep it warm while he tended the mother. Clyde waited in the plane as minutes passed, wondering what was keeping the doctor.

News of an emergency at the Peterson ranch spread quickly, maybe because the family was on a party line phone shared by a dozen neighbors. Soon Dennis Burghduff and Joe Painter arrived. Painter brought along two Mexican farm laborers. It took all six men to hold the plane on the ground. Finally, the doctor came out of the house carrying a bundle of quilts, with the newborn girl tucked inside.

Clyde suggested that they not fly back into the blizzard. It was a short discussion, however, when Dr. Betts explained that the girl weighed only three pounds and needed an incubator. There wasn't space for the mother or father, so the pilot and doctor got back into the cockpit with the doctor holding Marie on his lap, and breathing into her mouth to keep her alive. Clyde's first concern was getting the plane airborne in the gusty wind. He told the ranchers that everyone must let go of the plane at the same time, at his command, or it could tumble in the wind and crash. He was concerned that the Mexicans, who did not know English, would not understand the command; but their boss, Mr. Painter, said he could explain the situation.

Joe Heggem remembered that the weather would clear for a moment, and then "the next minute you couldn't see your hand in front of your face." He said when Clyde gave the command, everyone let go of the plane and it lifted straight up in the air. They watched as the little Cub fought against the west wind to fly south for Spearfish.

All the way back, the doctor administered CPR as Clyde battled the wind. It took two hours, Clyde estimated, to return. Again he followed the river and the phone line, the only visible landmarks. When he reached the airport, his son, Howard, had a dozen men waiting. They grabbed the plane even before its wheels touched ground. There was an incubator waiting at the airport. Little Marie was rushed to a maternity home, operated by a local nurse, Mrs. Calvert. Marie spent three months in the incubator and another few months in Mrs. Calvert's arms before she was big enough and healthy enough to go home.

Marie grew up, married, and raised a family in Rapid City. She stayed in touch with the barnstormer who saved her life. And when we met him in his ranch house near the Spearfish airport, he showed us her family pictures, tucked away with all the other photographs and momentos you'd expect a 96-year-old adventurer to be hoarding. He said that flight to Bullock was his proudest moment in 62 years as a pilot.

Nov/Dec 1985

In 62 years of flying, Clyde Ice said he never had an accident or an injured passenger. "Safe and sane flying" was his motto. "In all the years I flew, I only drew blood once," he said. "A young girl was climbing over a barbed wire fence to go for a ride with me and she cut her leg on one of the barbs."

CROP-SPRAYING MISHAP

Cliff Adkins, who sprayed crops for 36 years

I STARTED TEACHING Parkston guys to fly in 1949. We've never had anybody get hurt, which is lucky, since one guy I taught sat in the bar all day and came out to fly in the evening. I was a little worried about him. I busted up two planes bad. Once I was looking the other way at the end of the field and I didn't see the telephone wire behind a big cottonwood. I hit the wire and it busted off the carburetor. Gas sprayed out and caught fire and I set it down fast. I had a heck of a time getting out. I landed in a coyote den, which was lucky. My boy and I kicked dirt over the motor and put the fire out. All I got was a skinned shin. The other crash, the engine quit and I plowed into a coal chute.

Jan/Feb 2003

WHERE ELK SPEAK

Paul Higbee

KEVIN LINEBACK, I thought, was playing me for a greenhorn when he stooped, picked an inch-long elk dropping from the forest floor, and pronounced it the product of a bull elk rather than a female.

No, he assured me later, there's a difference in shape — Black Hills outdoorsmen can tell. I should have known Kevin was being straight with me. He has a fine sense of humor, but I've never heard him joke about elk, or about the special place he goes to watch them.

An hour before dawn that cold fall morning, Kevin and I bought coffee at Spearfish's Mini Mart.

"You didn't use any deodorant or cologne?" he asked, and I answered no. He'd told me the night before that elk can smell those substances at great distance, and that I needed to also avoid bright colors and freshly laundered clothes. So, appropriately muted in hue and naturally scented, we warmed ourselves with coffee as we drove from Spearfish up a gravel road a few miles. Then we hiked along a clear stream in a narrow draw. After 15 minutes, the sky was turning gray as we reached a pool fed by the stream; the mud had been gashed and marked with large hoof prints.

"A wallow," Kevin whispered. Here a bull elk had created its own cologne by digging up the soft mud, urinating in it, and then rolling in it. That's part of the rutting ritual each fall, when bulls show off by sight, sound and smell. Then it's pretty much the cow elk's decision with whom to mate and run.

From the wallow we made an aerobic climb out of the draw and walked through wide stands of aspen and ponderosa pine. Not far from where he picked up the dropping, Kevin motioned me behind a wide pine trunk and said, "With luck we'll get you face to face with a bull. Well, maybe not face to face, but real close."

He produced an elk call, an instrument with a latex reed that fits into the mouth, and a two-foot corrugated plastic tube — a "grunt tube" for imitating various snorts and growls. "Years ago, when I was learning to call, I sounded like a wounded animal from another planet," Kevin told me. "I drove my wife crazy, and my neighbors. The call fits way back by your wisdom teeth, so when you're learning, you're trying both to get the right sound and to prevent yourself from gagging."

The learning's behind Kevin now. He pierced the still air with a clear, high trumpet tone.

Silence.

Kevin waited a minute, then called again. This time, almost immediately, he was answered. Through the trees floated the sound most symbolic of the natural American West: the musical bugle of the bull elk. And music it is, too rich in tone to be called a moo, or screech, or anything else.

Kevin called again. He tries to mimic the sound of the elk he's calling, and each animal sounds different. He's been able to recognize certain bulls from year to year by their distinctive bugles.

Again Kevin was answered. How far away was the elk? Quarter mile? Half mile? I couldn't guess. But when it answered a sixth or seventh time, it was suddenly much closer. A couple minutes later we could hear branches and undergrowth snapping, maybe a hundred yards off.

Something huge was moving our way.

Properly speaking, these animals are called "wapiti." Once they ranged as far east as the Allegheny mountains of Pennsylvania and West Virginia. There, English settlers needed to distinguish them from small deer and took to calling them "elk," the term for a European moose. The name stuck. Although they are part of the deer family, they differ from white-tailed and mule deer common to the Black Hills in countless ways, beginning with the way they noisily crash through the forest, and their size. A half-ton bull elk weighs easily four times what a large mule buck would weigh. Also unlike deer, a bull elk mates by attracting a "harem" of 15 or 20 cows, then fighting off other bulls. That's partly what all the bugling is about each fall — the bull Kevin called thought another bull was challenging him for cow rights.

Kevin had told me that a bull's bugle, at close range, is a powerful statement, "a nine hundred or thousand pound animal proclaiming to the world that it's his mountain." It is powerful, and indeed majestic when you add the visual image of the bull moving in search of the caller, closer and closer, until he stands just 20 yards away.

That's how close the bull came to us that morning. Then he stood suddenly still, all 900 pounds of him; Kevin had explained they sometimes pose silently when they know they're near the competing bugler, as if to say, "Look. I'm a force to be reckoned with." I twisted around the tree trunk and snapped a photo, concerned that the bull's white rump would register bright in my picture while the rest of him, grey and brown, would blend into the forest background. And yes, his vast antlers were like a crown, six points on either side. With them he dug at the ground, sniffed the dirt, then sniffed the air. He was deciding something was wrong, that no other elk were present, though he hadn't spotted Kevin and me. Slowly he lumbered back the way he came, then ran. Beyond our view we heard him stop, and Kevin began "cow talking," a series of mews and chirps. In Kevin's experience, cow talk brings a bull back about nine times out of ten.

But not this one. He bugled back once, and then was finished with us.

The sun had climbed over Lookout Mountain's shoulder as we arrived back in Spearfish. "You know," I said as we drank Mini Mart coffee again, "we've had an experience some people would drive a thousand miles for, and save money all year."

Kevin nodded. "I can't imagine why everyone who lives in the Hills isn't out there. But I'm glad they're not."

March / April 1996

ELZADA MARSH AND BIG FOOT THE BOBCAT

Martha Linde

MY FATHER WAS operating a grocery store in Keystone in 1924 when reports surfaced of a big bobcat in Coon Hollow near Rockerville. Keystone was then a mining town. Mount Rushmore was still just a mountain so there was no need for the gift shops, eateries and motels that now line main street. When the mines closed in winter, the men often turned their attention to hunting as a way of feeding their families. When game became scarce at Keystone, they would ride by horseback to Coon Hollow. It was there that the Rockerville Bobcat was first seen by a man.

A miner's horse spooked when it saw the big cat perched on a limb over-hanging the trail. The horse snorted, bolted and scraped the rider off against a tree. The angry rider took off after his horse. When he saw the big cat tracks under the tree he never stopped running.

He caught his horse. Then he and a friend returned. The bobcat was gone but his large paw prints were visible in the snow. Soon, other hunters also saw the tracks. A Harney Peak ranger confirmed that the prints were from an unusually large bobcat, so it became known as Big Foot.

The cat was not a renegade predator like Three Toes, the bad wolf of Harding County. Still, stories of Big Foot's prowess grew, and they were not always negative. A big barn in Rockerville had become a haven for wild house cats. They were a nuisance. When they began to disappear, Big Foot got the credit.

Still, in the hunting culture of the southern Black Hills, Big Foot was fair game. Speculation grew as to who might be the lucky hunter to bag the cat. Jerry Spriggs, who often clerked at the store, thought the person with the best chance was not a miner, but his young niece Elzada Marsh. He had taught her to hunt and she was a good shot.

Spriggs knew about some wolf dens near Rockerville and he suspected Big Foot was using them. One day, he showed the dens to Elzada and they found Big Foot's paw prints there. Smaller bobcat prints were also present. They probably belonged to the bobcat's mate.

The big bobcat and his mate wanted only to be left alone. His diet was rabbits, birds and mice – perhaps an occasional weak or wounded deer. He hunted mostly at night, perched on a branch over a game trail. As game approached, the only sign of life on the branch was a tensing of his muscles and a nervous twitch of his stubby tail. With a leap, he would ambush prey before it could escape.

Elzada stalked Coon Hollow throughout the winter of 1924, studying the habits of Big Foot and his companion. Late that spring, she knew the mate was staying in a den with newborn kits. She did not go near them.

When winter returned, she knew the young bobcats were on their own and she continued the hunt. In January of 1925, she shot the light-colored mate. By March, Big Foot had left the six-mile area where he had always been safe and he came closer to Rockerville. Perhaps he was searching for another mate.

On a blustery day in March, Elzada came upon the big cat in a rocky valley just one and one-half miles from Rockerville. A shot from her .22 Stevens Special ended a pursuit that had begun more than a year earlier.

Friends and fellow hunters came to the Marsh home to see Big Foot. They were amazed by both his size and the quality of his dark fur. No official record was taken of his weight, but it was estimated at 40 pounds. A big rug was made from the hide. Elzada kept it at the foot of her bed.

Jan/Feb 1992

KILLING BLACK HILLS BEARS

Katie Hunhoff

IF WILD BEARS remain in the Black Hills they're well hidden and protected from hunters. It wasn't always that way. In August of 1874, Lt. Col. George Armstrong Custer was delighted when he and his men bagged a big grizzly. "I have reached the hunter's highest round of fame — I have killed my grizzly," he wrote in his journal.

Another grizzly was reportedly shot near the Wyoming border shortly after, and probably a number of black bears were killed. But both species were wiped out by the turn of the century. Though occasional sightings of black bears have been announced, none have been confirmed.

There was at least one more bear in the Hills, however. In 1968, Delmont farmer Roger Kaufman was hunting deer with his sons near White Tail Peak, south of Deerfield Lake, when they came upon a large black bear. Kaufman said he wasn't afraid of the black bear lumbering toward him, but worried for his sons' safety, he took aim. Two shots from his rifle brought the 500-pound bear down.

Custer's grizzly was harder to kill. Described as old and dark brown, he was judged to weigh about 600 pounds, only a bit bigger than Kaufman's bear. But grizzlies tend to be more aggressive toward humans. Custer and three other men fired shots at the grizzly before their Indian scout, Bloody Knife, cut its throat.

Custer's bear meat was distributed among his men, and the camp had a feed. Some complained that the meat was tough. Similarly, Kaufman's bear meat was served at an annual Izaak Walton League dinner in Rapid City. Kaufman, who ate a couple of steaks, said he had a good dinner. He described it as dark and lean. The bearskin was bought by Ted Hustead and still hangs in Wall Drug.

May / June 2003

Why Do Rodeo Cowboys Ride?

Jerry Wilson

CASEY TIBBS. Yakima Canutt. Tom Reeves. Whatever else they did in life, and they all did much, they were cowboys first, and maybe last. They climbed on top of a bucking bronc or a ton of bellowing bull, muscles straining for release. Not once, not twice, but again and again. They knew that unless a miracle intervened, their fate was a bone-crunching ride for a second — or if they were lucky, eight — a crazy launch to a dust-filled sky, a rolling dive past hooves and hide, an ungraceful crash on churned-up earth.

Why do they do it? For some, it might be the gleaming pot at the end. But just one man comes out on top. Only one collects big pay. The rest get pay dirt, and they're still spitting it out at breakfast. Why do they do it? You'd have to ask a cowboy. Maybe it's tradition, honoring a fading way of life. Maybe its laying out a saddle bag of skills. Maybe it's having a fast horse between your legs. Perhaps it's embracing a code, impossible standards chalked up by legends of the past. Or maybe it's testosterone, the same that powers the raging bull and the never-ridden bronc. Maybe there's a woman in the stands, tight jeans, saucy eye, a whiff of perfume. But what kind of girl would want a guy with bruised up flesh and busted bones and grit in his hair? You'd have to ask a cowgirl that.

They start out young, a rope in the hands, an oversized hat, a bleating bag of wool between their legs. If it's not in the blood from birth, it's inhaled with the dust that floats across signs for snuff and beer and Dodge Ram trucks. It's from tales told around campfires and bars and pickup trucks. It's father to son, uncle to kid, cowboy songs. And when they're old, too old to mount, limping from one fall too many, do they look back with regret, wish they'd passed up the ride? If they do, they rarely tell us so. They remember the bad ones, yes — Lucifer, Tipperary, Blazing

Blood. They remember their falls when the wet winds blow. They count the times they fed on dust. But they also remember when the rope hit right, when the steer went down, when they out rode the clock, when for a few ticks of time they beat the odds, when they clung like death to a thing that most can't comprehend.

July/August 2003

THE BULL AND MISS ADELINE JENNEY

Audrae Visser

ONE DAY ADELINE Jenney, former poet laureate of South Dakota, told her Campfire Girls to hop into her car and she would take them to the country for a picnic. The chattering girls were no sooner seated on a blanket under a big cottonwood tree in a river pasture, when an enormous bull crashed out of the nearby thickets and came lumbering toward them. Screaming with terror, the girls jumped up, dropped their sandwiches, and dashed off in three directions — some for the fence, others for low trees to climb, and two for the river.

Now, whether Miss Jenney felt that it was useless to run (she was old, short-legged, and fat) or whether she was going to test her faith in the Lord (she was very devout), nobody knows; what is known is that she did not run but stood her ground with arms akimbo and stared the bull squarely in the face.

"Run, Miss Jenney!" shrieked the girls who had climbed trees. "This way, Miss Jenney!" shouted the girl who had crawled under the fence. "Oh, Miss Jenney!" wailed the girls who stood dripping on the other side of the river. They doubted if Miss Jenney could swim.

But Miss Jenney paid no attention to any of the girls. She was busy staring down the old Hereford bull! The bull likewise glared at this audacious woman who dared to question his authority, and when he could no longer stand her haughty stare, he lowered his head and scraped the ground with his hoof, to scare her.

Miss Jenney, undaunted, continued to stare back. The Campfire Girls held their breaths. The bull, seeing that his pawing accomplished nothing, tried a new tactic. He let out a roar that seemed to shake the very ground.

But Miss Jenney refused to budge. The bull turned, retreated a short distance, and charged back, coming to a sudden halt immediately in front of Miss Jenney. Miss Jenney eyed the bull coldly, as a mother or teacher would eye an overgrown boy who is making a fool of himself. The bull didn't know what to think! Baffled, he stood confused. But apparently he decided this silly bunch of female human beings didn't threaten his status in life and that he might as well be gallant and leave them alone.

As he walked leisurely away, he turned his white curly head around and seemed to grin at Miss Jenney and the girls. He seemed to say, "Har! Har! Gave you a good scare, didn't I!"

Audrae Visser of Elkton succeeded Adeline Jenney as poet laureate.

March / April 1995

THE SUPER BOWL OF DRUG BUSTS

Bernie Hunhoff

JERRY GOETZ SPENT the afternoon of Jan. 20, 1980, ice fishing on the Missouri River with his sons, Todd and Tim, a cousin, Don Goetz, and Bowdle bait shop owner Rollie Rieger. They planned to fish for a few hours before heading home to watch the Super Bowl on TV. The fishing was better the previous Sunday, Jan. 13, when they were on the same stretch of river. On that day, a small plane flew over several times.

At about sundown on Super Bowl Sunday, Rieger said, "By God, we've been fishing all day and we haven't even seen a plane!" No sooner had he uttered the words than a large plane — much larger than the one they'd seen the previous week — came low over their heads. The plane made one bank and then landed about three miles north of the anglers along Swan Creek. The nearest community was Akaska, a little fishing village with about 30 full-time residents (the population quadruples in the summer when the fish are biting).

"At first we thought he was going to try to land on the river," Jerry said. "When he landed that — well if you want to see a cloud of dirt and dust, watch them land in a stubble field." Rieger and the Goetzes figured it must have been an emergency landing. The five anglers jumped in two pickups and headed for the dust cloud to see if they could lend a hand.

"It took us 45 minutes to an hour," Jerry said. "I'd just bought a '75 Chevy pickup and didn't have a CB installed or we could have called for help." When they neared the plane and saw that it had apparently landed without incident, Don Goetz grew suspicious. "Hey, this could be trouble," he told his companions.

Two men were standing by the door of the plane. One said they had engine trouble. The other mumbled something about being low on fuel. He complained about being cold so Rieger gave him his gloves. "They were really quiet," Jerry said, when interviewed by *South Dakota Magazine* in 1997. "We just tried to strike up a conversation. As we stood there visiting, we heard somebody hollering behind a huge hill, Capitol Hill. I told Don I was going to drive up and see if I could find out what was going on."

Don told one of the boys to let the air out of the plane's front tire. Then they parked their pickup in front of the plane so it couldn't take off. Meanwhile, Jerry Goetz and Rieger drove toward Capitol Hill where they saw a green Dodge pickup with Ohio license plates parked in the rough pasture. Rocks, gopher holes, shrub cedar and creek beds made travel difficult. The only way into the stubble field was through a rocky pass. Apparently, the driver was bouncing over the bumps when the battery came loose and shorted out the engine.

Smelling trouble now as well, Jerry worried about his cousin and sons back at the plane. "We'll go back to the plane and get a mechanic," he told the pickup driver. Jerry checked his .222 Remington and hurried back. The two men at the plane had fled on foot.

Meanwhile, rancher Tom Rivers, who lived on the opposite side of the Missouri, had seen the plane go down and telephoned Mobridge police at 5:25 p.m. to report a crash. Dispatchers notified Highway Patrolman Terry Mayes and Walworth County Sheriff Jim Spiry, who had arrived at the crash site before sundown. Sheriff Spiry saw a foreign flag on the plane. Grabbing his 12-gauge shotgun, he entered the aircraft and found it stuffed with bales of marijuana, twine-tied and wrapped in gunny sacks and plastic. The bales, 396 in all, were stacked window-high from the front to the rear. A grassy aroma filled the plane.

Jerry told the law about the Dodge pickup a mile away. The sheriff apprehended three men there without any struggle. Meanwhile, the fishermen helped authorities pick up batteries and lights that had been strung out along the stubble field for a nighttime airstrip. Attorney General Mark Meierhenry, DCI Assistant Director Bernie Christenson and other officials soon arrived. Christenson will always remember the scene: "Ranchers and farmers and law enforcement people were combing the area. They'd already rounded up three people."

The fishermen finally headed home. The Super Bowl game was over. But they'd had ample excitement for one night. Next morning, Jerry Goetz reported to his job at the farmer's co-op store in Akaska. He spent most of the day talking to reporters, law enforcement officials and others who wanted to hear the story. "I didn't know who was involved so I tried to keep my mouth shut," he recalls. But the neighbors, and the world, it turned out, wanted to know about the big drug bust in little Akaska. News reporters were calling from across the country. State authorities said it was the biggest drug bust in South Dakota history. Television stations sent photographers and reporters. A t-shirt business sprang up, of course. The favorite themes were "The Biggest Bust in South Dakota" and "Akaska International Airport." Several more suspects were apprehended in the area, including one who was walking toward Akaska. Two others were found hiding in a hay stack. Eventually, 17 were questioned in the incident, including some local people. Most were never charged.

Here's how the plan was supposed to work. The DC-7 left Columbia on a non-stop flight for the Akaska stubble field. It flew low to escape radar. The pilots and crew were drinking rum and smoking marijuana on the flight. Midwestern accomplices were employed to lay out a landing strip of temporary lights powered by 50 car batteries. Two semi-trucks were ready to haul away the cargo. The accomplices — including a minister, furniture factory owner and pilot — were apparently respected middle-class people who were offered $30,000 each. Sheriff Spiry said they might have been successful if southerly breezes hadn't pushed the plane ahead of schedule. Instead of arriving in the dark of night during the Super Bowl, it landed in daylight, and in sparsely-populated Walworth County it was a spectacle.

When the fishermen arrived, the truck drivers were alerted that the operation was in trouble. They never attempted to rendezvous with the plane. By that time, the big pay day became a nightmare for them. Officials figured there were at least eight Midwestern operatives. Six were apprehended and brought to trial. The attorney general's office and Walworth County authorities began to build cases. But before the trials began, all six reached plea bargains. The culprits received two to three year sentences and fines of $3,500 to $5,000. Seventeen days after the plane landed, its $18 million cargo of marijuana was burned near Pierre.

The drug bust remains a popular topic of conversation at the Sportsmen's Bar in Akaska. Experienced fishermen like to tell newcomers. That will continue for generations. However, as we sat around the Sportsmen's Bar and encouraged the storytelling, it seemed interesting that after 17 years the stories hadn't been embellished. That's unusual with any fish story. Perhaps in Akaska's case it's because the DC- 7 was the big fish that didn't get away.

Jan/Feb 1997

Snake Hunting with A.M. Jackley

Archie Gilfillan

A.M. Jackley became a folk hero to many in South Dakota when he became the state's official rattlesnake exterminator in 1937. He had already earned a reputation as a man who knew how to kill rattlers. He had hunted them for years as a favor to neighbors, and he knew their habits. Eventually, some individuals began to oppose his eradication efforts. Jackley had little time for them. "Those of us who have looked upon the still form of a child lying on the prairie with a rattlesnake coiled beside it, or have seen one bitten and suffer death, cannot take kindly this opposition," he said. He died in 1950 at age 70. Although he'd been bitten several times, he didn't die of snake bite, but of a heart attack in Hot Springs after he and his wife had returned from their first vacation since his appointment 13 years earlier. The following story was written by the popular West River humorist Archie Gilfillan following an outing with Jackley.

ONE SUNDAY ON the streets of Edgemont, I was hailed by a familiar voice that I had not heard for months. It was A.M. Jackley, variously known as "the snake man" and "the St. Patrick of South Dakota." He was the man who for some years devoted his entire time to the extermination of rattlesnakes in South Dakota; and if his simple and feasible plan were followed, it would result in the eradication of poisonous snakes from this state. It is said that the very thought of Jackley caused many a snake's blood to run cold.

Jackley told me that he was going snake hunting that afternoon and he invited me to go with him. I had had other plans, but the chance to spend the afternoon with the man who perhaps knew more about the life and habits of rattlesnakes than any other individual in the United States was too good to pass up.

After a good dinner we set out for the snake country. We pulled up near the first of the dens, and as I followed closely in Jackley's footsteps, I was conscious of a tingling along the spine. I had killed several rattlers a year during my 20 years in the range country, but this was different. We were about to call on the snakes at home and without invitation, with the express purpose of doing them great bodily harm. It was natural to suppose that the snakes might resent this.

Suddenly Jackley stopped and pointed to the ground in front of him. "There's a small one now," he said.

I looked in the direction he pointed but could see nothing. It was only after repeated pointings that I could make it out, unusually dark-skinned for a rattler and with his body folded together like a grass mat. As Jackley stepped forward to snare him, the snake dropped down a hole with incredible speed. The mouth of the hole had been hidden from where we stood. Jackley tip-toed away from the spot.

"We'll get him when we come back," he remarked.

We visited two or three other dens along the rocky rim without success. When we returned to the first den, Jackley stole forward, made a swift stab with the three-pronged hook that he always carried, and threw the snake some distance from the hole.

"Got him!" he said. I opened the mouth of the sugar sack I was carrying, to receive the snake.

"I don't want him," said Jackley. I was glad of that, because I didn't want him either. "I would hate to admit," remarked Jackley, as he dispatched the rattler, "that that snake was smarter than I am. It is a two-year-old female." To me it was just a small rattler.

We went back to the highway and Jackley said that at a certain point ahead of us, he had frequently seen snakes on the road. Sure enough, when we reached the spot there was a big rattler sunning itself. Jackley captured it without difficulty and popped it into the sack. I spoke of the remarkable coincidence of finding it where he had seen snakes before; but he told me that members of the state road patrol noted every place where the snakes crossed the highways, and called them "snake passes." We visited rocky points where Jackley had not been before and he discovered three new dens, But the temperature was not quite high enough and all the places yielded was some baby rattlers, only a few weeks old but full of fight. Something about the configuration of the big snake in the sack caused Jackley to wish to investigate. He pulled out a small pair of scissors and picked up the sack. For a moment I thought he was going to perform a vivisection, but he dumped the snake on the ground, picked it up with the snare, and snipped off its head as you would the head of a daisy.

As we drove back to town in the late afternoon, I couldn't help wondering why I hadn't been able to see that first snake, even when Jackley had pointed it out to me.

"It was just as natural for me to notice that snake," said Jackley, "as it would be for you to notice a pretty leg." I admitted candidly, "There couldn't be anything more natural than that."

As we parted in Edgemont, Jackley said, "Come with me, and you'll see snakes." I answered, "If I have to see snakes, I' d rather see them with you than alone."

Nov / Dec 1996

THE BATESLAND RAID

Bernie Hunhoff

JERRY GOETZINGER received one of those dreaded, plain and humorless letters on cold black and white stationary. It stated that an IRS agent would arrive to do an audit of his farm implement business in Martin. The agent showed up in a suit and tie on a Monday morning. He said the audit would take a number of days, so Jerry cleared a desk for him and produced the financial files. The grizzly, grease-in-the-fingernails implement dealer liked the baby-faced agent, so he invited him to join the boys at a smoker planned for the next Friday night at the Batesland Fire Department. Batesland is a town of about 100 people, a few horses and a lot of grain bins. Twenty miles west of Martin, it is located squarely on the Pine Ridge Reservation — a fact that worked greatly to Goetzinger's favor by week's end.

"What's a smoker?" asked the IRS agent.

Jerry explained that it was a fundraiser for the fire department. Poker, beer, polish sausage and all the mountain oysters you can eat. The agent knew about mountain oysters. He liked them, in fact, and said the smoker would be great. Unfortunately, as the week progressed, the very disagreements that one might expect did arise. Jerry's views on federal tax law and what constitutes proper expenses and deduction, while honestly developed, departed just enough from the young IRS agent's training that their initial friendship began to fade. On Thursday, the agent told Jerry he didn't think he would be able to attend the smoker.

On Friday afternoon, Jerry thought it would only be hospitable to extend the invitation one more time.

"Mountain oysters?" asked the agent.

"Yep, all you can eat."

"Do I have to change clothes?"

Jerry said it would be a good idea, so he waited at the shop while the agent dashed over to Harold's Motel and exchanged his suit and tie for more appropriate attire. Then they drove to Batesland and parked Jerry's Ford pickup a few blocks away from the fire hall. From there they walked to the white, cement-block hall where ranchers and businessmen were already gathering for the festivities. Smokers remain a common part of social life in rural West River. Fire departments, Legion clubs, VFWs and other respected organizations rely on the annual parties for a substantial part of their revenue. Selling alcohol of any kind is prohibited on the Pine

Ridge, but authorities generally take a "see no evil" attitude toward smokers and those types of events.

The agent liked the smoker. The fried mountain oysters were everything he had hoped. His beer glass was full and he had a pile of poker chips in front of him when tribal police stormed through the front door and announced that everybody was under arrest for illegal drinking and gambling. The agent reportedly shoved his chips to the center of the card table and announced that he was making a donation, as if that might take him off the hook.

Nobody is saying, even today, why tribal police raided the Batesland Fire Department on that particular night. It was related to some minor political disagreement. The agent knew nothing about local politics, of course. He only knew he was in big trouble. "You've got to get me out of here!" he pleaded to Jerry. "I'm a government agent. You've got to get me out of here or it'll cost me my job!"

Some of Jerry's friends think the implement dealer might have staged the raid. He says absolutely not. He insists he's not that smart. But he was smart enough, once the raid began, to see a golden opportunity to ingratiate himself with the young agent. The tribal police began to collect names and addresses of the 100 or more people who had been enjoying the smoker. It was a time-consuming process. And painful. The detainees had all been drinking beer, and the bathrooms were located outdoors. One man suggested that the next time the door opened they should all charge through. "Pretty soon, the door opened so I took the agent by the arm and we ran," remembers Jerry. "When we got outside we hid in the ditch. Red lights were going around and sirens were blowing. We crawled to my pickup, got in the cab and drove out of town with the lights off."

Jerry dropped the agent off at Harold's Motel just in time for him to hear the Rapid City television announcer report on the 10 p.m. news that 28 people had been arrested on the Pine Ridge Reservation for drinking and gambling.

The agent calmly showed up at the implement dealership the morning after. "We got along real good after that," Jerry said. Before long, the audit was concluded and the official IRS file on Goetzinger Implement, Ltd., was closed. At least for a while.

Jerry came across the agent in Rapid City several years later and they shared a laugh. Local people continued to tease Jerry about organizing the raid but he replied that he would never sacrifice 28 of his customers and friends. Not the way the farm economy was in the 1970s.

Nobody in Martin can afford to lose 28 customers.

Word of the Batesland raid may have sifted back to the IRS because a few years ago another auditor showed up at Goetzinger Implement. “That gal wouldn’t even have coffee with me,” Jerry said disgustedly. “She was quite precise.” Not that it mattered. The Batesland Volunteer Fire Department has installed indoor bathrooms. “We’d never get out today,” Jerry said.

Nov / Dec 2000

The Milk Bottle Gang

Robert C. Coney

BY 1940, THE DROUGHT in northern South Dakota was pretty much over. In spring it rained so much that the little WPA dam at Lake Evarts, where Timothy Clement Bailey and I and other Mobridge Boy Scouts camped, washed out. TC and I had finished our sophomore year in high school, and had just turned our newspaper routes over to younger brothers. We sat on the front steps of the library, wondering what to do in the long summer ahead. TC remembered a western we had seen a week before at the Mascot Theatre.

“Hey Bob,” he said, “wouldn’t it be great to work as cowboys?”

“It sure would,” I agreed, “but who would hire us?”

Trying to think of somebody who would hire a pair of greenhorns who had never been on a horse, let alone seen one up close, I remembered an uncle, Francis Lee, who lived in the Nebraska Sandhills. I had never seen him, but my mother had told me he’d inherited a ranch in Cherry County and was raising cattle. We immediately wrote a letter asking for jobs. The answer came in about 10 days. We would be hired at a dollar a day plus room and board, but we had to be in Valentine, Neb., in four days.

Early next day, we stood by the road with our thumbs pointing south. With $5 in our pockets and a small valise with extra socks and underwear, we were ready for anything, we thought. By late afternoon we found ourselves in Pierre, looking for a place to sleep. We found cots on a porch for 50 cents each, had a hamburger and malt down the street and went back to the house, ready to call it a day. While chatting with the landlady’s daughter and her friend, we heard the music of a carnival a few blocks away. Soon the four of us were riding the Ferris wheel, eating cotton candy and throwing darts at balloons. It was rather late when we got back to the house, but the next morning we were ready to resume our journey south.

"Hey Bob," TC asked, "how much money do you have left?"

I reached in my pocket and found a quarter. "How much do you have?" I asked. He opened his hand. There were two dimes.

"We've only got 45 cents left," TC said. "And two days to go. I could sure use something to eat." At a corner market down the street, we bought a loaf of bread, a small jar of strawberry jam and a quart bottle of milk. "That'll be 45 cents and 10 cents deposit on the milk bottle," the store owner said.

"We've only got 45 cents," TC told him.

"We're just going to the park across the street," I said quickly. "We'll bring the bottle right back." The owner, reluctant to let the bottle go without a deposit, said, "Well, all right."

We found a bench and had bread, jam and milk. Then we sat staring at the empty milk bottle. It was our only asset. Ten cents was a huge amount of money when you didn't have any. We sat there for the longest time, staring at the bottle. If we took it back, as we had promised to do, then we had two days of bread and water to look forward to, with a little strawberry jam to wash it down. If we didn't return the bottle, we might be able to sell it for a dime, and maybe we could work the disappearing bottle trick again. That was our dilemma. Boy Scouts promised to be honest. That meant we should take the bottle back. But Boy Scouts should also be prepared, and we had two long, hot days ahead.

We sneaked out of the park and headed south, thumbs frantically waving at every truck, car and tractor that passed. We were sure the store owner had called the sheriff. We wanted to get out of town, fast. Several hours and many miles later, we sold the bottle for another 10 cents and talked that grocer into selling us a bottle of milk for a dime, but foregoing the deposit on our assurances that we would return the bottle. It was easier to decide not to return the second bottle, and the third was even easier to keep. South of Vivian a salesman gave us a lift. He glanced uneasily at our two little bags, one of which bulged with an empty milk bottle.

"You boys don't have guns in those bags, do you?" he asked. We assured him that we didn't carry guns so he let us in his car, not knowing that we had already robbed three stores that day. Late that second afternoon, we were deep into the Rosebud Indian Reservation. It was growing late and we had seen no one for hours. Thirsty from a long hot walk, we drank from a windmill stock tank. We went to sleep on the cold prairie, our bags for pillows, convinced that no sin goes unpunished.

Stiff, cold and hungry in the early dawn, we had little hope of a ride.

Then an Indian family, whose car was already overloaded, stopped for us. We stood on the running boards and clung to the door frames, one on each side. Late in the day we arrived in the lovely town of Valentine. We had finished the bread and jam about noon, so we traded our bottle for a bottle of milk and drank it in the store. We found the hotel where we were to meet my uncle. Seeing the jail, we approached the deputy and explained our situation. Since he'd heard of my uncle, he let us sleep overnight in a cell, locking us in when he went off duty. Both of us were just about asleep when the deputy came back with fried chicken, mashed potatoes, green beans and milk.

Next morning we met Uncle Francis on the steps of the Valentine Hotel. He took us into the dining room and bought us a big breakfast. As we wolfed down pancakes, bacon and eggs, he asked us if we'd had any trouble getting to Valentine. "No, sir," we said. "No trouble at all. Scout's honor."

Nov / Dec 2000

Leaving Tracks

Phillip Hammes

I ONCE HOPPED a freight train in Portland, Ore., on a journey to Sioux Falls. I jumped on a flatcar and rolled into a white wall of pine boards, a sack of potatoes with initiative. I crouched behind my duffel bag to break the wind and watched the mellow woods flow by. A couple of days later I was in the rail yards in Rapid City. By then I did not resemble a Cornell undergraduate at a soccer game. My hair was matted and my clothes gave off a peculiar fragrance. I had the wild-eyed look of a man with habitual insomnia. I ranged down the tracks looking for someone who would talk to me.

Finally an older man in black overalls stopped. He looked tired himself, a day's growth of whiskers on his chin. "Where are you heading?" he asked, wiping his hands on a rag. "Sioux Falls," I told him. "I have a job waiting. But I'm broke."

"I've been there," he said. He told me which train I needed, and handed me a candy bar. "Stay low and don't get noticed," he advised. "No fires for cooking or heat."

I found an empty boxcar and climbed in. The train snorted and pulled out. On the edge of the city it crawled through a crossing. Vehicles were lined up behind a black and white barrier. A child standing in the back of a battered pickup, his arms on top of the cab, waved at me. I waved back. His father gave me a look of pure disdain.

As the train picked up speed, a young Native American man sprinted to the door and dove through. I pulled him inside. He wore a blanket roll on his back. His thick, black hair was tied in a long ponytail. He slid to the wall and caught his breath. We stared at one another without speaking.

"What do you say?" he asked at last. "Do you have a ticket?" I wondered. He hesitated a moment before answering.

"No," he said. "I didn't think you needed one back here."

"Where are you going?" I asked.

"I'm just going." He took off the blanket roll and stretched his legs. "My name is John." I told him my name and said I was glad to have company. John opened his blanket and removed a bag. "Are you hungry?"

At that moment I could have gnawed my way through a bowl of wax fruit, a paper-mache turkey and a plate of candied birch bark. "I could eat," I admitted casually. He pulled out cans of tuna fish, beans and roast beef hash and several chunks of buffalo jerky. I had a tin can I used for drinking. John emptied a portion from each container in my cup. We ate on the boxcar floor, saying nothing as the train rocked and rolled through gathering twilight. For dessert I pulled out the chocolate bar the yardman had given me and broke it in half.

I sprawled on the hard wood floor, my duffel bag under my head. The train pushed through tomb-like darkness, making a tunnel with its noise and speed. It swayed and sagged in arthritic accompaniment to the terrain.

The train halted on a side-track in some small town in the middle of South Dakota. It sat for at least 20 minutes; it was as if all living things, except the crickets, had deserted the land.

"Quiet," I remarked.

John nodded. "I can hear the owls breathing in Canada."

Sept/Oct 2000

CLIMBING THE NEEDLES

Jerry Wilson

TONI BRUMBAUGH is still at her desk in Rapid City at 4:45 p.m., — elegant, precise, professional — answering the phone, setting appointments, directing visitors, and making decisions as administrative assistant to the president of National American University. An hour later the same fingers that dialed the phone and danced the keyboard are dusted with calcium carbonate for gripping granite, her feet changed from office heels to soft-soled shoes for clinging to the almost 90 degree face of Gossamer, a giant, windowed upthrust slab of ancient Black Hills rock, not far from Mount Rushmore.

Her climbing partner is Mark Strege, a carpenter from Hill City. Mark will go first. He dusts his hands from a bag on his belt to keep them dry and adjusts his gear. "Belay on?" he asks. "On belay," Toni responds. She holds a nylon rope, the lead end of which is attached to Mark's harness. She will feed it out as he climbs.

"Climbing," Mark calls. He reaches high for a grip, sets a lead foot and pulls himself up. He "boulders," climbing freehand to a steel eyebolt anchored in a crevice about 15 feet up. He detaches one of several carabiners from his gear loop and snaps the oblong ring to the bolt, then passes the rope through the carabiner eye. Anchored at that level, Mark scrambles toward the next bolt, where he repeats the process. In five minutes, his rope is looped through half a dozen eyes; he pulls himself up, anchors to the top, stands on the needle point and shouts down, "off belay."

For the first time the five other climbers on the ground — Chris, Robb, Paula, Rob and Joelle — speak. "Very nice," one shouts. "Good climb!"

"Belay off," Toni calls. Mark pulls up rope. "That's me," Toni hollers when the slack is gone. Mark tosses the lead end of the rope to the ground. "OK, put me back on," he calls down. "You're on," Toni answers, holding the rope taut.

He steps off the peak, his body perpendicular to the face, and launches himself into space, gliding, lightly touching, rappelling back to Earth. "That's the fun part," he calls from his glide.

Now it's Toni's turn. She begins to climb, her slender arms and calves defined by firm, tense muscle. She reaches the first bolt, removes the carabiner and clips it to her gear loop, then moves on. As she goes she "cleans the gear," reversing the process, removing the protection Mark had placed.

Toni's Rapid City office is less than a distant memory now. Her concentration is absolute, a fly on a wall, eyes intent on the pinnacle above. Bolt after bolt she climbs, fingers clutching the rock. Soon she is on top. She pauses to enjoy the pinnacle — and to assess clouds boiling in from the west. She grasps the rope, backs herself into space and skips off to the ground.

July/August 2002

Harry Truman's Gregory Adventure

Jeff Johnson and Roger Holtzmann

SOMETHING for nothing always gets people's attention, even if it's only a hot dog or a free car wash. Imagine the reaction, then, if someone took it in their head to give away 160-acre farms. That happened in South Dakota in the early years of last century. As was generally the case, this largesse was made possible by first dispossessing Indians. Under the Dawes Act of 1887, tribal members on South Dakota's reservations were each assigned a specific tract of land. All that remained was declared surplus, and distributed by lot.

Land lotteries drew thousands of land-hungry folks to South Dakota. Temporary land offices, where people could register for the lottery, were established in Bonesteel, Chamberlain, Fairfax and Yankton. Tens of thousands of hopefuls showed up, many arriving on special trains. Among them was a future president of the United States, Harry S. Truman, who in 1911 was an unhappy farmer in Missouri, striving to make himself worthy of Bess Wallace, the woman he hoped to marry.

"I'm getting ready for South Dakota today," Harry wrote to Bess on Oct. 16, 1911. The man who would be the Man of the People was distressed about what he was sure he'd find in Dakota. "I bet they'll be more bohunks and 'Rooshans' up there than white men," he went on. "If they had only stopped immigration about twenty or thirty years ago, the good Americans could all have plenty of land and we'd have been an agricultural country forever." Harry arrived in Gregory late at night on Oct. 18, and sent Bess a postcard the next morning. "We are here and have registered," he wrote. "I suppose we'll all draw No. 1." He followed that with a more detailed account of the journey. "We managed to get seats in the last coach. There were 687 people on the train and nearly all were nice looking Americans. I only saw about a dozen bohunks all the way there and back."

Harry and his traveling companions played pitch and seven up all the way, and took turns eating lunch because they couldn't risk giving up their seats all at once. "At nearly every station we met trains coming back," he wrote. "People on them would yell 'Sucker! Sucker!' at us and men on our train would do the same. One fellow hollered for us to go right on through to a very hot place. It sounded like a pretty place to be, it was so cold up there. We got to Gregory at about 10:30 p.m. Then began a chase for a place to sleep. The hotel man finally agreed to give us a cot apiece in the waiting room, which was some luxury I tell you. There were people who sat up all night."

Gregory had built its own Corn Palace, complete with towers and minarets, to use as a registration center. But the man from Missouri was not impressed. "After we'd cinched our rooms we went and registered at the Corn Palace, a wooden shack. It takes about one minute to do it. There were about twenty notaries in a hollow square. I bet there was more swearing going on there than ever will be in one place again. I really don't know what a Quaker would have done." Truman strolled around Gregory, which struck him as "a strictly modern town," then it was back to the hotel. He didn't get much use out of the cot he'd rented. He was back on the train at 6 a.m., having spent just over seven hours in town. Harry Truman Slept Here indeed. That's about all he did.

In the end, the whole expedition really was "fifteen good dollars thrown away" Harry later wrote. When the drawing was held, his card stayed in the barrel. "I never could draw anything," he wrote to Bess when he got the news. "Not even the lady I wanted. You see, I am born under Neptune or some other far distant and unlucky star. I guess it's good for me that I haven't [a] pessimistic disposition. It seems best to be silly and grow fat. Just keep imagining that my luck will change someday."

Nov / Dec 2002

FOSSIL HUNTERS ON CROW CREEK

Bernie Hunhoff

ANCIENT SEA MONSTERS buried in eroding shale on hillsides of the Crow Creek Reservation are playing a role in cultural reconciliation. South Dakotans Jim Martin and Lee Azure, if they both lived to be 100, probably would never have met at a cocktail party or a pool hall or golf course — or any of the other places men become acquainted. But once they were introduced by a mosasaur they became fast friends. Azure is an Indian from Crow Creek who cleans classrooms for a living. Martin is a white guy who lectures in classrooms in Rapid City as a professor of geology. Azure grew up in Montana and came to South Dakota as a youth to attend Fort Pierre Indian School. Martin was born in Wyoming, the son of a coal miner, and came to South Dakota at age four when his father died of black lung disease.

Martin is especially interested in mosasaurs and plesiosaurs — big lizard-like creatures that inhabited this land 75 million years ago when it was an inland sea during the Late Cretaceous period. Thanks largely to his friendship with Martin, the scientific names for those reptiles roll off Azure's tongue like he was also a scientist. But before he befriended the professor, he knew little about the fossil bones he was finding in the hills around his hometown of Stephan. "I took them to the science lab at the high school but nobody knew what they were. I thought maybe some cow died there years ago," he said.

Still, Azure gained a reputation as a fossil hunter, and when the professor showed up on the reservation a few years ago and expressed an interest in helping the tribe preserve its fossil resources, the tribal chairman didn't introduce the scientist to the local teachers. He sent him to the football field where Azure, the school maintenance man, was mowing grass. Martin and Azure soon found that they had more in common than just old bones. They also shared a belief that the fossils belonged to everyone and shouldn't be sold for a profit. During their first conversation on the football field, Azure told Martin he didn't want anybody to gain financially at the tribe's expense.

In most of East River country, the shale and its fossils are buried beneath corn and bean fields. Throughout most of West River, the Pierre Shale which dates to the Cretaceous Period (and is the region's most common soil formation) is buried beneath topsoil and grasses. But in some areas, shale lies exposed on the surface and that is where Azure and other fossil hunters, commercial or scientific, do their searching. Erosion, a scourge to farmers and ranchers, is a friend to the paleontologist because it exposes what has been buried.

Nobody is any better than Azure, the 66-year-old Indian, at finding fossils. A heavy smoker, Azure usually leaves behind several cigarette butts when he scouts a site. His paleontology pals joke that they can usually find a fossil by looking for the cigarettes. "Smoking wasn't any good for the mosasaurs, either," somebody always quips. Actually, it was a smoking volcano that may have killed many of the sea animals. Research at the S.D. School of Mines, where Martin does his teaching and research, indicates that volcanic eruptions sometimes left ash a foot or more deep on the ocean surface; when the animals tried to break through to the surface for air they breathed the ash and glass shards into their lungs. The ash is easily visible in some areas today as a one or two inch layer of yellowish bentonite. An inch of bentonite probably constituted about eight inches of ash.

Azure says that even if he were not searching for fossils, he could stroll for hours through the hills, soaking in the beauty. Some days he witnesses nature's fury, like the time he saw a badger killing a rattlesnake. But the landscape here is usually gentle and quiet, interrupted by the honking of geese on the Missouri more than anything else. He once hunted the hills with a rifle, but now he carries a magnifying glass that he uses to examine tiny finds like the petrified fish gills he recently discovered. He is seldom seen without a walking stick, which he fashioned from a willow branch. He jokes that the stick starts to shake when he gets close to a mosasaur. Scientists sometimes call him a fossil-witcher. "In the last three years, Lee has found more specimens than anyone else in the last 100 years," said Professor Martin. "We wouldn't be nearly as far along without his eyes and leg work."

Excavating sea creatures on the Crow Creek Reservation also demonstrates how much all of mankind has in common. On the black hills of the Crow Creek, people from universities and reservation towns, big cities and tiny hamlets, Caucasian and Native American, young and old, work together toward a common goal of preserving the lessons locked in bones from another age. People of various races and cultural backgrounds alive in the world today seem not very different from one another, not when seen in perspective with the last 100 million years.

Nov/Dec 1995

ON THE TRAIL OF LORD GRIZZLY

Ried Holien

THE SPOT WHERE mountain man Hugh Glass was mauled by a grizzly bear is now beneath Shadehill Reservoir, south of Lemmon. How he survived that attack is among the great adventure stories of all times — it was the subject of several books, including *Lord Grizzly* by Frederick Manfred — but Glass' life to that point was a tale all its own. It is believed that Glass left a wife and two children in Pennsylvania to sail the seas on a merchant ship. When his ship was captured by the notorious pirate Jean Lafitte, Glass joined the pirate crew to avoid death. Months later he escaped off the coast of Texas and swam to shore; from there he walked to Kansas, where Pawnees captured and held him for years. Escaping once again, he headed up the Missouri River as a fur trapper.

Among mountain men, Glass had the reputation of a man who could be counted on when someone else was in need. That only magnifies the crime he suffered at the hands of those he thought were his friends. After

Glass was attacked and mauled by the bear — leaving him with his right leg broken, several ribs shattered, skull exposed and bloody, foot-long gashes down his back — his companions broke the mountain man's sacred code by stealing Hugh's "sack of possibles." Bereft of rifle, powder horn, bullets, and blanket, he was left to die.

Glass crawled across almost 200 miles of rugged country to Fort Kiowa, near present day Chamberlain, dragging his broken leg, traveling at night to avoid detection by Indians, living on berries, ants, mice, rotting buffalo meat, whatever he could find. In the course of researching Lord Grizzly, Manfred discovered that Glass hunted down the two men who had abandoned him. Revenge could well have motivated him during the long, arduous ordeal, but Glass spared both men, proving yet again the strength of character that had pulled him through.

Sept / Oct 1998

SAILING FRANCIS CASE

Thomas A. Dempster

IN MARRIAGE, IN religion, in nature and in sailboats, wisdom has more to do with submission than with strength and verve. When I can't sleep at night, I imagine myself at the helm of Dutch Treat, my 26-foot S-2 sailboat. The sails are up, the engine silent; the boat, a ballerina, curtseys before the wind and the waves. Like an eagle aloft over Lake Francis Case, she fills her wings.

From the marina west of Platte, 40 miles of navigable water shimmer south to Pickstown, another 40 beckon north to Chamberlain. Head to open water, and turn left to port, and you're headed south under the bridge to prairie estuaries, big bays and sandy beaches. If the helm turns you to starboard, you're off to Red Rock and purple pinnacles that fade majestically into the distance. This 80-mile stretch of water is perfect sailing, the shores laced with bays and inlets, anchorages that offer refuge from marauding storms. When the sun rises and sets, whitetail and mule deer lap their fill at the edge of bays.

One of my family's favorite bays is 10 miles upstream, a bay dubbed Scorpio's Howl. My three daughters, my wife and I sailed for a day, set anchor in lee of a ghosted bluff, and grilled a sirloin at the back of the boat. As darkness fell, the giant star Antares throbbed red to the south, pumping its blood through the constellation Scorpio.

Coyotes yelped and howled as we went below, a shrill chorus you hear through your spine. Tucked away in sleeping bags, we rocked with Dutch Treat, tugging at her anchor like a golden retriever begging for a walk. Early in the morning, I pulled the hatch covers shut as a shower cleansed the boat.

Bathing in the cool Missouri water is bracing, but idyllic. Only once in 10 years of sailing Francis Case have I shared an anchorage with another boat. Brew a cup of coffee, suck in its heat and steam, check for fishing boats, then strip, lather and jump in.

Hills, their crowns rounded by age, surround my anchorage. Before anyone else is up I take my dingy to shore and creep to the hilltops, keeping an eye out for thistles, cacti and rattlesnakes. My boat slumbers, too, tethered to the river bottom gumbo. The air is sparse and clean, fragile as an icicle. Wild turkeys parade on hillsides, buzzards and hawks circle overhead. One morning, as the sun pushed against the eastern hill, the ground began to shake. A young whitetail buck thundered past, so close I saw the velvet of his antlers. When he finally saw me, he stopped cold, eyeing me, the intruder, then disappeared into a cluster of trees.

There is mystery in sailing, an alchemy that returns at unexpected moments. I can be walking down Phillips Avenue in Sioux Falls on a winter day and feel wind across my cheek. I glance at the flag on the bank building and feel exactly the heel and motion of a boat the wind in the flag would create. Driving down an interstate alone, some might suddenly crave clam linguini, or a lover. That is what sailing is like. It is an internal experience, a quickening, the same yearning you have when you remember the high cheekbones of your wife or catch a daughter's goodbye as she runs out the door. "It's as if I'm back in my mother's womb," a friend said, "warm, bathed in motion in her amniotic fluid."

A sailing vessel adds to those sensations freedom and refuge — and at least the illusion of controlling the forces of water and wind. Raise the sail, and you convert wind to torque. Pull your boat so its bow faces directly into the wind. Pulley up the sails as you would a flag, first the mainsail, then the jib. Before the sails are set and the mainsheet hardened, a sail quivers in the wind as surely as a thoroughbred shivers its mane, eager to taste freedom and wind. Take the tiller in your palm and push until the boat lies 20 degrees off the wind. Pull the mainsail line and tighten it down, then cleat off the line from the jib. It is then that the boat, creaking like a cottonwood rooted to the prairie floor, heels over slightly. The sails, white sheets on a clothesline, stiffen and fill.

Never could I write a sheet of music or conduct a symphony. But I think I know how that might feel. There is a certain perfection in the pitch, roll, yaw, and heave of a boat as it balances momentum and drives with sails overhead, keel or centerboard underneath, all in balance with the spinning and heated Earth that created the winds that fuel the boat, in precise tempo, in perfect symphony with everything.

May/June 2002

CALAMITY JANE, THEATER CRITIC

Ried Holien

THE MOST FAMOUS derogatory review of Deadwood theatre in the days of the opera houses was delivered by the renowned Calamity Jane at the play "East Lynne." Charles E. Chopin, a child actor at the time, wrote of the experience years later.

Chopin recalled, "She and Arkansaw Bill, a famous stage robber, occupied front row seats in Deadwood. Calamity dolled up for the occasion in a corduroy suit and sombrero and appeared particularly vain of her green kid gloves. Soon as she was comfortably settled, she bit a chunk of tobacco and chewed as industriously as any miner throughout the evening. She and her escort clapped in noisy appreciation until Lady Isabel eloped with Sir Francis, and then Calamity showed her disapproval of the erring wife's conduct by marching down to the footlights and squirting a stream of tobacco juice over the front of Lady Isabel's pink satin evening gown." A fight nearly broke out when Mr. Lord protested the insult to his wife. Only after Calamity tossed a handful of gold coins onto the stage to pay for the damages did the actors continue the performance. Chopin recalled that thereafter, "she chewed her cud in courteous silence."

March/April 1997

Calamity Jane died in Deadwood in 1903. Old-timers asked the Rev. Charles Badger Clark, the father of poet Badger Clark, to come down to city hall and say a few words over her body. "That's no place for anybody to be buried from, not even a sinner like Calamity Jane," he replied. "Bring her to the Methodist Church and we'll give her a real funeral." That's how Martha Jane finally got to church, a place she'd taken great pains to avoid while she was alive.

May/June 1987

Buck-a-roos' Annual Ride

Jerry Wilson

IN HIS YOUNGER days, Jim Ramey ran 5,000 steers on his ranch near Wanblee, so his wife Myrtle couldn't understand why he'd want to take what she called a "busman's holiday" — why a guy who rode a horse every day of his working life would want to ride on his vacation.

Women just don't get some things. Ramey, now 85, was a charter member of a group known as the Western South Dakota Buck-a-roos. They set camp for the first time in 1966, and have gathered on a trail in western South Dakota the third weekend in September ever since. There are real cowboys, ranchers with leathery faces and barbed wire hands and the demeanor of men who've passed lots of time alone with the wind and sun, plus some weekend wannabees — lawyers, businessmen, doctors and retired guys who like horses and the camaraderie of a few days with friends. Without their wives, of course.

When the group formed it was a few dozen guys, mostly cowboys. "We all slept on the ground around a big fire and lied to each other," Ramey said. They cooked their own meals, and entertained each other with skits, some even dressing like women to play their parts. "About the fourth year, in the Badlands, 300 guys showed up, doctors and lawyers and such. That's when we put a limit on the number. Now lots of guys stay in motor homes. They don't rough it like we did." Ramey said there's less drinking now than when he was in his prime. "In the old days we'd be out at 10 o'clock at night picking up guys that had fallen off their horses," he said.

Every old Buck-a-roo whose name comes up elicits some kind of story from Ramey. There was Ross Hamm, "a whale of a cowboy," who liked fast horses. "It was Ross Hamm that roped the coyote. He jumped a coyote and everybody had their ropes down, running into each other trying to catch him. Ross roped the thing and rode his horse right into the tent and tied the coyote down. Before supper they auctioned him off. I think he brought $75. The auctioneer said 'he's yours.' The guy took the rope off and the coyote ran out and was gone."

Even Ramey's hat, which looks like a museum relic from the Chisholm Trail, has a story. "I bought it in 1947," he said. "After the war, cattle were selling for 12 cents a pound. I told my wife, 'I'm gonna' drive the steers to Interior and put 'em on railroad cars and I'll ride down with 'em to Sioux City. If I can't get a good price there I'll take 'em on to Chicago.' I got to Sioux City, and that morning the government took the lid off and prices shot up. I sold the steers for 24 cents. I called Wanblee, 'cause we didn't have a phone. They got word to Myrtle. We had an old beat up Chevy. I said 'come down to Sioux City and pick me up. We'll buy a new car and drive to Chicago and see the International Livestock Show.' I bought a Chrysler straight eight, a New Yorker. I bought this hat for $100, and we headed for Chicago."

Sept/Oct 2002

No Mosquitoes, but Lots of Trout

Roger Holtzmann

FANCY TALKING AND an invitation from the State Legislature eventually persuaded President Calvin Coolidge to vacation in the Black Hills in 1927. In the end, it seems he chose the Game Lodge at Custer because of its lack of flying insects. South Dakota's U.S. Rep. William Williamson was making still another tourism pitch to Coolidge when the president asked whether there were many flies and mosquitoes in the hills.

"In the mountain-proper, few or none," answered Williamson.

"That's good," said Coolidge. "Last place I went they nearly pestered me to death." Soon thereafter, he chose Custer State Park's Game Lodge as his summer White House.

Black Hills promoters, hoping to establish the Black Hills as a fishing haven, persuaded the president to try his luck in Squaw Creek. Wearing a suit and straw boater, no angler in history every looked the part less, or had a better chance to catch fish. His hosts did everything but throw the trout in the basket for him. About a mile above and below the lodge, park officials had installed fish nets across the creek. Into this pen they had dumped more than 2,000 trout from the state fish hatchery in Spearfish. They were not small-fry, either. They were, "tired old breeding trout ... (that) the hatchery had been planning to get rid of anyway," wrote Rex Allan Smith. "Years of lazy living on ground liver and horsemeat had left them fat and flabby. But they were big, fearless and eminently catchable."

Despite the fact that Coolidge "handled his fishing rod as gingerly as he might a red-hot poker," he caught five fish, one right after another. Another outing that afternoon yielded equally spectacular results, and Grace Coolidge later remembered that Cal was "as pleased as a boy with his first pair of red-topped boots."

March/April 1996

Shark Hunting in South Dakota

Richard L. Wadleigh

"HOW WOULD YOU like to hunt for sharks' teeth?" I said one Sunday afternoon. "What is this, a South Dakota version of the snipe hunt?" our friend Darlene, from Illinois, asked. "Get in the pickup and I'll show you," I said.

The South Dakota terrain hasn't changed much for as long as we can remember, so we assume it has always been this way. But if we scratch just below the surface we find glacial sediments, sands, gravels and clays deposited by glaciers 10,000 years ago. Dig deeper, and we find sediments from the upper Cretaceous period, over 65 million years ago, evidence that the place we know as high and dry was once covered by a wide but shallow sea — a sea which harbored fearsome creatures, including sharks.

When these large predator fish died, their remains were either consumed by other predators or fell to the sea floor. Their bodies, composed of flesh and cartilage, soon decayed. All that remained was their teeth. But how could even teeth survive for 65 million years? To become fossilized, material must be durable, rapidly buried, and undisturbed. The sharks' teeth were very hard, and the shallow seabed provided the necessary climate for their preservation. Millions of years later, the area was uplifted, exposing the sea floor to air. Plants emerged, followed by animals, and much later by glacial ice. When the ice melted 10 millennia ago, streams and rivers cut through the ancient sea bed, exposing what remained of the sharks — their teeth. Eroded from ancient moorings, the teeth floated down flooding streams. When the waters subsided, they were deposited on stream banks and gravel bars. One such stream is Firesteel Creek, which drains Jerauld, Aurora and Davison counties before emptying into the James River east of Mitchell.

With permission from the farmer who owned the property, we set out on an expedition in search of ancient teeth. We parked by a gravel road and hiked half a mile to the creek. For Gail, who knew the hectic pace of Denver, we had traveled back to the prairies of 1860. At the creek bank everyone went to work, intently searching the shoreline. "I've found one!" Darlene yelled, and everyone rushed to see.

After finding a few fossils, the youngsters got more interested in splashing water. That's when someone yelled "Look out, there's a shark!" They almost left a hole in the water, they got out so fast. Sharks' teeth range from a quarter inch long to three quarters of an inch. They are shaped like an arrowhead, or like a stubby, pointed nail. Their charcoal color blends with the sands and shales; the smaller ones are difficult to spot. After an hour of serious searching, we relaxed on the creek bank and ate our lunch. Then we hiked back to the pickup and drove back to the 21st century, bringing with us the fearsome arsenal of the monsters that once ruled the South Dakota sea.

July/August 2001

A LION'S DEATH IN GARY

Mildred Reinhardt

IT WAS 1928 in Gary. I was eight years old, and had never seen a circus. I could think of little else. At last the day arrived. The big tent was staked out on the hill by the railroad track. There would be a parade before the performance. Hours earlier, hundreds of people gathered along main street. At last we heard the cheery music of the shiny red and gold calliope coming down the hill, playing "Yankee Doodle Dandy." The parade had begun.

The elephant plodded slowly, swaying, tasseled and grand with a proud, turbaned rider. The crowd applauded, and kept cheering as the acrobats in sparkly outfits of pink and yellow and blue performed fantastic feats. After the acrobats, three trick dogs and their beautiful lady trainer came along, dancing on their hind feet, jumping through hoops and rolling over so fast you could barely see them.

Behind the dogs were cowboys and Indians riding, shouting and whooping on their spirited horses. Next, tumbling and joking and doing silly tricks, were gaily dressed clowns. Then, most wonderful of all, came six tiny white ponies with red harnesses, their red, feathered headdresses bobbing jauntily with each dainty step. They were pulling a rig with a lion in a cage. The crowd applauded uproariously.

Just as the ponies were directly in front of where brother and I stood, the wagon came loose, and the door of the lion cage sprang open! In an instant the creature leapt out onto the street. With shrieks of terror the crowds fled indoors. Brother and I raced to the display window in Dad's drugstore. Disoriented, the lion streaked down a side street, then returned and attacked the pony nearest the empty cage. Spectators gasped as the jungle beast clawed at the helpless pony, gouging and tearing its flesh. The little red harness and feathered headdress lay in shards amidst the blood. Someone shouted, "Get a gun!" Then the lion attacked another pony.

The hero of the day grabbed a gun from the hardware store, loaded it, ran to the scene and shot the lion. It lay dead on the street. The injured ponies were carried away, and spectators rushed to help the driver quiet the remainder of the crazed team. The calliope in the distance bravely wheezed out the tune of "America" as it wound its way back up the hill. The circus performers stoically followed the procession back to the Big Top. The show went on.

July / August 2001

LEAD-FLAVORED BEANS IN CENTERVILLE

Roger Holtzmann

DURING THE EARLY 1930s, some of Chicago's lawbreakers apparently thought Centerville was an ideal spot to get away from it all. Some people affectionately called the southeast South Dakota town Little Chicago. For one thing, the visitors could be sure of having access to alcoholic beverages. It has been estimated that the town of 900 and surrounding parts kept 20 or so bootleggers in business.

Fred Mart wasn't one of them, though he admitted later to having sampled their wares. His field was electricity, bringing more than 60 area farms their first wiring during his early years. Fred also worked on radios in those days, and that's what he was doing at Ole Knutson's farm one evening in the spring of 1934. It was nearly midnight when he arrived back in Centerville, but he thought he would look in on his friend Bert Hart, who ran a coffee house and card room on main street known as the Bloody Bucket. Fred had an appetite for a specialty of the house, baked beans. He was surprised to find the front door locked. After a short time, a nervous Bert Hart appeared.

"Geez, I'm glad you're here," he told Fred. "Can you stay for awhile? I've got some characters in the back and I might need some help." Bert added that a batch of beans was almost ready. He led Fred toward a back room where three men were rolling dice, a pile of money between them. There was also a knife and "an awful big gun" on the floor, Fred remembered. He recognized one of the men as Mike Mee, owner of a local bank. Mee's position was ironic considering the identities of the other two men. Years later, Bert told him who they were — Baby Face Nelson and John Dillinger.

The three men greeted Fred and continued their game. Mee and Baby

Face were drinking near beer spiked with something from another bottle. They offered Fred one and he accepted. Fred was flat broke so he couldn't join the dice game. He stood around waiting for Bert's baked beans, sizzling and popping away in the wood cook stove in the corner. After a time, Baby Face Nelson noticed the stove for the first time and he asked what was cooking. Beans, Fred said.

"Well, let's flavor them up!" he said, and he fired his gun into the stove. Bang, bang, bang!

Bert came running from the front, crying, "What happened, what happened!" Steam and smoke were billowing from the punctured stove and bean juice was flowing out on the floor. Bert was furious, but it doesn't pay to get too angry at a man with a gun. There wasn't much he could do.

"I never did get anything to eat that night," Fred said many years later. "I decided I didn't want any lead-flavored beans." With nothing left to stick around for, Fred decided to call it a night. As Dillinger let him out the back way, he reminded him that he had gone straight home that night.

"I don't know anything. I didn't see anything," Fred told him.

Jan/Feb 1993

FROM CLODS TO CLOUDS

Jerry Wilson

JOHN SPADER, A flying farmer from Oldham, died in 1985, but photos in his children's family albums still stir the urge to defy gravity. "Dad didn't get Mom's permission to buy a plane," said son Dean Spader. "And he bought it with borrowed money. She apparently wasn't too pleased. I remember her standing in the kitchen saying, 'Dad's up there flying around in his airplane, and I'm down here with 15 kids.'"

John Spader and two neighbors, Wallace Brown and Dale Wells, hired a pilot to teach them to fly, Dean said. "He landed in an alfalfa field, gave them a couple of lessons, and they were on their own. They all went out and bought planes."

It wasn't all for fun. John Spader did aerial spraying, and when Dean was 10, he helped his dad plant flax seed from the air. "When he got over the field, I'd pull a plug in the back and seed poured out through a gasoline funnel," Dean recalls. "When he got to the end he'd yell, and I'd put the plug back in. We flew low, under power lines at the ends of fields."

John Spader took his wife, Catherine, on numerous trips in the plane, Dean said, which must have softened her resistance to such an expensive toy. "They flew all over the country, without a radio — Florida, California, Canada." In 1954 they flew to the national Flying Farmer's convention in Wichita. The master of ceremonies called for the woman with the most children to stand up. Nobody could match the Spaders' 15, so they brought home the grand prize: a freezer, a set of encyclopedias, a table, chairs and kitchen utensils.

John Spader "never crashed to wreck the plane completely," said another son, Darrel Spader, "but he did have some experiences. Once in winter he nose-dived into a snowdrift and broke the propeller off. About three times he ran out of gas. Once he landed at an airport, just 50 feet from a gas tank, but the other times in fields."

"In tough times he did a lot of hunting," Darrel said. "We have pictures of a hundred foxes and coyotes. In winter he put skis on the plane. He'd land and pick them up and turn them in for the bounty. Sometimes our hired man, Vincent Spry, went along to do the shooting, but a lot of times Dad would do both the flying and the shooting. He was pretty handy."

Darrel also flew with their neighbor, Dale Wells. "He flew so low, it was scary," Darrel said. "And he'd buzz us in the field. One day when I was a kid I was driving the tractor and day dreaming about being in the forest, surrounded by lions, when he came over about 30 feet up. He scared me so bad I jumped off the tractor with it still going. He was a crazy man."

Flying, even in small airplanes, is relatively safe today, probably safer than navigating city streets in a car. But in the early Flying Farmer days, that wasn't the case. There must have been a grain of craziness in all of them, a lust for adventure not present in every farmer's breast. Otherwise, how could they have taken to the skies in primitive machines, with minimal training and no instruments or ground support, depending on luck as their copilot to keep their wings amongst the clouds?

Maybe it was their occupation, an occupation only those who have passed countless hours behind a team of horses and a plow or lulled by the drone of a diesel engine and the slow passage of a million miles of stubble and soil could understand. Perhaps only those whose clodhoppers have sunk into the earth with every step can appreciate the freedom of the hawk soaring overhead waiting for the dispossessed mouse, riding the furrows of cloud and air, liberated from the soil, and weightless in the universe.

From a Piper or a Cessna or a cobbled-together plane, the horse was the mouse, the plow a mere speck, the field and the home a clod, the county a farm, the Earth the domain of animals plodding without imagination toward their graves. For long moments, the Flying Farmers escaped all that; they had what men had dreamed of long before Leonardo da Vinci fashioned his first wings 500 years ago.

March / April 2003

SOLDIERS STARTED GETTYSBURG

Bernie Hunhoff

CIVIL WAR SOLDIERS learned to appreciate a good hill. How better to stop the enemy? Maybe that's why the grizzled Union veterans who came to Dakota Territory in 1883 liked Potter County. The Yankees camped at a place called Eagle Peak, the highest point between the Appalachian Mountains and the Black Hills, and then staked out a town site two miles south. They called the town Gettysburg, after the great battle site of their war 20 years earlier.

The Civil War colony had a population of 211 in its infancy. Veterans and their families started farms and businesses. They were a fiery bunch, as neighboring Forest City citizens soon learned. When Gettysburg won an election over Forest City as the county seat in 1884, Forest City refused to hand over the records. The feud ended when about 100 men from Gettysburg (including many of the veterans) armed themselves and stole the safe and papers at dawn.

If the old soldiers were alive today, South Dakota might look a little different. Who knows where the state capital or Citibank or Ellsworth Air Force Base might be if the Union loyalists were still marching around South Dakota with their muskets?

May / June 1995

BUFFALO 4, BULLS, 0

Jim Dickson

James "Scotty" Philip was a Scottish immigrant who came to western Dakota in the 1870s as a mining prospector. He served as a military scout, cowboy and freighter before settling on a ranch in the Pierre area in 1890. Realizing that the buffalo were nearing extinction, he began to raise them along the Missouri River. Some say he saved the species.

SCOTTY PHILIP, WELL-KNOWN Stanley County cattleman and buffalo fancier, was in Texas when he encountered a couple of sports from Juarez who boasted about the fighting heart of the sharp-horned bulls they bred for combat. Philip politely suggested to the boastful Mexicans that he had any number of ordinary buffalo that could mop up the ring with the finest of those so-called fighting bulls. He furthermore offered to ship one or more of these buffalo to Juarez to prove his point, and solidified his proposition with a substantial wager.

The Mexicans had seen only pictures of buffalo. The prospect of one of the awkward, shaggy creatures challenging their fast-stepping, muscled beasts translated to them as an opportunity for "mucho dinero." Philip's sporting proposition was quickly joined, and arrangements were made for publicity and use of the Juarez bull ring. Unfortunately, a severe blizzard required Scotty Philip's presence on the ranch that January, so he was unable to make the trip to Mexico. He dispatched his nephew, George Philip, to look after family interests and those of the local community who had accumulated a sizeable pot to be wagered on behalf of the buffalo. Cowboys Eb Jones and Bob Yokum were sent along to tend the livestock.

Philip selected two run-of-the-herd buffalo bulls, an eight year-old and a four year-old, for the contest. He called the older one Pierre; the name of the other isn't recorded. Murdo, perhaps. They were loaded into a specially reinforced boxcar, and the entire party made the trip to El Paso and across the Rio Grande to Juarez in seven days, amidst a generous amount of hoopla due to the advance publicity. When they got the buffalo to the bull ring on the designated Saturday, George Philip and company were surprised not only at the size of the facility, but at the number and fervor of the partisans from both sides of the border who had gathered for the spectacle. When Pierre ambled into the arena, the crowd emitted a buzz of anticipation. But the buzz became a groan as the shaggy bison reached the center of the ring and — tired from his long trip — calmly flopped down. There was a reverberating roar as the Mexican bull was turned into the ring. Enraged by darts that had been plunged into his shoulder to enhance his fighting spirit, the snorting, pawing bull launched himself at the unkempt mound in the middle of the arena like a 1,500 pound juggernaut from hell.

Pierre managed to get to his feet in time to take the bull's charge head-on. There was what sounded like an underground explosion, and the dust cleared to reveal the unmoved Pierre stoically contemplating a surprised and slightly dazed bundle of bovine bewilderment that had bounced back a rod or so from the point of impact. But the bull's momma hadn't raised a dummy. He sidestepped to a position that gave a clear shot at the buffalo's uncovered flank, lowered his head and charged for the midsection. Alas, the bull's momma hadn't told him about a major difference between bulls and buffalo; namely, that buffalo turn on their front, rather than rear, legs. This ability allowed Pierre to pivot at the last minute and once more absorb the bull's charge with his massive skull. And this time, the buffalo put some thrust behind his counter-blow. The bull was knocked backwards and put down on his haunches. Several fruitless repetitions of this maneuver were met by increasingly powerful counter-blows. After the final encounter had brought him to his knees, the once-fearsome fighting bull fled to the nether regions of the arena and tried to climb out of the ring. Failing that, he could only stand shaking as the catcalls of the angry crowd rained down.

Claiming a fluke, the Mexican breeders called on George Philip to allow them to try one of their "best" bulls against the buffalo. Ever willing to go the extra mile, George agreed. A fresh contender roared out of the corral directly at Pierre, who stood patiently at ring center. The outcome was the same as before. No matter which direction the bull charged, he was met head-on. That scenario was replayed that afternoon with yet two more bulls. By the time the sun started to sink, four battered and shaking Mexican fighting bulls huddled in the shadows by the west wall while the pride of Stanley County rolled contentedly on his back in the arena sand. George Philip offered the younger buffalo in combat the next day, but all the heart had gone out of the Mexican breeders, and they declined. They desired no further decimation of their prize stock.

It would be nice to report that the buffalo were given heroes' welcomes back home in South Dakota; but to save transportation costs, they were sold in Juarez. One hopes they were used to enrich the fighting bull genetic strain, but the likelihood is that the burrito might have been replaced by the buffalito as the fast food mainstay in old Juarez for a time.

March / April 1995

BADLANDS BACKPACKING

Kim Ode

SOMETIMES YOU WONDER who you're trying to impress. It begins when you tell people you're going backpacking in the Badlands National Park. The Badlands often spur harsh memories. Travelers are usually trying to reach the Black Hills by evening, thus they see its lunar landscapes in the white heat of mid afternoon. So friends tend to be skeptical. You flatter yourself that they wish they had the guts, the daring, the very stuff that you're made of. You buck up their flagging spirits with a modest, "Well, it's not for everyone."

It's hardly for anyone. We deduced this after picking up one rock from the thousands on the plain we were crossing and discovering it was too hot to hold. In shimmering waves of heat, we saw the faces of those we sought to impress, laughing maniacally; raising glasses of iced tea in mocking salute. To be fair, we didn't expect hospitality from the Badlands. That's part of the reason for going — to place yourself in a foreign environment and to suffer a bit for that opportunity. But it's one thing to anticipate suffering and quite another to be in its clutches.

The Badlands are the headstones of the Oligocene Epoch, between 23 and 37 million years ago. The land rose from a giant saltwater sea to form a broad marshy plain that was home to countless mammals. Toward the end of the epoch, volcanoes to the west began dumping ash on the region, forming the whitish layer near the top of Badlands formations. Over the centuries, rivers flowing east from the Black Hills ate into the sediments, through the ash and into the mineral deposits of purplish manganese and orange iron oxide, creating the eerie escarpments that Indians named *mako sica*, or land bad.

Despite its forbidding face, the park cradles a wide variety of life in its craggy arms. Prairie dog towns are heard before they're seen, the small rodents popping from their holes like hand puppets, barking their annoyance. A coyote lopes across the plain. Vultures and hawks hitchhike on the thermals. Meadowlarks trill. Pronghorns and mule deer pace the park. The ground bristles with prickly pear, but mostly it is covered with a shaggy mat of grass tacked down in the few hollows by cedar and cottonwood. Every so often, you see a buffalo wallow, a small pool of dirt where the animals have rolled for sheer pleasure.

There is a reward for enduring the Badlands' day. It is the night. The hours between dusk and dawn have a mystical quality. The dense smell of pure heat fades to the scent of sage. The wind calms. The sun drops like a coin into a slot on the horizon, triggering a jukebox of coyotes. The full moon rises so huge and fast, you unconsciously brace yourself against the rotation of the Earth. Stars burst into view.

You wouldn't be anywhere else. There is nowhere else. One measure of a successful vacation is feeling that you've been away far longer than the calendar would indicate. The Badlands can do that to you. You forget about impressing others and just sit back. Impressed.

May/June 1990

AN ELEPHANT HUNT IN ELKTON

Bernie Hunhoff

ELKTON HAD A rollicking start. In 1893, during a national depression, the local businesses printed their own aluminum money and a federal agent came to town and confiscated $15,000 worth of the coins. Three years later — seven years before the Wright brothers took flight — Henry Heintz got a patent for what may have been the United States' first airship. Built by Frank Woulf of Aurora, the contraption rose in the air but wouldn't move forward. But Elkton's biggest adventure happened May 15, 1916, when a large elephant named Hero escaped from the circus.

Hero had balked at his job of pulling up tent stakes. His trainer, who had been drinking, began to beat the elephant. Hero knocked the man to the ground. No matter where the trainer tried to hide, Hero followed, tipping over equipment and leaving a trail of debris. The beast went into Elkton's business district, pushed his head through the milliner's window and charged through a pool hall. Eventually, he ran east of town, ripping out fence posts as he went. Perhaps he thought that, having been beaten for being slow at pulling up the stakes, he could appease his pursuers by yanking out the posts. One hundred men finally joined the chase. Many had guns and they took numerous shots at the terrified beast. Paul Hohnke finally killed the big animal with his Savage big game rifle. An autopsy later revealed 200 small bullets and 100 large bullets in Hero's hide. The Elkton hotel took some of the meat, and the college at Brookings took the bones for study. The remains were long forgotten by the 1960s, when they were rediscovered by nursing dean Inez Hinsvark. The bones were dusted off and moved to the W.H. Over Museum on the University of South Dakota campus in Vermillion.

Hohnke's rifle is in the Elkton museum, along with other memorabilia from the circus, but some in the area think the bones should also be returned to Elkton. Nobody at the W.H. Over in Vermillion seems concerned, not even if the Elktonites bring an elephant gun. "We paid for the bones. I've seen the paperwork," laughed Dorothy Neuhaus of the Over Museum. "And we give Elkton due credit. The exhibit includes a photo of the men from town standing over the elephant like they are on an African safari."

Hero was killed in Elkton and forgotten in Brookings, so it's not likely he would want to travel north if he had his choice.

Sept / Oct 1995

BOUNDARY WALKER

Jerry Wilson

FOR 25 YEARS Emmett Bennett walked the streets of Rapid City, delivering the mail. On weekends, he and his wife Mary Ellen took a hike. Before he delivered his last piece of mail in 1970, he found a new reason to walk. He learned that a century before, surveyors had marked the boundaries of the state with cottonwood, iron or granite posts at every mile. So he went to the southwest corner and began a trek around the state. Using maps and a compass to guide his feet, he walked several miles of pathless terrain a day.

In 1995, having walked the southern, northern and western boundaries, Bennett set out in Jones County, south of his boyhood home of Ft. Pierre, walking west along the 1877 surveyor's base line to where that line meets the Black Hills meridian on the Wyoming border. By 1998 he still had not found the monument marking the site. On August 17, darkness fell, and Bennett had not returned. After a frantic night, Mary Ellen called the sheriff. Searchers found him the second night, wandering the 6,600-foot Limestone Plateau, disoriented and dehydrated.

Annoyed at getting lost so near his prize, Bennett spent two weeks studying maps, then set out again the last day of September. Again, he did not return. This time Mary Ellen was even more alarmed, especially when the night turned cold and rain began to fall. For two days, dozens of people combed the rugged state-line area. On the third day, a Colorado team with dogs found Emmett Bennett's body at the bottom of a brushy ravine in Parmlee Canyon, a quarter mile across the Wyoming line, just beyond the mile post he sought.

Why Emmett Bennett's passion to walk? Perhaps it was his birth on Earth Day. Or rather, Earth Day was born on Emmett Bennett's 60th birthday, April 22, 1970. Millions of Americans celebrated the day as he did, by walking — marching to protest pollution. To celebrate the 20th Earth Day and his 80th birthday, Bennett climbed Harney Peak, the highest point between the Big Horns and the Pyrenees.

The truth is that when Bennett walked he was only pacing himself, reining in his natural tendency to run. Speed was in his blood. From 1926 to 1930, he earned 12 athletic letters at Rapid City High School in football, basketball and track. In 1929 he placed sixth in the nation in the 440-yard race in Chicago.

At 74, Bennett rode his bicycle across Nebraska and twice across

Minnesota. Then he renewed his track career. He entered a triathlon in Minnesota, beating not only every man over 70, but everybody over 50. At 85 he was still running. At the 1995 Senior Olympics in St. Louis, he competed in eight events and set new records in five.

So this was the Emmett Bennett who, that late September day in 1998, set out on his last walk. Perhaps he became disoriented again, fell or blacked out. Possibly he simply lay down to rest. The first chill of winter came, and by morning he was dead.

Walking was as natural to Emmett Bennett as breathing air. But why the attraction to boundaries for a man whose very life said movement, independence, speed? For a quarter century Bennett walked the line. To earn his bread, he traversed the same prescribed path, day after day. But for 88 years he also pushed the line, lunged toward freedom. He was a man who defied boundaries, pushing himself to the last ounce of endurance.

And yet, perhaps there was within him some need for the line, even if artificial or imagined, something to keep him in check, to give life order. Something epitomized by a boundary marked at regular intervals with granite posts. Otherwise, he might not have returned. He might have simply kept walking. Somehow, it's comforting to know that the night Bennett died, he was across the line, beyond the boundary marker he sought, doing what he loved doing — putting one foot in front of the other, his eye on some goal ahead, a mail box, a finish line, a six-foot granite post, the summit of the next horizon.

May / June 2000

THE BRONC FROM BUFFALO

Gary Licking

YAKIMA CANUTT was the only man who ever rode Tipperary during the horse's prime, though the top riders of the day tried. Tipperary was foaled in 1905 near Long Pines, west of Camp Crook. His owner, Elmer Wickham, tried to break him when he was a four year-old, but Tipperary bolted on his first night in the corral.

No one else tried until 1915, and that attempt lasted only a few seconds. Ed Marty was chosen to get in the saddle. Frank Latham pulled a blindfold from Tipperary's eyes, and the horse promptly showed Marty what he would later do to the best riders in the country. Ed was thrown to the street and then said the words that would give the horse its name: "It's a long, long way to Tipperary!"

Wisely, his owners decided Tipperary's talents lay in being other than a saddle horse. From 1916 to 1926, he threw 91 riders. Canutt was considered the best rider in the world in 1920 when he climbed aboard the bronc from Buffalo at the Belle Fourche Roundup. He had been warned by Tipperary's other victims to watch out for the third jump. As Tipperary reached that third buck, Yakima said, "he practically exploded!" Canutt's head was popped and he was loosened in the saddle. But he wasn't thrown and he made a qualified ride. He was invited to return to Belle Fourche in 1921, where he repeated his success of the year before and received $500 and a gold token inscribed, "Tipperary Medal, Belle Fourche, S.D., presented to Yakima Canutt, Making the only qualified ride ever made on Tipperary."

Harold Eckberg successfully rode Tipperary in 1926 when the horse was 21 years old. After that Tipperary was put out to pasture in the jump-off area west of Buffalo, and died in a blizzard in October of 1932. A monument to the horse was erected in the Buffalo City Park in 1955. But it didn't require a stone marker to keep Tipperary's name alive in the minds of rodeo cowboys who saw him buck.

Nov / Dec 1987

THREE TOES AND THE CUSTER WOLF

Archie Gilfillan and Martha Linde

FEW CREATURES evoke a more emotional response than wolves. Our fear of them is deep-seated, almost instinctive. They live in our fairy tales and nightmares, but to some they were more than an abstract symbol of peril. Grey wolves, larger and stronger cousins of the timber wolf, lived along the river breaks of western South Dakota during the early years of white settlement. Stock growers considered them a plague and hunted them nearly to extinction, but not before two wolves achieved a horrific notoriety and exacted the only revenge their kind would ever get.

The Custer Wolf, who roamed Custer County during the early part of last century, was a finely tuned killing machine — a beast that once killed ten steers in a single night, leaving only one partially eaten. He eluded capture for years, until H.P. Williams came to the area in 1920, fresh from a successful hunt of the Split Rock Wolf in Wyoming. Williams coated his boots with the scent of that female and traversed the Custer Wolf's known range. From that point on the animal's behavior became erratic. He began digging a den in a dry gully about 20 miles northwest of Custer, hunting only enough to stay alive; after his death, the den was found to be almost 50 feet deep. Williams closed in. On a rainy, windblown October day he found the wolf dragging a trap that had been scented with she wolf. Williams waited for a clear shot, and ended the creature's killing days.

Three Toes was a 75-pound gray who, "for 13 years laughed at poison, traps and guns, lived in and off enemy country with the hand of every man against him, a cunning, bloodthirsty killer, a superwolf among wolves, and the most destructive single animal of which there is any record anywhere," wrote Archie Gilfillan in his 1929 classic, *Sheep*. Where and when he was born is unknown, but by 1912, Three Toes had established a reputation. He was so named because he lost a toe to a trap early in life, "and the mark of this maimed foot he subsequently left in the dust of many a sheep corral, a print as legible and damning as any fingerprint." That distinguishing characteristic enabled exasperated ranchers who were his victims to track the destructive swath he cut through Harding County: An estimated $50,000 worth of cattle and sheep before he was finally brought to ground.

In the spring of 1925 Three Toes was on a rampage, killing but not eating his prey — killing for the sheer joy of it. County commissioners increased the bounty to $500, which encouraged numerous hunters to try their luck. Early in July, federal wolf hunter Clyde F. Briggs set up shop on a ranch near the center of Three Toes' hunting range. For two weeks the trapper and wolf sparred. Briggs patiently set and reset his traps, using every trick he'd learned hunting wolves across the West. Three Toes' tracks were seen around the traps on several mornings, but he was wily enough to elude their grasp. For a time, at least. Three Toes was found in a cleverly concealed trap on July 23, the ground around him torn by his frenzied efforts to escape. Briggs muzzled him, and put the exhausted beast into the back of his car, intending to bring him to Rapid City. Before they'd gone three miles one of the party shouted, "I think he's dying!"

"Briggs stopped the car, and looking around, found the wolf's eyes fixed on him. But the eyes did not see him, for the wolf was dead," wrote Gilfillan. "Call it a broken heart, or what you will — something of this sort is what killed the old wolf. He was resting easily when found, his wounds were superficial … but there was something in his grand old spirit that could not brook capture, and Nature, more merciful than he had ever been, granted him his release."

March / April & Sept / Oct 1990

RAPID CITY'S BATMAN

Phil Henry

JOEL TIGNER doesn't wear a mask or a cape, and his wards are the furry creatures that make some people scream. Tigner ventures out at night to work long, solitary hours while most people are tucked in bed. A stocky man with black beard shot with silver, he sets up strange-looking devices called mist nets and harp traps in marshlands, secluded streams and the mouths of caves. He crawls into the bowels of the earth and wades through waist-deep, murky water in abandoned mines. He has encountered rattlesnakes and even a mountain lion that came to drink in a forest pond where his nets were set.

Tigner is worried about Townsend's bats. People have locked them out of their winter homes. For eons bats slept long winters in Black Hills caves, and since the 1800s, in mines. They have been excluded from tourist caves, and many abandoned mines are collapsing or have been sealed to avoid liability.

Some people believe bats attack people and other animals, others that they carry rabies, the most frequently-cited reason for their wholesale extermination. Tigner says both beliefs are false. Some see them as flying mice, too scary-looking to behold, vampirish and evil. Hollywood helped give bats a bad name. The entertainment industry has long associated bats with vampires and the evils of midnight. In a 1960s television movie, millions of rabid bats roared from caves, searching for anything or anyone to attack in a frenzied attempt to cool the red fever in their brains.

Joel Tigner harbors no such phobias. He has been fascinated by bats since elementary school. Today the Batman of Rapid City studies bats and their shrinking world. He works with government biologists to preserve and restore bat habitat. He presents bat slideshows at the Cleghorn Fish Hatchery in Rapid City, Badlands National Park, and the Booth Fish Hatchery in Spearfish. Sometimes he puts a favorite bat in his pocket and goes to schools to educate youngsters about the importance of bats in the natural order. His goal is to save bats from defamation and destruction.

To keep people out of known bat caves during the crucial spring maternity and nursing season, Tigner installs gates. As bats open their eyes on summer evenings, he sets up aluminum poles on the banks of forest streams, unfurls mist nets and stretches them across a body of water. He arranges his equipment on a tarp — a clipboard and forms, pen, small scale for weighing bats, and a micrometer to measure forearm length.

As he works, Tigner gives a seminar on bats, the dozen species that inhabit South Dakota, how many mosquitoes a bat might consume in a single night, their important place in a balanced ecosystem. Understanding of his nocturnal friends has grown since Tigner began his work in the Black Hills. His colleagues at the South Dakota Bat Working Group have now launched a website dedicated to bats, and to spreading the word that these furry little night flyers are worth their keep.

May / June 2002

SAM BROWN: A PRAIRIE PAUL REVERE

SAM BROWN WAS a young scout at Fort Sisseton in Dakota Territory. On April 19, 1866, he learned of a suspected Indian raid. Fresh moccasin tracks had been discovered near present-day Jamestown, N.D. Brown told his commanding officer of the tracks and was instructed to ride to Elm River, near Ordway in Brown County, to alert scouts to the danger. Donning a buffalo coat to stay warm, he saddled his horse and left at sundown.

He galloped into the night, covering a distance of 55 miles in five hours. However, upon his arrival, he learned that the passing Indians were peace messengers. In a newspaper interview many years later, Brown noted, "I was struck dumb with surprise and mortification, for I was satisfied I had come on a wild goose chase and the alarm was a false one; that no war party was coming, and that the tracks or the trail of these Indian messengers had been seen and supposed to be the tracks of hostile Indians. I at once decided to return to Fort Wadsworth (then the name of Fort Sisseton) without delay. I deemed it my duty to return at once and intercept the communication which I had sent in previous to my departure relative to hostile Indians ... so as to not create unnecessary alarm at headquarters in St. Paul and throughout western Minnesota."

So the prairie "Paul Revere" mounted a fresh pony and retraced his trail in the black of night. A wind and rain storm overtook him and nearly blew him from the horse. Soon the rain turned to snow and a spring blizzard set in as he reached the James River. He became lost in the blinding snow and went too far south. When he reached Waubay Lake, he knew where he was and he turned north into the wind. It was 8 a.m. when he reached the fort and alerted officers that military action was not necessary. Brown's legs were frozen and he was paralyzed for the rest of his life. He had ridden 150 miles in 15 hours through snow and sleet. Many people felt his ride saved lives and unwarranted escalation of hostilities between the military and the Santees.

Brown died at age 80 in 1925 at Browns Valley, Minn., where a museum was established in his honor.

May/June 1993

IN SEARCH OF THE MOREL MUSHROOM

VerLynn Kneifel

MOREL MUSHROOM hunters are a tight-lipped bunch — they guard their favorite locations like state secrets. "It's six mosquito bites and four woodticks up the creek," said one vaguely. They will offer specific, if contradictory, advice about where to find them, however. A professor of botany and mycology advises looking under recently dead or dying elm trees. Another mushroomer says they favor north slopes. Another says look near oak trees. One says the biggest mushroom he ever found, seven inches across, was found near his doghouse, leading him to favor animal droppings as the most likely site. Less adventurous sorts might prefer to find a comfortable chair and wait for friends to call and invite them to a mushroom feast.

May/June 1986

THE FLIGHT OF EXPLORER II

Karen Paige

AS TOPOGRAPHICAL FEATURES go, it was interesting, but not particularly striking. Not like Bear Butte, or Devils Tower. It was a big hole in the ground, a steep-sided, natural depression about 11 miles southwest of Rapid City. No mapmaker had thought to give the spot a name until someone figured out it would be a fine place to launch a balloon. The bowl afforded protection from surface winds, and the hundreds of miles of flat, open prairie to the east offered good landing possibilities.

The first flight from the site, launched by the National Geographic Society in 1934, ended badly. An explosion ripped the hydrogen-filled balloon apart, destroying the scientific instruments on board and forcing the pilots to bail out. A second attempt, on Nov. 11, 1936, gave the Stratobowl its name and earned it a place in aviation history. *Explorer II*, filled with non-explosive helium, carried army pilots Albert Stevens and Orval Anderson to 72,395 feet, establishing an altitude record that stood for 21 years. After eight hours aloft measuring cosmic rays and photographing the earth's curvature, *Explorer I* returned to earth near White Lake, having traveled just over 200 miles. There were other launches from the Stratobowl: A manned flight in 1956 reached 76,000 feet, establishing a new altitude record; three years later, an unmanned, 10 million cubic foot behemoth left from the Stratobowl to attain a height of 120,000 feet. As rocketry developed, putting satellites in orbit around the earth, there was no further need for stratospheric balloon flights, and South Dakota's Stratobowl is once again a peaceful hole in the Black Hills.

Jan/Feb 1986

Claremont's Mighty Bill Prunty

John Andrews

AN EXHIBIT IN the South Dakota Baseball Hall of Fame honors what was perhaps the most dramatic moment in state tournament history — the 1938 championship game between Claremont and Aberdeen. The game was tied 4-4 and was headed into extra innings. The field in Aberdeen had no lights, so umpire Tommy Collins declared that if the game wasn't over after the 10th inning, it would be replayed the next day.

Aberdeen went scoreless in the top of the inning and Claremont had two outs in the bottom. That's when Bill Prunty stepped to the plate. After working the count to 3-2, he cracked a long home run that disappeared into the night and gave Claremont the championship. The ball was found the next day and now resides in the Hall of Fame at Lake Norden.

May/June 2002

Western Democracy Began at Elk Point

Jerry Wilson

WE CREDIT THE ancient Greeks with inventing democracy. But the first vote by American citizens west of the Mississippi was held at Elk Point in 1804. The vote was to elect a replacement for Sgt. Floyd, the only casualty of Lewis and Clark's expedition up the Missouri to the Pacific Ocean.

According to Capt. William Clark's journal, Floyd was "taken very bad all at once with a bilious colic," probably appendicitis. He died the next day "with a great deal of composure," and was buried on what we still call Sergeant Bluff south of Sioux City. Three days later the Corps of Discovery landed 30 miles upriver, by a lone cottonwood on the north shore. A herd of elk lazed on a sandbar, and the men fired at two swimming in the river. There, at "elk point," the explorers set up camp and held an election to replace Sgt. Floyd. Lewis and Clark proposed three candidates, and 19 of the 27 men voted to elevate Pvt. Patrick Gass to sergeant.

Almost two centuries later, the late "mountain man," Ole Olsen, decided his town's role in history had been overlooked too long. "When I found out Elk Point wasn't included on some Lewis and Clark maps, it kind of teed me off," Olsen said. "I kind of promised we'd have an election on August 22 every year." The corps' landing site was pinpointed on the southwest edge of town where the river ran in 1804, near what is now Heritage Park. In 1998, Olsen and fellow history buffs staged a black powder rendezvous to reenact the first election in the Louisiana Purchase. *Elk Point Leader Courier* editor Kelly Kruithoff discovered Eugene Gass Painter, the great grandson of Sgt. Gass, living in Avella, Pa., who flew to South Dakota to be elected sergeant. Remarkably, only four generations in the Gass family have passed since the days of Lewis and Clark. Explorer Patrick Gass didn't settle down to family life until he was in his sixties, when he married a 20 year-old woman; his very young, 84 year-old great grandson planned to get married after being elected sergeant.

July / August 2002

WE'RE SURE GLAD YOU RETIRED, CASEY

Bev Pechan

WHEN HE WAS 13 years old, Casey Tibbs hitchhiked to White River, thinking he was going to enter his first rodeo. Officials told him he was too young to compete, but they allowed him an exhibition ride. Tibbs got so mad he never went back to White River. Once each season, at least, the rest of the cowboys on the circuit had a chance to win.

Casey Tibbs won his first trophy saddle in 1946, at age 16, earning the nickname Kid Wonder. Between 1949 and 1959, Tibbs was nearly unbeatable. He won eight championships from the Rodeo Cowboys Association and ten world championships from the International Rodeo Association; his lifetime total of 42,065 points still stands as a record. Tibbs' dominance was so remarkable he even managed to bring the sport of rodeo into the mainstream, appearing on Ralph Edwards' "This Is Your Life" television program in 1958. Tibbs retired from competition in 1964 and launched a second career as a stunt rider for movies and television. When a producer told him he didn't look the part of a real cowboy, a miffed Tibbs un-retired and won top money at nine of ten rodeos. Having proved his point, he retired again.

To the relief of his fellow competitors, it took this time.

May / June 1990

CROUSE & CREW CLOWN COMPANY

Bernie Hunhoff

DON AND DOROTHY Crouse were running a drug store in Willow Lake when the town celebrated its 75th birthday in 1957. Every business wanted an original parade entry, and the Crouses settled on the notion of rebuilding a Model T. As word got out, people brought Tin Lizzy parts from their garages and barns.

"We wanted something that would make people laugh, so we bolted a post on the back with a saddle," Don Crouse explained. "Then we had the wheels welded off center so it would bounce up and down as it went down the street." One of the guys dressed as a woman. (Laughs come easier in Willow Lake than in some places.) The car was a smash, so the Crouses drove it in other area parades

They kept the car close to home until 1960, when they were persuaded to enter the National Legionnaires Parade in Denver to help promote South Dakota. Men dressed like women were prohibited, but the Willow Lake clowns did so anyway and no one objected. Sioux Falls promoters were releasing pen-raised pheasants and shooting at them with blanks directly in front of Crouse and two friends who had joined the clown act. It was a hot afternoon and the pen-raised birds were so tired that they began to walk ahead of the Model T. People lined the 24-block parade route, so the pheasants could not escape to either side of the street.

"We also brought a few live pheasants. We had our birds tied by their legs to the running boards," Crouse said. "The people watching the parade thought the pheasants walking ahead of us were also part of our act, and they could not imagine how we'd trained them to walk down the street."

Yes, humor is unexplainable, even accidental. But if you don't paint your face and find some trick or skit, like a crooked-rolling Model T and a man in a dress, you don't have a chance.

Thirty-two years after the Denver parade, the Crouse & Crew Clown Company, headquartered in Watertown, continued to entertain parade audiences.

July / August 2002

TYLER'S BACK FROM TEXAS

VerLynn Kneifel

Somehow the right girl never came along
to melt his guard, for Tyler is shy.
He tended his cattle and read a lot.
Smithsonian, Michener. Time went by.
Tyler never said much what he thought.

Somewhere along the way, he got older.
The summers got shorter, the winters colder.
The windmill creaked and the wind blew.
His oldest friend got older, too,
and died down south in Texas.

Even in letters someone else had the say.
He sent her words by Edna St. Vincent Millay.
"Michael spoke of you so often," came her reply.
Black and white, funeral colors, unheard sigh;
"It looks like an early winter in Texas."

That winter he thought of her now and then,
and finally Spring arrived in Dakota again.
He wondered how she was, finally wrote to ask.
She answered in tentative and delicate hue, in lavender like prairie pasque.

She wrote again in springtime apple-green;
"No, the pasque is a flower I've never seen."
The windmill creaked and the wind blew.
Birdsong, too, he rarely heard, and this, too,
went into all those letters to Texas.

She replied in pink, replied in blue.
"Won't you come to Texas, Tyler, my dear?"
"I know of a good specialist here."
Now Tyler's back from Texas with a hearing aid,
and by his side, his Texas bride.

March/April 1992

Humor & Craziness

HUMOR IS A delicate and unpredictable emotion. You learn that when you publish a magazine. Once we accepted a story about a hog butchering that went badly. It seemed the pig was unfazed by the bullet to the head and escaped back into the herd. The shooter couldn't identify which pig he had shot, so he went through the hog yard calling, "Here, piggy piggy .... here, piggy piggy." Something about the contrast between shooting a pig and then, a minute later, calling endearments to it struck our editors as funny. Our readers didn't see the humor. We were deluged with irate letters and calls.

We've had similar results with rattlesnakes (even if you paint an olive branch in their fangs, most people just don't find them funny). We hope to have better luck with these excerpts. Some are obviously funny (to us, anyway). Others are just weird and crazy. But isn't that life?

Don't worry. "Here, Piggy Piggy" didn't make the book. I'm not that stupid. I don't even think it's funny any more. But wait 'til you read about those turkeys in Gettysburg.

— Bernie Hunhoff

WHY I DON'T UMP BASEBALL GAMES

Colin Kapitan

Colin Kapitan of Yankton had long established himself as one of South Dakota's most versatile and best-known sports officials when he explained to our readers why he quit doing baseball games.

IN 1962 I WAS looking for a basketball referee partner. A friend, Darrell, was seeking a baseball umpiring side-kick. We compromised. Darrell would work basketball with me. Together, we would work college baseball.

I worked a lot of games. Southern State, Yankton, Wayne, Morningside and the University of South Dakota. Three, sometimes four doubleheaders a week. For three years. Three long years. I don't know why, but I couldn't get into balls and strikes. Certainly it wasn't that I didn't love the game. Or that I didn't know the game. Maybe it was those doubleheaders. Start at noon and go 'til dark. No daylight savings time back then. Maybe it was the dreary weather. Wind and rain. More wind. More rain. I wore more clothes on the diamond than when shoveling snow.

My last afternoon was a day much like just described. Riverside Diamond in Yankton. The wind was whipping off the river, bringing slow and steady precipitation. The temperature was mid 30s. Your regular college baseball doubleheader. The Yankton College Greyhounds were entertaining John F. Kennedy College of Wahoo, Neb. Both schools are now defunct. I was behind the plate for the first game and should have suspected this would be worse than your ordinary game when the JFK catcher came out for the bottom of the first. Despite the weather, he wore a t-shirt. Maybe he figured all those tattoos would keep him warm. He looked 35 and sounded like a Marine drill sergeant. Jose was his name. Jose didn't like most of my decisions. His coach agreed with him. The coach? Bob Cerv. Not a name that rings a bell with your average baseball fan, but Bob Cerv was a good player on the New York Yankee teams of the mid-1950s. He played with Mickey Mantle. He had several World Series championship rings. This day he was as big as a house. Three hundred and fifty pounds, plus. Over a 6-foot-4 frame. With a growly voice and a vocabulary that put his foul-mouthed catcher to shame. He visited me often during the first game.

The seven innings went pretty fast. I figured I had it made. Just seven more innings on the bases, collect my $30, and get home to a hot bath. It wasn't that easy. I forgot Murphy's Law. First play of the second game. A bangbang at first base. My call went against JFK. Here comes Cerv across the diamond as fast as a 350 pounder can make it. I made up my mind right there. Before the ex-big leaguer could utter a word, I had my say! To my surprise, Bob Cerv grinned. He left the diamond, never to return that afternoon.

Darrell could hardly wait to get to me after the game. "What happened?" he asked. "What transpired that Cerv never again left the dugout?"

As Cerv approached in that first inning, I chose my words carefully. "Excuse me, Mr. Cerv, but this isn't Yankee Stadium. Don't think you'll make it there as a manager nor I as an umpire. But I will tell you one thing. If you leave me alone the rest of the afternoon, I promise you that I'll never umpire another baseball game so long as I live."

The lumbering giant stopped. He looked dazed for a moment, then gathered himself and smiled. "You got it, kid." He kept his word. And I have kept mine.

May / June 1994

MY RODEO DEBUT

Bernie Hunhoff

I HADN'T MILKED a cow in 25 years, so when two friends asked me to join their team for the Wild Cow Milking Contest at the Irene rodeo, I felt it was an opportunity for nostalgia. After all, I figured, how wild are the cows in Yankton County? Our neighbors butcher anything that looks cross-eyed or jumps a fence. With that type of selective breeding, their mother cows are as tame as the burros in Custer State Park.

I was a little surprised to arrive at the rodeo grounds and see a big stock trailer rocking back and forth. I peeked in the rear of the trailer and a big black cow with red eyes and pointed ears charged the door. These were not Yankton County cows! Apparently the frugal Rodeo Committee figured they could save the $225 purse by going West River to find some critters that had never see anything on two legs but cowboys carrying hot branding irons.

Being a man of words, I suddenly realized why the word cow is a prefix for the word coward. In all our years of milking Holsteins on the farm, I'd never made that connection. Anyway, as I watched that trailer rock I suddenly remembered that I'd left the water hose running on the trees back home, but just as I walked a few steps toward the car, my team — Junior Rasmussen and Kurt Johnson — came rambling over. (That's what real Wild Cow Milkers do — they ramble.)

Kurt and Junior were all smiles. Obviously they hadn't seen the cows. They were outfitted for battle, with leather gloves to prevent a rope burn. And since they had gloves, they said, "Bernie, you can do the milking." (I made a mental note to bring gloves if there was a next time.) The Rodeo Committee held a meeting to explain the rules. We start with a rope halter on the cows in the bullpen. When the gun sounds, the cows are released and whoever gets a squirt of milk into a plastic pop bottle and races it and the halter across the arena to the judge wins the $225.

"If nobody does it in five minutes, time's up," said the Rodeo Committee. "We don't pay anybody." They didn't discuss the subject of disability compensation or survivor benefits. But one of our competitors, a young man from Nebraska with several missing teeth, said he and his friends had done this before and he recommended that everyone watch for flying hooves.

After the instructions, we waited. We watched the bucking broncs toss the young cowboys hither and thither and step on them. The broncs looked like the black cow in the trailer, I thought. We watched the bulls — and they didn't seem as mean as that black cow in the trailer. We watched little kids ride sheep. Those old ewes acted like Yankton County cows to me. They seemed milkable.

When it was time for the Wild Cow Milking Contest, Junior and Kurt and I rambled into the arena. I was grateful to see that our cow had a white face. The team with the black cow could hardly get a halter on her head. Our girl didn't like the bullpen but she quieted down a little when we whispered niceties in her ear and rubbed her tummy. I told her we didn't have a branding iron.

When the gun sounded, Kurt and Junior — fathers of 4-Hers with beef steers — led her out of the pen and put the famous 4-H neck crunch on her. She froze in her tracks. "Milk her, Bernie!" yelled Junior.

I stood about three feet away from her hooves and reached out for the closest teat. Milk squirted into the Mountain Dew bottle. Kurt pulled off the halter and we raced lickety-split for the judge. The black cow with red eyes passed us along the way, with three men chasing behind her. We were easily the first to arrive with milk. The Rodeo Committee kept their word and paid us the $225 — more than any of us had ever made on a cow.

Five minutes later a pretty girl in a halter top who hadn't risked anything but a sunburn all afternoon won a big vacation to Las Vegas when her name was drawn in the raffle. Had the Rodeo Committee gone nuts?

Then we learned that everyone expected us to defend our Wild Cow Championship at next year's rodeo. I'm spending my winnings on leather gloves … and raffle tickets.

Sept / Oct 1995

ALL THEY HAD TO DO WAS SLEEP INSIDE A DEAD HORSE

Roger Holtzmann

REMEMBER THAT old pioneer tale about the guy who gets trapped in a blizzard? He's lost, can't get a fire started and is unable to find shelter. As a last resort he shoots his horse (or in some versions, a cow) in the head, cuts open the belly, and survives by utilizing the warmth of the animal.

Luckily, no one had invented animal rights yet. Aside from that, I've always had problems understanding that story. What exactly is the procedure? Do you climb in the animal's stomach? Or do you just stick your head in for a while, then alternate with your feet? Maybe you stick your feet up through his neck, running your torso through his stomach, which would put your head right about ... no, that can't be right.

Doesn't the carcass freeze up after awhile anyway? So there you are, covered with blood, your head (or whatever) stuck where no man has gone before, and you're still freezing. Right about then, more than one immigrant probably thought, "Gees, I should have stayed back in Europe. Starving to death in a potato famine wouldn't have been all that bad."

Unless some of those pioneers were world class liars, which is a possibility, somehow it got done, and here we are. When we think of stories like that we sometimes feel a little twinge that we whine about piddly things — we wonder if maybe that pioneer gumption hasn't been diluted by central heat and factory-rolled cigarettes. In defense of modern men and women, though, just let me say this: Sleeping inside a dead animal is an accomplishment, all right, but there are few things that will test the mettle of humanity more than today's favorite winter sport, Getting The Car Stuck.

There are all kinds of variations on the theme *automobilae immobilicus*, winter variety. There's one which happens right outside your home that even novices can enjoy since this version doesn't require you to do anything at all. It occurs when you awaken to find your car — or rather, a tiny portion of your car — peeking out from a gigantic drift. If you live in a city, and your car is parked on the street, you'll find that for the first time in history they plowed your street early, piling up additional snow and leaving you a $25 ticket to boot. If you live in the country, you'll notice you parked your car with the engine side north. This allowed snow to blow in, completely filling the engine compartment and insuring your car won't start even if you do get it shoveled out.

For advanced grief, there's nothing like The You Bet Your Life Whirling 360 Spin Of Death. All you need for this is a plain old road, a coat of ice, and the foolish belief that you absolutely must be somewhere else. Someone who's enjoying this activity is easy to spot: They're in the ditch with a pulse of about 210, clutching their steering wheel, repeating their favorite expletive over and over. And over. After the heart attack phase, you sit there thinking should I try to walk for it or not? Every expert says stay with your car, but you know that advice is bogus. They assume you've packed an emergency kit in your trunk, but of course you never got around to that. You'll try to get a tow truck, but there will be three bozos in front of you. You'll try not to think of yourself as a member of bozodom but it won't work. That delay will leave your car out there becoming encased in its very own drift. Which will hide it from snowplows. As you sit in the gas station drinking vending machine coffee you'll ponder that: Large steel blades welded onto 20-ton trucks whose drivers have been living on caffeine for 48 hours. And your car — your nice, barely half-paid-for-car — on the same road.

"Boy, I wish all I had to do was sleep inside a dead horse," you'll say.

Jan/Feb 1993

NOW I'LL NEVER SELL MY HOUSE

Roger Holtzmann

LAST FALL THE South Dakota Supreme Court ruled on a case involving the sale of a house that had a problem with its foundation. Now the seller, herein known as The Seller, did cause to be affixed unto the disclosure form that there was "some crumbling" of the walls behind the basement paneling. An engineer who testified put it another way: The basement walls "could collapse at any time." Justice David Gilbertson made note of The Seller's "colorful attempt" to sort of tell the truth, but he and the rest of the men in black weren't amused. Fudging on known defects is not allowed, they ruled.

I can tell you what I thought when I read that story in the newspaper. No fudging? Are they serious? They could just as well have called this the "Anybody Who Lives In An Old House Might As Well Get Used To It

Because There Is No Way In Hell Or Halifax That You Will Ever Be Able To Sell The Darn Thing" ruling. Let's say you are a homeowner looking to move. You're sitting at the kitchen table with your disclosure form, wrestling with how to tell the home-buying public that your roof leaks. How about, "Roof leaks only when it rains." Or, "Roof leaks, but you only really notice if you're on the second floor. Most of the time it stays dry on the main floor." Or, "Roof leaked last week but I'm pretty sure it has fixed itself by now." Or, "Roof leaks, but you can get lots of apples off the trees in back."

How far does the fudging rule extend? After all, "New carpet installed three months ago" sounds straight-forward. But with this new ruling it will have to read, "Cheapest carpet we could find installed three months ago. Did it myself one weekend. I can't measure worth a darn so there's a highly irregular seam being hidden by the couch. Stuck it down with industrial strength glue that will create a horrible mess when you try to pull it up next year, which you're going to have to do because the carpet will be disintegrating by then."

No fudging? This could be a problem, but I for one promise to do my part. So here goes: House for sale. Lots of little things wrong. A couple big things wrong which I am trying not to think about. Many things waiting to go bad.

Just like the place you live in now.

May / June 1996

DON'T JOSH THE TOURISTS

Bernie Hunhoff

AN ABERDEEN MAN likes to kid visiting tourists that rock piles in the corners of our farm fields are there because the farmer just hasn't had time to spread them yet. Why do they spread rocks, the tourist asks? He lifts one up and shows how it conserves moisture in the soil. That makes sense to city-bred visitors. They see other fields with rocks scattered everywhere — farms run by more progressive farmers.

Joshing urban tourists can be fun. I know of another northeast South Dakotan who tells out-of-staters that our entire region was once a mountain range, much like the Rockies and the Black Hills. But, he explains, a massive agriculture improvement project known as the Mountain Leveling Act (MLA) reduced the peaks to today's rolling hills. Then there's the character in central South Dakota who tells guests on his treeless ranch that his land was a thick forest until the State Deforestation Project (SDP) was initiated. People will believe almost anything if you say the government paid for it.

Probably we shouldn't confuse our guests. They arrive here already perplexed about our language and ways. A young lady from Omaha who settled near us in the country says she couldn't follow some of our conversations when she first arrived. When a neighbor said he was going home to "walk the beans" she asked, "Where are you going to take them?" When someone else mentioned he was going to have his kids "pick rocks" she wondered, "What are you going to make with them?"

Ted Hustead, the founder of Wall Drug Store, didn't like to confuse visitors. Quite the opposite. He wanted tourists and newcomers to learn more about South Dakota so he asked me to write a brochure explaining the scenery along Interstate 90. I wrote about livestock and small towns and grain fields. On the front, we put a cute picture of a pig and titled it, "Buffalo Don't Oink." Boy, did my phone ring. Buffalo do oink.

South Dakotans who raise buffalo called me and Ted to point out that buffalo make a grunting sound just like a hog. Ted continued to circulate the brochure but we probably should have reprinted the cover. Still, it was an honest mistake. There's no excusing the joker who claims that all those threshing machines you see along South Dakota highways are not really cheap billboard backstops, but actually serve as radar for detecting Canadian livestock being trucked southward without legal inspections.

Wait a minute, that's not a bad idea. And I'll bet the ag department would pay for it.

May/June 1995

MELLETTE COUNTY'S HORSE TRADER

Roger Hutchinson

THE AUCTIONEER chattered as the sorrel mare reluctantly trotted into the sale ring. A young lady neck-reined her in each direction. "I got forty fi, fifty, now fifty fi," the auctioneer chanted. Somebody bid $60, and the auctioneer was about to close when the owner stood up in the crowd. He was a cowboy named Frank Krogman, from White River, who knew every horse in Mellette County and owned most of them.

Frank said, "Boys, this is a family horse, and I can't let her go that cheap!"

"You say she's a family horse?" someone asked.

"She sure is," Frank replied, "she's definitely a family horse."

The bidding quickened. "Sixty dollars for the sorrel mare. I got sixty, now seventy, now seventy fi," barked the auctioneer.

"Eighty dollars," shouted one bidder.

"I got eighty, now eighty fi, now ninety dollars." The crowd quieted. "Going for ninety dollars, once, twice, sold for ninety dollars to the man with the good lookin' wife and kids."

The family, delighted at their bargain, took her home in their pickup, and turned her out in an acre of fenced pasture. The farmer couldn't wait to saddle her up the next day. However, he couldn't catch her to even get a halter on her. He called his wife to help and finally recruited the whole family. The mare wouldn't be caught. In anger the farmer sought out Frank Krogman and shouted, "I thought you said this was a family horse!"

Frank calmly replied, "She is. It takes the whole family to catch her."

Everything was quiet in Mellette County until the next horse sale. A roan, bob-tailed appaloosa gelding was ridden into the ring. It was spring and the horse looked rough with spots of long winter hair not yet shed. The rider's leg brushed against the gate as the horse entered the ring. The first steps into the sale ring seemed uncertain as though the roan gelding was unsure of whether or not to enter at all. It had been a tough winter, and he looked thin as though his winter diet had been thistles and cactus.

The horse appeared friendly enough as he brushed against the side of the ring several times, seeming to be eager to be near the crowd. The auctioneer got only scattered bids. The owner — you guessed it, Frank Krogman — shouted, "Boys, he's a good horse. He just don't look too good." With this assurance, the bids began.

"Sixty fi, seventy, I got seventy fi. Eighty, eighty fi. I got eighty fi. Going once, twice, sold for eighty fi' dollars."

When the rancher arrived home, he thought he would saddle and try the horse out to see how it rode. To his amazement, the bob-tailed roan appaloosa gelding walked square into the side of the barn with such a jolt that it nearly broke both of their necks. The farmer got off and waved his hand in front of the horse's eyes. The roan didn't blink. Needless to say the rancher went looking for Frank and said, "That damned horse you sold me is blind as a bat!"

"I know he is," Frank replied. "I told you he don't look too good!"

Sept / Oct 1995

SOLITUDE WITH PAULIE AND CHARLIE

Bernie Hunhoff

THOREAU SAID he would rather sit on a pumpkin and have it all to himself than be crowded on a velvet cushion. He is a man who would appreciate South Dakota's wide open spaces. One benefit of living apart from the crowd is realized on those rare occasions when we get involved in a foolish or embarrassing situation. Former South Dakota resident David Wagner, now a glass artist in Singapore (where he is elbow to elbow with people) made that point in a recent letter to a friend in Rapid City. Of course, his friend, having nothing better to do in January, forwarded a copy of the letter to us and now David will be embarrassed anyway.

In the letter, David told a true story of when he was a young man near Mitchell and often stopped to visit an old bachelor farmer named Paulie. The fellow was great at fixing machinery for his neighbors, but beyond that he was laid back in his farming methods. Nine of the old bachelor's cattle got lost in an early blizzard, wandered onto a big, frozen pond, and fell through. The next spring, David stopped by to get his roto-tiller fixed. Paulie and his brother, Charlie, were in the farmyard. Here is David's version of what happened.

"After drinking the obligatory beer from the trunk of the car — it was in the 80s and somehow they could drink this hot Schlitz all day — the wind happened to shift and a strong aroma was detected. I inquired about the enlarged brown floating mounds on the pond. Paulie, who was playing a sort of accordion, suggested shooting the bloated cow corpses so they would sink and end the stench. So it happened that we pushed off in a rotting little skiff with Paulie playing the accordion in back, myself rowing in the middle, and Charlie loading his .44 in the bow and singing in some Eastern European dialect. (Their parents were Czech immigrants.)

"Basically, the procedure would entail Charlie blasting the Angus balloons at close range while I, having positioned the vessel, would be bailing with a coffee can and the bachelor accompanying me on the squeezebox. The magical thing about this little hunt was its placement in the shade of a sunken forest and junkyard. The trees had been pretty thick around the pond years ago, and people naturally pulled their old farm equipment up next to a tree when they dropped it off. The pond had swelled up and engulfed most of this, so now we drifted through the tops of old combines and tractors, rusting and almost architectural in ambience under the shade of elms and cottonwoods.

"Only about half the cattle sank, and Charlie miraculously stayed on board, standing in the bow, until just before we landed, when I bumped a cultivator, awash near the old Buick which served as a dock, and he fell into about four feet of water."

Moments like those wouldn't be the same in a Singapore crowd.

Jan/Feb 1993

ROY'S STORIES

as told to Norma Wilson

ROY JOHNSON WAS born on Independence Day, 1922, and lived out most of his years on a farm near Westreville, just north of Vermillion. When Jerry and Norma Wilson built their home just across the road from the Johnson place in 1982 they became good friends with Roy, and fans of the stories he spun about days gone by.

KIRBY BOUGHT SOME bottom land from some Nebraska farmers across the river. He was trying to beat the accretion law. One day he walked into the law office of Olsen and Flynn and started shooting. He hit Olsen, but he missed Flynn. Well, he had some reason for being mad at them, but not enough to shoot them.

So it went to trial, and Kirby was sentenced to five years, He had to serve two before they paroled him. One afternoon I ran into Kreuger in Wakonda. He'd served on the jury that sentenced him, and I told him, "You folks were too hard on Kirby."

He answered, "Aw, we didn't sentence him to five years for shootin' Olsen. We figured he deserved it for missing Flynn."

Drinking was never Norman Johanson's problem. His problem was staying sober. He was always a bachelor — never had a wife. Well, back in the 50s I needed a hay baler one time and I heard another bachelor who lived over at Gayville had one, so I went over to see Johanson and asked him to go over there with me. So he did. And on the way we stopped at Merle Jensen's, another bachelor's place. Well, we went on to Gayville, and I got the hay baler, but I thought I was going to hear some wild stories. I could have got more enlightenment from the Ladies Aid Society. All those bachelors talked about was cooking.

When I got to their houses, Johanson was making apple pickles, Merle was making apple sauce and Vernon, the guy in Gayville, was making apple pies. He was complaining that he couldn't get the crust just right.

So Johanson said, "What kind of shortening do you use?"

And Vernon said, "Crisco." "Oh, you should use lard," Johanson said. Merle was sitting in the kitchen when we got there. He had dirty dishes all around him, all over the counter, and the sink was full. Johanson said, "Merle, why don't you wash dishes?"

Merle said, "Winter's the time for washing dishes." He'd bought a whole case of dishes. He showed it to us. I bet he had 500.

July/August 1989

TURKEYS CAN FLY, CAN'T THEY?

GETTYSBURG'S BUSINESS group heard about a successful promotion in which free turkeys were given away. As they understood the concept, a pilot was to fly over main street at an advertised time and his passengers would toss six live Easter turkeys out of the plane at about 3,000 feet or so. If you caught a turkey, you had your holiday dinner. However, when the birds were pushed from the plane they dropped like rocks. One hit the bank roof. Five splatted on the pavement. Nobody was hurt, but a lady was drenched in blood and fowl parts.

The well-intentioned businessmen contacted the town that had previously tried the stunt to see what went wrong. Ping pong balls were the answer. Whoever finds a ball gets a turkey. Turkeys don't fly that well, said the advisor. A local humorist, Terry Williams, later suggested that the Chamber of Commerce plan a ham give-away next time. After all, he said, hogs fly about as well as turkeys.

July/August 2000

SNOOSE JIMMY'S VICTORY

Chuck Cecil

SOMETIMES EVEN today, in the pool halls of Brookings, someone mentions Snoose Jimmy's name. Jimmy didn't like his nickname, but the pool room athletes who whiled away the summer after World War II pushing cue balls around in the saloon up the block from Nick's Hamburger Shop and the I-X-L Grocery liked him.

Snoose Jimmy made his daily rounds regular as a clock, walking from the house where he and his sister lived on Fifth Street to the I-X-L to make his small purchase, and with sack in hand, walked buoyantly down one side of Main and back up the other. He stopped at the pool hall until one day the teasing got so intense he unbagged his whole load of groceries — except the snoose can — on the taunting crowd. Jimmy marked the pool hall off his regular ports of call.

Jimmy was nearly 50, and he had imagined nearly all of his life that people were stealing things from his house. Maybe that's why he'd developed a powerful fascination for spectacular crimes — especially bank robberies. He read all he could about every one. He was the town historian when it came to bank robberies. His other great interest was Stradivarius violins. He didn't own one, couldn't play one, and never had seen one. But he loved Stradivarius violins and classical music. Not even music professors at the college knew more about the Stradivarius violin than Snoose.

One sluggish day the idea of giving Snoose Jimmy an experience he'd never forget was hatched among the beer flies at the pool hall. The manager of the bank, located where the Ram Pub now resides, thought the idea was harmless, and the police and sheriff approved, as long as Jimmy didn't get hurt. Jimmy arrived right on time at the I-X-L Grocery, then began his migration south on Main, visiting with all who would listen to his unending string of facts about bank robbers and Stradivarius violins. Three of the pool room boys were hiding behind the bank door in black, pinstripe suits with wide lapels. They wore masks and carried loaded cap pistols. One carried a violin case for an imaginary sub-machine gun.

Another sat at the wheel of the getaway car, purring by the curb. Across the street, by Kendall's Drug, was a fifth, waiting in a huge, 12-cylinder Lincoln Continental his old man had let him use, provided he pick up the dry cleaning. Just as Jimmy's feet touched the opposite curb, the boys in the bank dashed out, twirling around like robbers were supposed to do, checking all points for danger. They backed Jimmy against the bank's cool, sandstone wall. Jimmy stood motionless, eyes as big as his snoose can. The robbers jumped into the getaway car and headed south.

Within seconds, the Continental glided across the street from Kendall's and stopped near Jimmy. The driver yelled for him to get in and help trail the robbers. Jimmy pried himself off the wall, swallowed hard and climbed in. Off they went. Jimmy bounced in the passenger seat, holding onto the grocery sack and the door strap. Guns poked out of the robbers' car. Little puffs of smoke appeared from the chambers. But the feeble explosions of caps must have been what tipped the bank robbery expert off that something was fishy.

The pursuers lost the getaway car as planned, and the Continental headed back to the bank. A crowd of chuckling onlookers — now in on the joke — clapped and cheered as Jimmy emerged from the vehicle just as the getaway car rounded the corner. But something was wrong. There was blood on Snoose Jimmy's chest — lots of blood. His face reflected great pain. He staggered, reached for an imaginary hand of help, then pitched over onto the curb. He didn't move. And neither did the pool room athletes, now as white as tapioca pudding. Then somebody looked inside the Continental and saw the I-X-L grocery bag tipped over on the seat. On the floor mat was a half empty ketchup bottle.

Down on the sidewalk, Snoose Jimmy, bank robbery and Stradivarius expert, beamed. Finally, he'd won a round. A big round.

Jan/Feb 1999

BARBER SHOP HUMOR IN CLARK

Bernie Hunhoff

A DOZEN OR MORE gentlemen gathered in the back room of a Clark bakery for a New Year's eve cocktail. They were swapping stories at the expense of Roger Chapin, the silver-haired barber who has been cutting hair for 40 years. "We all had hair before you came to town," said one balding fellow — and with that, all the other follicly-challenged males lifted their caps and their drinks in unison.

Then another told the story of when he sat down for a haircut and was asked by Chapin, "How do you want it cut?"

"I told him I wanted it high on one side, short on the other and uneven across the back and front," said the jokester.

"Well, I can't do that," answered the barber.

"You did last time I was here!" said the jokester. Everybody laughed and lifted their drinks.

Not to be outdone, Chapin told a true story about an elderly customer who slumped over in the chair while getting a trim. "He hadn't looked in the mirror yet, so it couldn't have been the hair cut," he said.

Chapin didn't have a phone in the shop, so before he ran next door he tied the customer to the chair with a strap to keep him from falling forward. When he returned a minute or two later, the customer was awake and healthy and quite perplexed over why he was tied into the barber's chair in an empty shop.

"That took some explaining," Chapin said.

March/April 2000

TESTING TRUE LOVE IN FAITH

Irean Jordan

ONE OF THE MOST colorful characters of Faith was Jens Peterson, a.k.a. Rattlesnake Pete. He came from Nebraska with a carnival about 1909. He drove a race horse and chariot, and between acts ran a concession stand.

When he got to Faith he liked what he saw, and decided to stay. For years he lived in a sheep wagon, killed and skinned rattlesnakes to make belts and hat bands, stocked ponds and fished, and raised goats. Now and then Pete gave a kid goat to a neighbor kid for a pet. In the early thirties he brought a pair of baby goats to my friends Bernard and Eldora Thomas. As they grew, the goats lost popularity with Bernard and Eldora's mother, especially when they ate the garden and the flower bed. But in the middle of the Depression, children had few toys, and the goats brought some fun.

One afternoon I was playing with Bernard and Eldora when a shiny new car pulled up the wagon trail from the south. A tall young man got out, stepped back to admire his car, and hollered up to us, "You kids stay away from my new car, ya hear?" It was a gleaming brown Whippet coupe with a tan canvas top. The young man was Gene Baker, who worked at Gilbert Lee's garage in Faith. He'd come to take Bernard and Eldora's visiting Aunt Melissa to town for a dance.

When the sun set, I headed over the hill toward home, long before Gene and Melissa returned in the wee hours of the night. They got out of the car and went to the house, where Gene would spend the night. The commotion woke the two little goats, who slept in the yard. They apparently decided to inspect the new car. They leapt onto the running board and climbed the fenders to the hood, their hooves furrowing the shiny paint for traction. From there they hopped to the canvas top, where they romped and butted in a game of king on the mountain, their hooves poking holes in the canvas. Then they nibbled the fabric until they'd ripped a gash big enough to drop through to the shiny, patent leather seat. There they danced, pottied and chewed. But even fun can be tiring, so eventually they settled down to nap on the torn cushions.

Exactly what happened when Gene went out to his car early Sunday morning I know not, though Monday morning at school Eldora and Bernard told the terrible tale of the ruined Whippet. When, in the spring, Gene asked Melissa to marry him, she had no reason to doubt his love.

Nov / Dec 2002

LUTEFISK: NOT FIT FOR MAN NOR BEAST

WHEN IT COMES to food, here's a rule of thumb: If somebody says, "You have to acquire a taste for it," you know they're talking about something which tastes truly awful. That's what they say about the Norwegian delicacy lutefisk. And worse.

There once was a man, goes the story, who had problems with skunks taking up residence under his front porch. He called the county extension agent and asked him what to do about it. "Put some lutefisk under there," advised the agent, and so the man did. A week later he called the agent back.

"How is your skunk problem?" asked the agent.

"Great, they're all gone," said the man. "Now can you tell me how to get rid of all the Norwegians under my porch?"

Rev. LeeRoy Eikanger told that joke when he was pastor of the Bethel Lutheran Church in Lead. He liked lutefisk. And he wasn't alone. Bethel Lutheran annually kicks off the opening weekend of the Black Hills deer season with a lutefisk dinner, and they go through 800 pounds in an average year. But if you mention lutefisk to almost anyone who isn't a fan, the reactions range from laughter, to a wrinkling of the nose, to, "Yuuck! Soak fish in lye and then eat it!?!" Back in the old country, people used to preserve cod by drying it. When the time came to use the fish they would soak it in lye to soften it — hence the name lute (lye) fisk (fish). One local rancher, who attended the Bethel Lutheran supper every year to support the church, had a suggestion: "If you're going to soak something in lye, why don't you start out with something good. Like steak!"

Author and humorist Bob Karolevitz, who is more Polish than dill pickles or sausage, is another fan of lutefisk. His wife, Phyllis, on the other hand, who is of impeccable Norse ancestry, can't stand the stuff. Every Christmas Bob suggests they host a lutefisk and lefse party to mark the season. Every year he gets shot down.

"First of all," Phyllis fairly shouts, "I don't want my kitchen smelling like a fishwife's laundry room. Secondly, I think all that lye will melt your stomach just like it does that stinky fish." She has even gone so far as to accuse Bob of not really liking lutefisk. It's just a good excuse to eat lots of melted butter, she insists.

Even those who can't stand the thought of eating fish soaked in lye might be able to enjoy it using Red Stangland's recipe. Step 1: Get some lutefisk. 2: Get a pine board. 3: Lay lutefisk on the board. 4: Flatten lutefisk with a cleaver. 5: Sprinkle with pepper and salt. 6: Pour on melted butter. 7: Heat in stove for two hours. 8: Allow to cool down a bit. 9: Throw away lutefisk. 10: Eat the pine board.

Some have gone so far as to suggest that lutefisk should be made illegal, or at least regulated like other toxic, dangerous substances. But as a sign in the Hetland Post Office said: If you outlaw lutefisk, only outlaws will have lutefisk.

BADGER CLARK AND LIPS OF FIRE-ENGINE ENAMEL

Roger Holtzmann

WHEN AVIS OSLAND heard Badger Clark deliver a lecture at Sisseton High School in 1931, she was not impressed with the man, his words, or his title as poet laureate. "He was just another speaker, and like the other students, I was glad to have someone deviate us from the monotony of daily routine," she remembered, speaking for generations of teenagers. Four years later she found herself in English IV class, where her teacher tasked the students to write a poem and submit it to two state poets for their evaluation.

Avis sent along a paraphrase of Joyce Kilmer's "Trees" that she had written. Hers was entitled "Girls," an ironic commentary on makeup that ended with the lines: "Poems are made by fools like me, But only makeup maketh thee." Quite unexpectedly, she touched upon a notion dear to Badger's heart.

"Dear Avis," he wrote in reply. "Your paraphrase of "Trees" tickled me so that I am going to keep it and read it to sundry people of my acquaintance. You see, I'm hopelessly old-fashioned ... I hate sham in general, and get wolfish at the sight of anything that's imitation, for an imitation in the nature of it is bound to be shoddy and cheap. I always growl at the sight of girls — young and healthy girls who, if they applied mere soap and water to their faces would make them as fair as they could be — going about with their cheeks smeared with barn paint and their lips shining with fire-engine enamel. I have lived a bachelor life thus far and don't anticipate the slightest difficulty in maintaining that status to the end, for lo, temptation will not come nigh to me so long as the present fashions last. There seems to be more pretty girls to the square yard than ever before, but I walk among them with perfectly cold eyes. Their lips! Oh their lips! The fascination of them! The allurement of them, wooing me to wistful dreams! It would be exactly like pressing my lips tenderly to a newly painted gasoline pump!"

Just as he predicted, Badger Clark did indeed remain a bachelor all his days, though he wavered a time or two. He went so far as to give a ring to Miss Helen Fowler of Deadwood, but the match was opposed by her ambitious mother. The elder Mrs. Fowler didn't see Badger Hole — Clark's cabin home near Custer, which lacked electricity and indoor plumbing — quite as romantically as the poet did, apparently. Helen returned his ring by mail, and Badger may have thought better of his proposal as well. "The altar is a halter," he scribbled later, "a place where freedom ends."

Jan/Feb 1989

FEELING THE HEAT

THIS SUMMER'S SCORCHING heat elicited some of the craziest "How hot is it?" jokes we've heard in years. The best was about three Swedes who settled on the Great Plains — one in South Dakota, one in North Dakota and the third in Canada. Many years later, all three happened to die on the same day, so their families decided to cremate them together. The Canadian became ashes in an hour. The North Dakotan was reduced to ashes in two hours. After three days in the fire, the South Dakotan poked his head out and said, "You know, another week of this heat and we won't have much of a corn crop."

WHAT'D YOU GET OUT AT YOUR PLACE?

Roger Holtzmann

CONSTANT REFERENCES to a recession in the media finally spurred me to do my bit for the nation's economy: I bought a rain gauge. Actually, I didn't do it just to enable those good folks at the Chaney Instrument Company of Lake Geneva, Wisc., to hold on to their homes. I did it for me. I can now take part in the number one topic of conversation in South Dakota during the summer: rainfall totals.

It was quite a moment when I brought my Acu-Rite Gauge home and tacked it to a fence post near the garden. What a relief to know I could now speak with authority on this vital subject. Anybody can talk about the possibility of rain, or how much rain they got in the storm that "went by to the south of us," but to enter into real weather talk, you absolutely have to have a rain gauge. For the last few years, it seems, I've been living on the edge. Every time it rained I was condemned to the conversational sidelines for a couple of days. In South Dakota, if you aren't prepared to expound extensively about rainfall amounts, you might as well stay home and talk to your spouse.

"We got 46 hundredths," a friend would say. "What'd you get at your place?" Note the units of measurement used: Hundredths of an inch. You can build a grandfather clock and never need to use hundredths of an inch. But try to use "six-tenths of an inch" in a rainfall conversation and see what it'll get you.

"We got a pretty good shot," I'd say vaguely. "There were puddles in the fields."

I don't exactly know what "puddles in the fields" signifies. Since I've been using that line, which I overheard a long time ago, I have gotten several interpretations. One lady stated it means at least a half-inch. Another fellow said it indicated more than an inch. Yet another acquaintance insisted it doesn't mean anything other than it rained a lot, but I always suspected that man was hiding a weather ignorance as deep as my own.

During my time in exile, so to speak, I spent a good deal of time analyzing weather conversation since I couldn't be a part of it. What I have learned is very disturbing. Several years of dry weather have destroyed the common references. Our conversational standards are clearly eroding. In days past, less than a quarter-inch of rain would have been "just enough to settle the dust," or "a sprinkle." If the person were having a bad day, they might even have called it "hardly enough to bother with." Greater amounts were referred to by specific phrases, handed down from generation to generation. "A pretty good shot" was an inch of rain; "it rained like a son of a gun" was used from one to two inches; "water was running over the road" signified two to three inches of rainfall; and the venerable "gully washer" was used for everything above that.

Nowadays, a quarter-inch falls and people are calling it "a pretty good shot." Three-quarters of an inch comes down and people swear "there was water running over the road." More than an inch falls and people just go to pieces. Farmers start casually inquiring about the price of land that adjoins theirs, city dwellers wonder about flood insurance and everybody refers to it as a "pretty good gully washing son of a gun." Rainfall isn't the only area of weather conversation affected, either. Mild winters of late have left us adrift, conversation-wise: how can we complain about the weather if it's nice all the time? Forecasters have tried to lessen the climatic changes' impact by inventing Wind Chill Factor. When it's 20 degrees above they tell us it's 95 below or some such thing. But it's just not the same.

I'll worry about that season when it comes. In the meantime, I've got my rain gauge. If it ever rains again, I'll be ready.

May/June 1990

Notes from Jim River Country

Bob Karolevitz

"Once during my 20 years wandering, I actually pounded my fist on a table and shouted, 'Wild horses could never drag me back to South Dakota!'" wrote author/humorist Bob Karolevitz. "I call that my unenlightened period." Like the Prodigal Son, Karolevitz eventually returned, and has been telling South Dakota's stories ever since — from Where My Heart Is, *his award-winning biography of Harvey Dunn, to his downright goofy observations of everyday life in* Tears in My Horseradish. *He was an early contributor to* South Dakota Magazine, *and following are some excerpts from his jottings.*

I WAS TWELVE when I dug the worms and was picked up at the Deep Rock gas station by a young man in a white 1934 Ford V-8 with balloon tires. Gaudily painted on the side of the car were the words, 'Lawrence Welk's Honolulu Fruit Gum Orchestra.' Away we went — America's soon-to-be favorite accordionist and I — off to the Jim River to see what we could catch. I don't rightly recall if we hooked anything, but I do know that I ended up with plenty of free samples of Honolulu Fruit Gum which, incidentally, tasted like Juicy Fruit for about 15 seconds and then like the back of an old school tablet.

———

Among the things I'm not very good at is checking the anti-freeze in the tractor and pickup. The bouncing beads in the gauge don't tell me much, and the only time I really knew for sure that I didn't have enough Prestone in a particular vehicle was when the engine block cracked. That, of course, is not a practical system of measurement.

———

Farmers concentrate too much on raising corn and soybeans, in my opinion. I think they should diversify into the dandelion business. Without half trying, I've got a lawn that would produce five tons to the acre, and I didn't even have to cultivate. Dandelion leaves can be made into salads, or cooked like spinach, and they supply more than twice as much Vitamin A as Popeye's delight. I read where the seeds are edible, too, but it takes a couple weeks to pick enough for a good meal. There's always dandelion wine, and the Russians apparently figured out how to make rubber out of the roots during World War II. Those ubiquitous yellow flowers have to be good for something. Eighty million bees can't be wrong. William Allen White was right when he wrote: "Sin and dandelions are very much alike. To get rid of them is a lifetime fight, and you never quite win it."

We may have to quit farming here in Jim River Country. No, it's not because of economic conditions. We're almost out of used baling wire, that's why! Now that they're putting up hay in big round bales tied with plastic twine, the once plentiful strands of baling wire are going the way of the whiffletree and the whip socket at our place. A farmer can get by without fancy tools, a new tractor or even a pickup topper, but take away his all purpose fix-it wire and you've crippled his operation. When it's gone, how will we shut gates, repair fences, string up morning glories, reinforce trailer hitches, bundle old magazines, tie down tarps, replace broken chain links, make bucket handles, mend screen doors, etc. etc.? Like so many other good things — fire, water, sunshine, castor oil — baling wire has a few drawbacks. It gets lost in high grass easily. However, it is also easy to find — wrapped around the shaft of your power mower. I suppose if worse came to worst, I could buy a new roll of the stuff. On the other hand, it doesn't seem quite right to use NEW baling wire for fixin'. As the song goes, baling wire, like love, is lovelier the second time around.

THE REAL REASON BULLS LIKE TO FIGHT

Newt Hicks

THERE'S AN OLD story about a rancher who had a Hereford bull, a Shorthorn bull and a little Angus bull. The bulls heard through the grapevine that the rancher had gone to town to buy a new Charolais bull. The Hereford bull said, "I'm the boss bull and the new guy isn't getting any of my 50 cows." The Shorthorn bull said, "I'm number two bull around here and the new guy isn't getting any of my 35 cows." The little Angus bull didn't say anything.

About that time, the rancher pulled into the yard with the stock trailer. The Charolais bull filled the entire trailer. It was rocking and swaying, and the white bull was snorting and stomping and bellowing. The Hereford bull took one look at the Charolais and said, "I could probably give him 10 cows." The Shorthorn bull said, "I can probably give him 10 of my cows." However, the little Angus bull ran up on the dam grade and started snorting and bellowing and pawing dirt.

"What are you doing?" asked the big Hereford.

"I just want that guy to know I'm a bull!" replied the Angus.

March/April 2002

ON THE DIFFICULTY OF RETIRING RED CLOUD

Roger Holtzmann

APPOINTED TO THE newly-established Pine Ridge Agency in 1879, Valentine T. McGillycuddy was an exception to the rule of Indian agents in that he was basically honest. Unfortunately, he and Red Cloud were like oil and water. Red Cloud was "a disagreeable, arrogant old man," according to McGillycuddy; for his part, Red Cloud considered the 30-year-old agent, "little more than an obnoxious boy."

Many years after the fact, McGillycuddy gave an account of how he was compelled to assemble all the Oglala and confront the disruptive chief. "Red Cloud and his two hundred young men came dashing over the hill in their flaming war gear whooping like demons and firing their revolvers," wrote Doane Robinson in his retelling of the story. "Down they came to the council place, rode three times around it and, in their most insolent way, slumped down in the circle." Unfazed by this bravado, McGillycuddy boldly approached him. "'Because you have defied your agent and insulted the Great Father, I now break you of your chieftanship. You are no longer chief of the Oglala. Red Cloud, to your teepee.' Red Cloud turned and slunk out, with the contemptuous eyes of all of his people upon him. His influence was broken and gone forever."

McGillycuddy must have enjoyed his moment of triumph. So much so that he broke Red Cloud on a regular basis thereafter. McGillycuddy's monthly reports almost invariably told of how he had defanged the old Oglala, followed by complaints that Red Cloud was interfering with his plans. "To be eternally harassed by this old man is getting to be monotonous," he wrote three years after Red Cloud had been broken forever.

Jan/Feb 2000

SETH BULLOCK'S HAPPY HOUR

Adapted from Wit and Humor in Business (1904)

ONE OF DEADWOOD'S fanciest hotels bears the name of Seth Bullock, an early-day horse trader and town marshal, but Bullock couldn't have afforded to stay in such a place back when he was a young placer gold miner in the 1860s. In those days it took a bit of doing, in fact, just to get himself a drink. Entering a saloon in Helena, Montana Territory, one afternoon, Bullock told the bartender, "George, I'll tell you what let's do. If you will furnish the sherry, I'll furnish the fresh eggs and we'll mix up a drink that is out of sight."

Liquor wasn't cheap, but eggs were $2 a dozen, so the bartender thought that sounded like a bargain. Seth went to the grocer across the street and said, "Willard, if you'll furnish the eggs, I'll provide the sherry and we'll have something worthwhile in the line of fancy drinks." The grocer agreed, and the two went to the saloon, eggs in hand.

The concoction was duly prepared, and the three began to absorb it. Seth had already swallowed his share when an idea struck the bartender. "Say," he demanded of Seth, "Willard provided the eggs, and I provided the liquor. Where do you come in on this deal?"

"Oh," Bullock replied, "I'm the promoter."

May / June 2002

THE CRY WOLF ACT

Roger Holtzmann

NO MATTER WHAT issue comes up in South Dakota, sooner or later someone is bound to say that it is (a) nothing more than an insidious attempt to enact an in**me t*x, (b) will inevitably result in an in**me t*x, or (c) is the moral equivalent of an in**me t*x. It doesn't matter if it's a question of what color to paint the stripes on the road, somebody will swear this is so. And we all know what that means. In South Dakota, accusing someone of favoring an in**me t*x is tantamount to calling them a crack-dealing, neo-Nazi child pornographer. This must stop. If we continue to indiscriminately use this Big Bertha of insults it will lose all impact. We need to enact a law that would prohibit using the term "in**me t*x" in public discourse unless the subject under discussion is a bona fide, hand-in-your-wallet inco … well, you know what I mean.

Jan / Feb 2001

How Long Does a Pig Live?

MOST PIGS ONLY live a few months before being becoming bacon or pork chops. But when hog prices plummeted in 1999, farmers began to wonder how long a pig might live before it had to be slaughtered. Could they live long enough to ride out the price debacle? A veterinarian, speaking at a hog farmers' rally at the Sioux Falls Stockyards, says he was asked that question by a producer. "I told him that I know of some hogs that have now lived for 27 years," said the vet. "I vaccinated them as baby pigs, and the farmer said he'd pay me when he sold them. That was 27 years ago!"

March/April 1999

Literate Deer At Risk

MARK HAGEN, A Sioux Falls area journalist, wrote about a lady who called her township board to request that the "Deer Crossing" sign be removed from her road. Her reasoning? Too many deer were crossing at that point and being hit by cars, so she no longer wanted them to cross there.

May/June 1999

When Wetonka Made Letterman

SOME FOLKS LONG for stardom while others have it thrust upon them. The ten residents of Wetonka, S.D., fit in the latter category. When David Letterman's late show producers looked for a town to feature in a "Top Ten Reasons For Living In A Small Town" segment, they settled on Wetonka, population 10. Each Wetonkian read one of the reasons, for which they received $321, a Letterman t-shirt and their cue cards as souvenirs.

Among the reasons:

- If you get a busy signal you can just yell out the window, "Get off your damn phone."
- It takes Domino's seven hours to get here so the pizza is always free.
- If your wife gets flowers from a guy named Roger you have a pretty good idea who he is.
- You can open a burger stand and your slogan can be Best Burgers In Town even if they are really bad.

'NO SALE' MEANS MORE FUN

THERE'S THE TALE of an old rancher whose wife kept him on a short leash. He seldom got to socialize with the boys. When a horse auction was scheduled in the nearby town, his wife suggested that they take the opportunity to sell their extra horses. The old rancher quickly agreed. He called a neighbor, who had a trailer, and they loaded three horses and headed for town. When they arrived at the auction barn, they were told that it would be late in the evening before the horses would be sold.

Not disappointed in the least, they drove downtown and proceeded to play cards and enjoy all the merriments of the local tavern. Several happy hours later, they returned to the auction barn barely in time to watch the three horses come up for sale. The first horse sold for $500. The second sold for almost $600. The final bid on the last horse was $710, but the old rancher jumped to his feet and hollered, "No sale, no sale!"

"What are you doing?" asked his neighbor. "It brought more than the first two!"

"I know," said the old fellow. "But if I sell them all I won't have any excuse to come back next month!"

July / August 1999

THE MOONSHINER AND THE RIGHT OF SELF-INCRIMINATION

A MAN WAS hauled into a South Dakota court for illegally making whiskey during prohibition in the 1920s. The judge asked him, "What's your name?"

"Joshua," he replied.

"Well, Joshua," said the judge, "did you make the walls come tumbling down?"

"No," replied Joshua. "I made the moon shine."

BANKERS AND THE LETTER OF THE LAW

Bernie Hunhoff

BANKERS GET RIBBED for the hours they work, but the late Alfred Anderson, a banker at Okaton during the Dirty Thirties, didn't even take time off for the President of the United States. Anderson was running the bank when Franklin Delano Roosevelt declared the Bank Holiday in 1933 in order to give financial institutions time to regroup and stay open.

Anderson, a conservative financier, was not in danger of insolvency. "No #@*!@*# Democrat is going to tell me what to do!" he reportedly commented.

Still, he felt an obligation to obey the law. So he hung a sign on the front door: "Closed By Law, Come Around Back."

Horizontal Painter

A WELL-LIKED ALCOHOLIC who frequented the bars of downtown Yankton was notorious for evading work when it was offered by good-intentioned friends. He was enjoying an afternoon at the historic Walnut Bar when the phone rang. The station manager at WNAX Radio was calling to ask if anyone there wanted a job painting the 927-foot tower east of town. "Hey," the bartender teased the alcoholic, "You want a job painting the WNAX tower tomorrow?"

"You bet!" answered the inebriated fellow. "Tell 'em to lay 'er flat on the ground and I'll be there first thing in the morning."

What to do when the Governor Stops by

TOM BERRY, South Dakota's "Cowboy Governor" from 1933-37, once visited a farm where a large group of men were gathered for threshing. Perhaps he knew lunch was about to be served, or maybe he was campaigning. Or both. In any case, he was invited to sit down. The farmer's wife was very pleased to have such a distinguished guest of honor, and she tried to keep the conversation lively. She also worried what might happen after dessert, when the men generally took a nap on the porch. Surely, she thought, they wouldn't do anything so rude and embarrassing on this special day.

The men, of course, weren't burdened with such a strong sense of propriety. Once dessert was over they retired to the porch, and soon were snoring. Berry sensed the dismay of the missus, and assured her there was no reason to apologize — then he took off his cowboy hat and got down on the floor for a nap along with the threshers.

RULES OF THE ROAD

RULES POSTED IN the Dakota Stage Line coaches that once served Yankton: Abstinence from alcohol is requested, but if you must drink, share the bottle. Buffalo robes are provided for your comfort during cold weather. Hogging robes will not be tolerated and the offender will be made to ride outside with the driver. In the event of runaway horses, remain calm. Leaping from the coach in panic could leave you injured, at the mercy of the elements, hostile Indians, or hungry coyotes. Forbidden topics of discussion are: Stagecoach robberies and Indian uprisings.

HOW YOU CAN TELL YOU'RE IN A SMALL TOWN

Roger Holtzmann

BACK WHEN Charles Kuralt was on the road, he'd roll into a different small town every show and find that everything there was really profound. But by South Dakota's standards, his definition of a small town was way off. He would call a community of 5,000 a small town — even though people here would call that "pretty good-sized." For Charles' sake, here are three ways to know if you're in a real small town: a neighbor stops by to chat, you have banana bread and coffee, and it gets written up in the newspaper; the café has self-serve coffee, and customers feel free to make a new pot when the cook is busy; the street department and water department are the same guy.

HOW TO ESCAPE JURY DUTY

Paul Higbee

I WAS SERVING on jury duty in Rapid City when a lawyer questioned another prospective juror during the selection process. "I see on the pretrial questionnaire you completed that you list rattlesnake milking as a hobby," began the lawyer. "Yes, sir," answered the prospect.

"I assume 'milking' means extracting venom from the fangs."

"Yes, sir."

"Are there any uses for this venom?"

"No, sir. I just like catching rattlesnakes and milking them." The lawyer glanced at his client, and the snake milker was home before the rest of us had our coats off.

I WAS A CAR THIEF

Helen Kohler Noyes

MY DAD CLOSED his candy store in 1927 and started a car business in Madison. I was studying bookkeeping in high school, so Dad said he could use me at the agency. I was able to "borrow" a car for running errands around town. I seldom drove the same car two days in a row, and sometimes I would come out of school and not be able to remember which car I had been driving.

Once, Dad told us he would leave a car for my mother, sister and me on the street in front of our apartment so we could go to our Lake Madison cottage for spring cleanup. We loaded our supplies into a gray Willys-Knight, picked up my girlfriend and left for the lake.

Dad arrived late in the afternoon, took one look at the Willys and asked, "Where'd you get that car?" We decided we'd better return it at once. My girlfriend and I started for Madison and hadn't gone a mile before we spied the chief of police coming toward us. We knew what he was after so we pulled to the side of the road.

The chief pulled over to the other side. With him was an irate farmer who screamed at me. They had been all over town looking for the Willys. Luckily the chief recognized me and I was able to explain how it happened. With no more questions, he took us back to the cottage.

Doing Business

IN "NEW YORK, NEW YORK," Frank Sinatra sang "If I can make it there, I'll make it annywheeerre...," I always thought it was a catchy tune with a faulty premise. Surrounded by millions of people and all that money, who couldn't make it in New York? The real challenge is making a living in a place like South Dakota. Twenty years of exploring the state with South Dakota Magazine *and learning about the way our people survive financially, has left me convinced that songs should be sung about the acumen of our people.*

We aren't songwriters, but we've written many stories about the business of work. We are not going to declare that South Dakotans are smarter than people in other states. But working here — whether on the land or in a store, factory or office — has its differences. We don't have a long tradition of business and industry. We have few large corporations. We have vast rural spaces where customers are few and far apart. Other than the Black Hills, glacial lakes and river valleys, we don't have natural features that attract throngs of visitors.

Despite these obstacles, our economy continues to grow. Our cumulative brilliance may be part of the reason, but as you read our business stories, you'll likely spot other good qualities — like tenacity, sheer luck, love of the work itself, eagerness to provide a service, and a determination to stay in South Dakota.

Now those are things worth singing about. Here are excerpts from a few of our favorite stories on the business side of South Dakota. You'll have to provide the melody.

— Bernie Hunhoff

A Cattleman's Homecoming

Col. Jon Phillips

TO THE UNINITIATED, it's a scene every bit as mysterious, as seemingly chaotic, as the trading floor of the New York Stock Exchange: sale barns, where buyers and sellers of cattle meet to do business, sharing a culture and speaking a language all their own. I spent the first 20 years of my adult life among such characters, crying cattle auctions in South Dakota and Nebraska. Before that I chauffered my grandfather, Skinny Pfeil, a cattle buyer, from sale to sale over that same circuit. I drove the car while Skinny and his old pal Nils Callison sat in the back seat, barking out orders of where to drive, which market report to turn to on the radio and, "slow the damn thing down!" While most old men were playing shuffleboard and card games, those two tough old geezers were on the road every day, buying cattle and consuming everything Carl Tucker Foreman said would kill them, including strong cigars. They never did quit that schedule, and died one night in a car-train accident while coming home from a cattle auction. Skinny was 74 and Nils was 76 when they hit that train. The night they died, both of them had bought a lot of cattle. I'm glad they went out of this world with steaks under their belts and cattle on their trucks. That's the way they would have liked it.

Long after I'd hung up my auctioneer's microphone and turned to broadcasting and trading commodities for a living, I found myself on Interstate 90, heading west, when I saw the exit sign for Presho. My first thought was, "It's Saturday, and the cattle sale is going on right now!" My car was like a horse getting close to the barn. All I could do was drop the reins, give it its head, and it took me right to the sale barn. Drawn inside by the auctioneer's tuneless, relentless song, I found the uniform of the day just as I remembered it. Faded shirts, shop-worn blue jeans and overalls, and boots that hadn't seen shine since the store. They wore brown or tan hats with sweat stains around the band — if the band hadn't been torn off — and big wide brims shaped to suit the cowboy. The older ranchers with crows' feet at the end of sun-beaten, squinty eyes, weather-worn faces and tough gnarled hands rolled their own cigarettes and pulled the strings on the tobacco pouch with their teeth. Down in the front sat men with newer hats and shirts, pressed pants and polished boots. Their pockets bulged with buyers' cards and pencils, while their hands held pocket calculators or telephones. These men were the order buyers, cow buyers and traders. They were the objects of everyone's attention because the movement of a finger or wink of an eye made the difference between a good year and a bad year.

Down in the box, beside the auctioneer, stood Delmer Vollmer, his strong chin set hard, ready for action, his hands pointing for bids, and his voice demanding attention every time he shouted a command to the ring man or extolled the crowd to bid a little higher. Then he hollered, "Doggone it, Charlie, tell 'em about those high-priced bulls you bought last year. Remember, fellows, Charlie's been raising these fancy cattle for 45 years."

A bandy-legged little rancher stood up and, in a nervous voice, said, "Well, Delmer, you know they've had the seven-way shot, too," and then went into the rest of his spiel. Everybody answers to Delmer. He runs the show, has the first word and the last. Most of the big sales have strong men like Delmer, who run the auction with an iron, honest hand.

May / June 1985

THE DAY DOC MILBURN DECIDED TO STAY

Cathleen Curry

WHEN SIDNEY MILBURN graduated from veterinary school and moved to Elk Point in 1957, folks wondered if he'd last long. Would a black man be able to earn a living in an all-white farm community? Doc must have wondered himself whether he'd made the right move. Would he be accepted? Would anyone patronize his clinic? What would life be like for his wife, Corinne, and their children, Sidney Jr., and Deb? Union County had been homesteaded by European immigrants nearly a century ago — and sometimes the Norwegians and Swedes and Germans and Irish didn't get along so well. How would they take to the community's first black family?

The answer to all those questions came long ago. But for anyone who wasn't paying attention, it was made clear when Doc Milburn died, and the Norwegians and others filled the Catholic church on Elk Point's main street to say their goodbyes. Stories were told and retold, and one of the most telling concerned a dairy farmer who called Doc to his place to treat a sick cow shortly after the Milburns had moved to town — the very time when they were surely wondering if they had been smart to start a new life in a northern farming town. After working all night, the cow died. Doc reached in his billfold for a $20 bill and he gave it to the farmer.

"What's that for?" asked the bewildered farmer.

Doc explained that where he came from, when a black veterinarian lost an animal, he was required to reimburse the white owner.

"Get the hell out of here!" was the dairyman's shocked reply. He refused the $20 and insisted on paying Doc for his all-night vigil.

"That," said Doc Milburn many years later, "is when I knew I was going to stay."

May/June 1995

MIDLAND: HOT WATER AND A HOTEL

Bernie Hunhoff

JACK STROPPEL had pneumonia as a child. He found relief by soaking in hot baths at Capa. Convinced of the warm geothermal water's healing properties, he purchased the Bastion Roadhouse Hotel in Midland, and then drilled 1,784 feet until he found a free flowing well of the hot mineral water. He built a hotel addition to provide three dressing rooms and three baths of the 119 degree water.

The elder Mr. Stroppel found an enthusiastic clientele. In the 1940s, several thousand people came to the hotel to soak in the baths. His son, George, bought the family business in 1972. One of his first customers asked if he gave back rubs. He had taken a course in massage several years earlier, so he said, "I guess I could maul you around a little."

George had big plans. "When I first came here, I wanted to make a real nice spa out of the place, but I never did have the money to carry it through," he said. When Interstate 90 was built, it missed Midland by 13 miles and business was never the same; or, you could say, it stayed about the same. Nestled in the Bad River valley, the peacefulness of Midland is nearly as restful as a soak in the baths. Small white houses and old brick storefronts, most of them dilapidated, blend with brown hills that surround the town.

"We've had them come in here that couldn't walk," Stroppel said. "They've come on crutches, in wheelchairs — one on an ironing board — and I believe they've all had relief. This isn't a cure, but it provides relief from the pain and suffering."

Guests' ailments often include backaches, rheumatism, arthritis and kidney troubles. A combination of soaking in the hot mineral baths, blanket sweats and massage seems to help many of the guests.

"It makes me more mobile," said long-time client Rena Nemec, who suffered from multiple sclerosis for many years. "For me, it's temporary but it does give me some relief." Others seemed to find more permanent help. George Woods of Waupaca, Wisc., was "walking like a robot" when he first came 10 years ago. He stayed for a full 21-day treatment, and walked out with ease. He sent a letter several years ago that George keeps in a file cabinet:

"I came to the Stroppel Hotel at Midland, South Dakota, stiff and aching with arthritis. After a course of hot mineral baths, sweats and massage treatments, my joints are freed and I can move in comfort. My wife also enjoyed and benefited from the baths and massages."

March / April 1987

Sioux Falls: Like a Wealthy Uncle

Bernie Hunhoff and Jerry Wilson

DESPITE ITS SIZE, Sioux Falls doesn't dominate South Dakota like a pushy big brother. The city gains charm with every passing year, and part of its allure is the fact that it hasn't turned out to be a bully or braggart. Sioux Falls is not only the largest city in the state, but it is also the biggest place in the northern tier of states between Minneapolis and the West Coast. That size and momentum would be fodder for hard feelings in most regions of the country.

This city has largely avoided such troubles because, at least thus far in history, it hasn't pushed its weight around in the state or region. Like a wealthy uncle, it's just nice to have around. Sioux Falls doesn't overwhelm the state politically. Usually its citizenry votes much the same as their rural neighbors. Sioux Falls lawmakers are gaining numbers in the state capital due to the city's growing population, but they haven't been very successful at getting their way in the few instances when they've tried to band together.

The city also isn't the state's center for education. Culturally, the city isn't the epicenter of prairie life, either. It has too much concrete, too many lights, too much neon. South Dakota's culture is rooted in the bawdy Black Hills, the displaced Lakota and Dakota Indians, the struggling farmer and rancher, and the dwindling small towns. We write poems and songs about adversity and hard times. Sioux Falls doesn't seem to inspire those popular South Dakota themes. Economically, Sioux Falls is crucial to South Dakota. It has become the city of opportunity for thousands of young people who couldn't find a decent job in the small towns where they were born and raised. Their parents are glad their children didn't have to go farther from home to be successful. But again, Sioux Falls doesn't rule the state. We don't all cash checks at branches of Sioux Falls banks. We don't all eat at restaurants created and based in Sioux Falls. From a business standpoint, the city is important but not all-powerful.

Sioux Falls has a colorful history, but it lacks the characters that forever link places like Yankton and Deadwood and Pierre with the Old West. Sioux Falls didn't build its reputation on shootings and hangings, cattle and poker. In the early years, its leaders just tended to business and grew a city on the prairie.

So what does Sioux Falls mean today to the vast region that surrounds it? If it isn't our big brother in history, politics, media, culture, or business, what's left? Entertainment is the answer. Sioux Falls is best at entertaining both the locals and outsiders, and it gets better with every passing year. Just like the wealthy, kindly uncle who always has a good story, movie tickets or ice cream money, Sioux Falls knows how to make you feel good. It seems to have found its niche as the entertainment capital of a vast and hungry prairie.

Sept/Oct 1999

OSCAR AUSTAD'S SALES SECRETS

Bernie Hunhoff

MANY NORWEGIANS in South Dakota work too hard, shun alcohol and tobacco, shy away from golf courses, vote Republican and make lots of money. If they ever get under one roof and form an association, it is likely to be called the Oscar Austad Society. Nobody exemplifies their values like the mail order millionaire from Sioux Falls who started by selling cardboard golf club tubes from his car trunk.

Oscar Austad's early background seemed ideally suited for business mediocrity. His father wanted him to follow in his footsteps as a North Dakota carpenter. Oscar considered a law degree but quit college after three years. He was fired twice from the insurance business. He had the unpopular habit of advising superiors on how to run their firms. He disliked salesmanship, avoided social occasions where alcohol was served and couldn't resist telling prospects where to find the best deal, even if it wasn't from his company. Just the kind of guy you want to do business with if you're buying golf equipment by mail, apparently, because 770,000 people placed orders with the Austad Company in 1990, and total sales exceeded $50 million.

Austad once candidly told a writer that his weaknesses might have also been his strengths. "I had been a failure at a lot of things and I had five children to support (when he was fired again in 1963 as an insurance adjuster in Sioux Falls). But I had no antagonism ... it merely spurred me on. Anytime I got fired or had a bad break, it became a good break because it made me buckle down like nothing else."

While selling golf equipment for a brother-in-law, he got the idea of sending postcards to Minnesota bankers. When they bought, he added a few more products and mimeographed a flyer. Gradually he developed one of the hottest mailing lists in the sports world. In the early days of the business, his workers discouraged him from answering the phone because he couldn't shake that habit of recommending competitors when he thought they had the better product. "I never was much of a salesman," he claimed.

He can say it. But he isn't fooling many people today. The quiet Norwegian might be one of the smoothest salesmen of our times.

March/April 1991

Porcupine Quillworker

Alice New Holy, Lakota artist from Oglala

INDIANS BELIEVE that quill and beadwork is women's work. It was something I had to learn. All Indian girls had to learn quillwork, as well as taking care of the house and cooking. My grandmother cut out little moccasins for me to do beadwork, and I did little quillwork bracelets. It teaches you how to sit still and do something. Quillwork is the second oldest Lakota art form. Using earth paints is the oldest. The hardest part is taking the quills off the porcupine.

July/August 1991

Saloon No. 10 — Shooting (Film) Allowed

SALOON NO. 10 in Deadwood may be the only bar in South Dakota where you can shoot a camera flash and not cause a stir. It's a neighborhood establishment — locals call it the Old Style — but it's also the replicated site of the dastardly murder of Wild Bill Hickok by Jack McCall in 1876. People here are accustomed to tourists snapping pictures while they sip their taps.

May/June 1988

REDFIELD: PHEASANT CAPITAL

REDFIELD LEADERS crowned themselves the Pheasant Capital of the World soon after Spink County farmland became the first successful foothold for the hardy ring-necked import from China. That was in 1908, when three Redfield men released birds on a farm north of town along the James River. Other releases had been made in South Dakota, beginning with a stocking program by a Sturgis man in 1891. None of those lasted. However, the pheasant flourished in the thick brush of the James River valley. In 1919, state game authorities announced that there were ample birds in Spink County for a one-day season. It was set for Oct. 30. The momentous day was doused by cold and inclement weather and wardens estimated that less than 200 birds were bagged in a rather inauspicious start for what would become South Dakota's top outdoor sport.

Nov / Dec 1987

SCENIC: WHERE CHARACTERS HAVE A TOWN

Bernie Hunhoff

"EVERY TOWN HAS its characters, but in Scenic the characters had a town," wrote Philip Hall in the book *Reflections of the Badlands*. Traders, trappers, homesteaders, drunken monkeys, saloon-keepers, missionaries, rodeo champions, bikers, gamblers and other interesting sorts have called Scenic home.

The town site below Sheep Mountain has long been a "last stop" for travelers arriving in the Black Hills. Scenic's very first businessman, according to Hall, was bad-luck rancher Ab Jefferson. When a May blizzard pushed all of Ab's cattle over the edge of Sheep Mountain, he decided to open a saloon. Ab drank too much of his own merchandise, and sold some of the rest to his Indian neighbors. Selling alcohol to Indians was then a federal crime, so Jefferson ended up in jail.

All the flat land on the outskirts of the Badlands was claimed by the time Mary Hynes and her eleven children arrived. She was told that the only land not homesteaded was an inaccessible spot atop Sheep Mountain, so Mary and her boys clawed their way up the mountain, and were delighted with the view and the rich, flat grasslands. She brought her 20 cows up, staked a claim, built a sod house and made a life for herself.

Mary Avenell of Yankton, the granddaughter of Hynes, said growing up in Scenic in the 1950s meant living shoulder-to-shoulder with some of the most colorful people in North America. Mary's dad, "Happy" Hynes, ran a bar that competed with the Longhorn. Once, her dad bought "black market" meat and he felt guilty about it — maybe because he learned that officials from Rapid City were planning to investigate. "Hap," a non-Catholic, went to the parish priest to confess and ease his conscience. Meanwhile, her mother cooked and served all the evidence before the sheriff arrived.

Scenic is a company town these days, owned lock, stock and longhorn by a single corporation and run by a petite, pony-tailed woman who came to this windswept place against her will in 1963. Twila Merrill was riding rodeo stock, not barrels and poles that are usually the domain of the womenfolk, but the real thing: bucking broncs. She was mending from injuries in Omaha when her father, a longtime Pine Ridge Reservation trader and rancher, telephoned to say there was an emergency. Twila drove all night to get back to Pine Ridge, fearing someone had been hurt in an accident. "When I got home, Dad told me Bud (my brother) was going to show me a bar and a house in Scenic that I was supposed to buy," recalled Twila.

Knowing her dad's determined ways, she reluctantly agreed to take a ride. "There wasn't even a road all the way between Pine Ridge and Scenic then. We drove through Cottonwood Creek and mud was flying everywhere," she said. "The bar was a one-room affair with a nickelodeon. I didn't even look at the house. Tumbleweeds were blowing down the street and Scenic was the last place in the world that I wanted to live." She and Bud returned to their dad's Pine Ridge ranch, where a big argument ensued. She lost the argument but gained a town. Her family's corporation now owns all but one home in town. They also don't own the Congregational church, the school or the fire department. But they do own the land where the rented post office is located. And they own the Catholic Church, built in 1913 and now abandoned. Twila is considering a renovation project that would include "Michelangelo-style murals" in the interior. But the town's landmark — to some its very soul — is the Longhorn Saloon, little-changed since the 1960s when Twila's father persuaded her to come to Scenic. The front is lined with rows of skulls from longhorn cattle. Brands from area ranches are painted on the ceiling. Sawdust covers the floor. Oil barrels with metal tractor seats serve as sturdy bar stools. Twila has tried not to change the aura of the place. However, she did have the sign changed. It once read "No Indians Allowed."

She painted over the word "No."

March / April 1999

WHEAT DREAMS IN CLARK COUNTY

Marian Cramer

TELLING MOST BOYS they can't do something motivates them to go out and prove they can. That's how it was with 15 year-old Conrad Wertz back in 1934.

"I'll bet I can make a grain-puffing machine," Conrad told his friend, Edmund Rusche.

Edmund smiled. "I don't think you can."

When his dad got up at six the next day, Conrad was already at work. He and his brother, Miles, gathered scrap iron, tin, a pressure gauge and prestolite flues from a steam engine, some tubing and a couple of old gas burners. Soon they had a working model. In the winter of 1935 they set up shop in an empty building in Bancroft and began popping a pint of cleaned Durham wheat at a time.

"The owners kicked us out," Miles said later. "They were sure we were going to burn the place down." By then the boys' father could see that Conrad's machine had possibilities, but they needed bigger equipment. Before the summer of 1936 came around the brothers had built a new gun and installed it in an empty store in Melham. Conrad used a six-inch acetylene tank for the gun barrel, with an off-set bolt as a trigger. When the time came, Miles turned the bolt with a crescent wrench, releasing the gate that let the puffed wheat fly.

"When the thing went off, the recoil was terrible," Miles said. To contain the steam they sealed the contraption with babbitt and lead. Once in a while a chunk of lead flaked off — which might not meet FDA standards these days. Their new gun held five quarts of wheat, to which they added a quart of water, a tablespoon of salt and a half-cup of vegetable oil, applied with a fly sprayer. The wheat exploded into a screened cage four feet square and 40 feet long, then was sifted to remove old maids and chaff and dumped into a 100-gallon oil drum with a funnel shaped bottom that they used to fill individual sacks. A batch made 24 six-ounce bags of cereal, which the brothers sold in Melham for 12 cents each. With the drought years of the Dirty Thirties at their worst, making a living on the farm was an iffy proposition at best; at times it must have seemed like it was never going to rain again. Every bag sold helped.

The Wertz brothers were pioneers, not only in engineering but in processing and marketing grain. Even so, when it finally rained, they quit the cereal business and went back to farming. Anyone who ever loved the soil knows why. Sixty years later, South Dakota farmers still export most of their wheat to other states to be milled or puffed and packaged for sale by Kelloggs and Quaker. They still earn pennies on a box of cereal while processors and marketers earn dollars. If it hadn't rained in 1938, Clark County's grain-puffing Wertz brothers might have been cereal kings, New Deal Puffed Wheat might be the breakfast of champions, and Melham might still be on the map.

July / August 2000

Gregory's Oscar Micheaux

Ried Holien

LIKE EVERY SETTLER caught up in the Gregory County land rush of 1905, Oscar Micheaux dreamed of building a life in South Dakota. Like his neighbors, he struggled to break the prairie sod and raise a crop. He feared drought and grasshoppers. He prayed that rain and the railroad would come. In every way save one, Oscar Micheaux was like most South Dakota pioneers. In a region that welcomed immigrants from a score of nations, Micheaux was the only black homesteader for many a mile.

Today Micheaux is known as an author and filmmaker — America's first black filmmaker — but those were later careers. The fifth of 13 children in his Illinois family, he left home at 17 to shine shoes on the streets of Chicago, then became a porter on a Pullman railroad car, one of the best jobs a black man could hope for. He traveled the country, saving his money and waiting for an opportunity. His chance came when Rosebud Reservation land was opened to homesteaders. "I turned my face westward with the spirit of Horace Greeley," Micheaux later wrote, "the words, 'Go west young man, and grow up with the country,' ringing in my ears."

In 1910 Micheaux married the daughter of a Chicago minister and brought her to the homestead, but she stayed barely two years. Alone again, he began recording his experiences and wry observations of pioneer life, a process that resulted in *The Conquest*. When he couldn't find a publisher he printed it himself, and sold books door-to-door. Micheaux then started the Western Book and Supply Company to finance more books, selling shares in the enterprise to area farmers, and published *The Forged Note: A Romance of the Darker Races* in 1915. He followed that with the book that changed his life: *The Homesteader*, a reworking of autobiographical material from his first book.

Lincoln Pictures wanted to buy movie rights to *The Homesteader*, but

Micheaux insisted on directing the film himself and the deal fell through. So he started his own film company, again raising money door to door. He found the equipment and actors he needed in Chicago, bought a car, hired a white chauffeur, and drove all the people and equipment to Winner to film the movie. *The Homesteader* was the first full-length feature film written, directed and produced by an African-American, and it put Micheaux's name in the history books. With the movie's success, Micheaux was able to devote his energy to writing and filmmaking full-time. His days on the homestead were over, but he returned there often in his eight books and 43 films. Micheaux left South Dakota, but South Dakota never left him.

July / August 1998

THE BLACK HILLS' P.T. BARNUM

Anthony Petres

THOMAS SWEENEY settled in Hay Camp just as the shanty and tent town was springing to life, the right man at the right place. He quickly settled in and dedicated himself to building the city along Rapid Creek, which some had nicknamed "Little Denver," but we know as Rapid City. Sweeney was an early proponent of bold advertising, pre-dating later masters of the genre such as Wall Drug by decades. "Tom Sweeney wants to see you" was his well-known slogan, and customers came in droves. "Old Reliable," a moniker he borrowed from P.T. Barnum, prospered. By the turn of the 20th Century he was one of Rapid's wealthiest businessmen, an enthusiastic promoter of everything the city and the Hills had to offer.

Sweeney and other promoters took a page from Barnum's "there's a sucker born every minute" book when they faked a placer gold discovery in Rapid Creek to attract miners who had begun to leave the northern Hills as the easy deposits played out. But mostly he stayed above board, willing to do almost anything to advance his reputation. He welcomed all people to "his" town, and played a lead role in organizing the Stockmen's Days celebration, the seminal business and cultural event of early Rapid City that brought thousands of Indians and whites together in the tense period following the Indian Wars. Sweeney's plans for Rapid City were cut short when the Model T in which he was riding proved more risky than the bi-plane. On his way to a war bonds rally, he was struck by a freight train at a city crossing and killed in October of 1917.

July / August 2002

TY COBB AT CENTER STORE

Merland Howe

MY FOLKS, Ben and Mayme Howe, ran the country store at Center, in McCook County. There was relief from the grim thirties at the Center Store, especially during pheasant season, when hunters stopped for gas, soda, ice cream and shotgun shells.

Everybody knew Bob Feller, who pitched for the Cleveland Indians. He hunted every fall between Center and Howard with his uncle, who delivered gas and oil to the store. But nobody recognized a stocky, middle-aged hunter who strolled in one day. Kenny Knudson was there when the stranger appeared. Kenny had stopped on his way home from a baseball game in Salem, still wearing his uniform.

"I see you're a ball player," the visitor said. "I used to play a little ball myself." Kenny looked at the old hunter with doubtful eyes. "Yeah, when?"

"It was a few years back. Maybe you've heard of me. I'm Ty Cobb."

"Oh, sure," Kenny replied, "and I'm Babe Ruth."

Cobb, who had retired in 1928 after 24 seasons with the Detroit Tigers and the Philadelphia Athletics, and who in 1936 came in first in the first ballot for the National Baseball Hall of Fame, didn't say another word. He just pulled out his hunting license and presented it to the gape-mouthed Kenny.

July / August 2003

HOW AL'S BECAME AN OASIS

John Egan

IF SOUTH DAKOTA has a blue belt across its middle, Al's Oasis in Oacoma is the buckle. It marks the middle of the state, and the middle of the Missouri River as it winds across the state's midsection. Even the town's name comes from the Sioux word "okomo," a place between.

For those traveling Interstate 90 between Sioux Falls and the Black Hills, the buckle loosens up at mealtime. Vacationers as well as regulars have been welcomed to a respite from the road by affable Alfred Mueller at his "oasis" on the west bank of the Missouri for 47 years. Now, two sons and a daughter run the place. Al's late wife, Veda, her smile warm and her eyes twinkling like night stars over Lyman County, told me once how this South Dakota institution came to be. "It was noon on a summer day and I was on vacation from my teaching job at Oacoma. I used to go to the filling station we had on old Highway 16 to make sure that Al got a decent meal, since he was always there from morning to night. I had a couple of ground-beef patties on the hot plate in back and was about to bring the hamburgers to Al when I heard a voice. It was a man at the cash register paying for his gas. He must have smelled the frying meat because I heard him ask Al, 'Do you serve sandwiches here?' Never one to think twice about things like that, Al said, 'Yes.' And he came back and wrapped a napkin around the burgers and sold them. Things haven't been the same since."

May / June 2001

HOMESTAKE'S LAST OUNCE

Paul Higbee

BEFORE THERE was a South Dakota, there was a Homestake Mine. Four partners, exploring illegally in country not open to whites, dug a series of holes into a 500-foot stretch of rocky ground in 1876. The four — Moses Manual, Fred Manual, Alex Engh and Henry Harney — dug out $5,000 worth of gold that fall and winter, then congratulated themselves when they sold the mine to Californian George Hearst for a reported $100,000. Later that year the federal government broke the Fort Laramie Treaty and opened the Hills to settlement, and Hearst incorporated Homestake Mining Company. George Hearst's investment proved sound. When his grandson, Randolph Hearst, died in 2000, he was personally worth $1.8 billion, and Hearst corporate holdings were about $4.5 billion.

For 125 years, the fortunes of the town of Lead rose and fell with the mine that was its heart. Work there became a family affair, passed from fathers to sons, and eventually to daughters. Homestake was a leader in offering its workers benefits, implementing free medical services in 1910, and a pension plan in 1917. During the Depression, Homestake was one of the few South Dakota industries turning a profit; the gold tax it paid helped keep the state afloat.

In 2001, the mine shut down. For decades, South Dakotans boasted that their state ranked first in gold production, and Homestake mine was the western hemisphere's biggest, in continuous operation since 1876. No more.

March / April 2001

Mixing Sheep, Writing and Booze

Paul Hennessey

ARCHIE GILFILLAN started out as a sheep rancher, and ended up as an author and sagebrush philosopher. After a 20-year apprenticeship as a sheepherder in northwest South Dakota he penned one of the funniest, most perceptive works on early 20th Century West River life ever written. *Sheep: Life on the South Dakota Range*, first published in 1929, has been reprinted several times since, most recently in the 1990s. Stories from the book have been told and retold, especially in the bar rooms and around the kitchen tables of Harding County where he spent his shepherding days.

Archie Gilfillan was born in 1886, in White Earth, Minn., where his father served as an Episcopal missionary. As a teenager he worked on various farms, and his introduction to the world of animal husbandry came when he bought a sheep for $3, then sold it for $6, along with the wool, just a year later. "While I had never been especially good at mathematics, it seemed to me that 100 percent a year was a pretty good return on an investment and that if I could keep it up regularly I ought to be worth quite a bit some day," he wrote years later. "So I bought as many ewes as I had money for, and left them, supposedly, on shares, with a neighboring farm woman who had a few sheep of her own." The woman later mailed him a check for just $10, claiming the pasture bill ate up the rest of his investment. "I learned about women from her," he wrote. "I was wiped out. But while women are men's ineradicable weakness, sheep are not; and it was many a year before I again took up the trail of the Golden Hoof."

After graduating from the University of Pennsylvania in 1910, Phi Beta Kappa, with an emphasis in Latin and Greek, he followed his dream west and went to work on a ranch near the Black Hills. Gilfillan later moved on to homestead in Harding County, near Slim Buttes, and started raising sheep, but never seemed to find the rhythm of buying low and selling high; in three years he gave up ranching and decided to follow in the ministerial footsteps of his father and grandfather. He attended Western Theological Seminary in Chicago, an Episcopalian institution, and on the day before graduation had a change of heart: he joined the Catholic Church, and returned to Harding County.

In 1916 Gilfillan hired out to Almon Dean and herded sheep with him for 17 years, during which time he developed a problem with alcohol. Perhaps as a consequence of weeks and months spent with nobody but sheep to talk to, Gilfillan loved to socialize, and always found an excuse to drink. Poker was another favorite pastime, and he never understood that cards and whiskey did not mix. Dean let him borrow on future wages to pay debts, and the Ivy League sheepherder was always overdrawn. When Dean caught Gilfillan drunk in the wagon, he moved him to the home ranch to do chores. Such confined quarters proved unbearable to Gilfillan, and he soon retired from the sheep business to a log cabin in Spearfish.

For eight years, starting in December of 1924 when he was 38, Gilfillan kept a diary in cipher, a system of secret writing, filling over 9,000 pages. He wrote of daily happenings and hardships of his occupation — rattlesnakes, wolves, coyotes, two-legged camp robbers, seeking shelter from a tornado in an old well — and his three "secret sorrows." Sheepmen who didn't know as much about sheep as the herder headed the list, followed closely by cowboys who got all the glory while the sheepherder was looked down upon. "Is there any intrinsic reason why the man who takes care of cattle should be a romantic, half-mythical figure, while the man who takes care of sheep is either a joke or anathema?" he wrote. Gilfillan argued that the sheep herder was superior to the cowboy because he was his own boss most of the time while the cowboy "may be able to carry more than one day's orders in his head, but he seldom has the opportunity of proving it."

Gilfillan's other secret sorrow was women. He liked them; he just didn't think they were cut out to be sheep herders. "The truth is that in many respects they are unsuited to the work," he wrote. "With no more than a discreet allusion to the three quickest means of communication, can you really picture a woman engaging in an occupation which would leave her more or less in the dark with regard to the doings of even her immediate neighbors?"

In 1924 Gilfillan gave a talk to the Woolgrowers Association at Helena and caught everyone by surprise with an outstanding speech, "The Secret Sorrows of a Sheepherder." He never gave his name so he remained unknown for several years afterward, but it was the beginning of another avocation, public speaker. Gilfillan was equally at home before convention audiences and in smoky barrooms, always entertaining with his dry, self-deprecating wit. The herder-author referred to himself as a Phi Beta Kappa gone wrong. "I have the suspicion that Prof. Chanson has asked me to appear before these graduates to serve as a warning," Gilfillan said during a commencement address at Buffalo in1930, "so that they can see what may happen to them if they do not watch their step and be just a little bit careful."

At Spearfish, Gilfillan became a freelance writer for several South Dakota newspapers. In 1936 he published *A Shepherd's Holiday*, stories collected from his newspaper articles. Late in life, Gilfillan and his long-time friend Hoadley Dean wrote *A Goat's Eye View of the Black Hills*, interweaving legends from South Dakota's mountain towns with his personal perspectives and humor. He also explained why he remained a bachelor. "You profess sincere and unbounded admiration for the beauties of the opposite sex and you practically lay your heart at their collective feet; and then you meet some individual who combines the poorer qualities of a mama wildcat and a bitch wolf, with a voice like a buzz saw, the temper of a slapped hornet, and a disposition that would curdle the milk in four adjoining counties. And then you have to revise your opinion of the sex all over again and downward." In short, he never met a woman he liked who would have him as a husband.

Gilfillan worked with the Federal Writer's Project, a Depression-era work program that hired unemployed writers to interview old-timers, search files and records, collect folklore, and preserve the history, culture and contemporary life of American communities. He stayed until the project ended in 1942, then moved on to the Black Hills Ordinance Depot at Provo. When that job ended in he made his way to Deadwood; in failing health, he lived at the Wagner Hotel, where he could usually be found in a straight back chair, book in hand, or walking along Deadwood's streets. While enjoying a walk on Dec. 17, 1955, he dropped to the sidewalk, and moved on to greener pastures. Family and friends buried the old sheep herder at Belle Fourche, but it's not likely he's happy in his final resting place. They buried him beside two great cowboys, Paul Bernard and Joe LaFlamme.

Nov/Dec 1997

Drawing Pictures and Attention

Bernie Hunhoff

NEBRASKA AUTHOR Willa Cather once opined that art and economics have nothing in common. She never met Ray Kelly of Sioux Falls, who married art with economics and added celebrity salesmanship.

After college, Kelly sold cars on 41st Street, one man on a big sales team. He soon found it wasn't really a team game: it was sell or starve. He had to differentiate himself from a dozen other well-dressed, well-mannered salespeople every time a customer walked through the door. "So I wore the longer hair, the brighter suit, the $600 pair of boots with buffalo engraved on them," he said. "I knew I had to be a little more flamboyant. I couldn't just melt into the wall or I'd never sell a car. You have to expose yourself. You have to set yourself apart."

Kelly began to draw in 1985. Two years later he sold his first print, and art has come first ever since. He still works a day job to help pay bills, delivering cars for another dealer in Sioux Falls, but he doesn't allow that job to deter him from his passion for drawing the West.

Kelly seldom seems serious in public. His mustached and mischievous grin matches the boots. He's a showman, and proud of it. If most artists donned the boots, hats and jackets Kelly wears, they'd risk being dubbed a dude. Kelly doesn't care. Just notice him. Once you've met him, he figures, you're going to be interested in his art. Then you're only a few car salesman's questions away from a deal.

July / August 2001

MOVIEMAKING ON MINICONJOU CREEK

Bernie Hunhoff

WHEN KEVIN COSTNER and Jim Wilson went in search of a place to film their frontier epic, *Dances With Wolves*, they considered locations from Canada to Mexico. Once they'd narrowed it down to the northern plains they looked at Cherry County in Nebraska and Wyoming's Grand Teton National Park. Then they got wind of Roy Houck's Triple U Ranch, with something nowhere else in the world could offer.

"We had almost settled on another location, but I heard there was a large herd of buffalo on a ranch outside the capital of South Dakota," said Wilson, the film's producer. "It was really the buffalo that pointed us toward South Dakota. We knew we'd found it. As Kevin said, it was like gold dust suddenly started to drop on the project."

Dances' cinematographers were genuinely impressed with the Houck ranch's virgin appearance — no fences, roads or electrical lines. "At first they only intended to shoot the buffalo scenes here," said Roy's daughter, Kay Ingle, "but as they traveled about on the ranch they kept finding draws which they thought would work for other scenes." Nearly half the movie ended up being filmed on the Triple U; the open spaces, rolling hills and vivid sunsets provided the perfect backdrop for the story of Lt. John Dunbar, the Civil War veteran who wanted to experience the frontier before it was civilized out of existence.

"I thought [the ranch] showed up real well," Roy said after the movie, which was a considerable understatement. *Dances With Wolves* generated more favorable attention for West River's unique beauty than the Department of Tourism ever managed. Other scenes were shot in the Badlands, Spearfish Canyon, and on the Belle Fourche River north of Rapid City. Even the opening, Civil War action was shot in a cornfield about 25 miles southeast of Pierre, in the DeGrey area. In their quest for realism, the producers couldn't resist tweaking some scenes with wind fans, imported dust and painted trees. The buffalo couldn't be improved.

"The buffalo won a lot of respect. They're faster than horses, they run longer than horses, and they never backed down," said Costner. "They really fed our film, and in some way held it up spiritually." The herd's moment of cinematic glory was an action-packed sequence that recreated for theater audiences something not seen since the 19th Century: a full bore buffalo hunt. Ten pickups, 20 wranglers on horseback and a helicopter maneuvered 3,000 buffalo into camera range — in essence, they created a barely controlled stampede. Stockmen like Houck would be perfectly content to pass their whole lives without seeing a stampede, especially with buffalo, which are difficult to control in the best of circumstances. That it happened without tragedy was entirely due to Houck's years of experience with the animals.

Costner found more than just buffalo and landscapes in South Dakota. His quest for authenticity provided an opportunity for Doris Leader Charge, an instructor of Lakota language and culture at Sinte Gleska College. She was hired to help translate the screenplay and teach the actors enough Lakota to carry it off on camera; Costner was so impressed with Leader Charge's presence he gave her a part in the film. Cyvert Young Bear, a member of the Porcupine Singers, helped the production company choreograph buffalo and scalp dances that hadn't been recreated for more than 120 years. Costner also cast more than 250 Indians from reservations around South Dakota as extras. When the show premiered in Rapid City, audience members remained seated as the credits rolled, looking for names they knew.

Hollywood intruded upon the Triple U for but a moment, which was just fine with Roy Houck. "Some people probably thought we got rich, but it only amounted to a few thousand dollars altogether. It probably cost us money in the long run," he said, thinking back to four days of running the buffalo in the summer heat. But his big, brown grass-eaters and their native prairie are now part of Hollywood history.

March/April 1991

KING ZIEGLER'S OLD CAR FARM

Bernie Hunhoff

THE GOVERNMENT helped finance shelterbelts to slow the snow and wind. But there was another benefit. The trees also provided rural people a place to hide broken-down vehicles. Maybe rural South Dakotans aren't the mechanics they think they are, because most farms and ranches have junkyards behind the elms. Few people collected more old cars in the trees than King Ziegler.

In a 30-acre field west of Scotland, Ziegler earned his living from a crop of rusted iron and nostalgia. People came from miles around — some from as far away as Europe and Asia — to search for treasure. King's real name was Alfred. But if you asked for Alfred Ziegler at a café in his Bon Homme County town locals would look puzzled, until you added that he is the guy with all the cars. "Oh, you mean King," everyone would say in unison. "King Ziegler."

King ran a place some people would call an auto junkyard. In the phone book, it was called King Ziegler Salvage. So you expected to arrive and find workers removing parts from car carcasses. Grease. Oil. Sweat. Noise. None of the above. Blackbirds sang in a near-by cornfield. A herd of sheep grazed between rusting automobiles. A rooster crowed on a nearby farm and a donkey brayed in reply. That's about as noisy as it got at King Ziegler Salvage. King didn't remove parts from the cars. He never believed in removing parts before they were needed. "I have the customer take the parts off," he told us. "I tell them if they take it off they'll know how to put it on."

Most customers didn't mind the work. However, a city boy did object, according to King. And then he had the audacity to dicker on the price. And in a final insult, the city customer looked down his nose at the sheep that were grazing between the rusting cars. Then he reached down to pick up one of those pea-size pills that often follow sheep and he asked, "What's this?"

"That's a brain pill," replied King.

"A brain pill?" the customer asked. "What's that supposed to mean?"

"You eat it and you get smarter," King said.

So the city fellow put the "pill" in his mouth. He immediately spat it out and said, "It tastes like shit!"

"See," said King, "you're smarter already!"

A business school grad might think the Scotland salvage yard needed more modern management and customer relations. But after spending an afternoon at King's field, we wondered if maybe the rest of the world has gone overboard in those areas. After all, his system worked. He spent nothing on advertising, yet customers came from all over the world. He had only an eighth grade education, yet he made a good living without getting grease in his fingernails. He had no labor costs. No labor worries. No stress. No office expenses. No signs. The 1950 Chevrolet wrecker he used to hoist or haul cars had a phone number painted on the side. But it was not his phone number. He spent nothing on mowing, thanks to the sheep. He closed when the weather got bad. He closed for much of the winter. Customers could call him in an emergency. But it's hard to imagine why there would be a critical need for a 1949 Studebaker carburetor.

Nov/Dec 1996

All Signs Point to Wall Drug

DOROTHY HUSTEAD decided to take a nap. That's how it all began. When she awoke from her siesta, the first thing she heard was the jalopies trundling past on nearby Highway 16. The year was 1936, one of the hottest, driest years on record in South Dakota. It occurred to her that those passing motorists might be thirsty. Why not offer free ice water to lure them into the family pharmacy? Dorothy wrote a seven-line advertising verse, and her husband, Ted, put one line on each of seven signs. Before he got back to the store from putting them up, passersby were pulling in. With a little help from friends and fans, those "signs of success" have spread across the state and around the world. Wall Drug signs were sighted in Vietnam during the war years, and from the French Riviera to Antarctica and Africa.

March/April 1988

Let's Try Prosperity

PERHAPS IT'S TIME we tried prosperity. To some, it's a novel thought. Jon Hunter, publisher of the *Madison Daily Leader,* joked in our magazine that some South Dakotans seem adverse to success. "At the coffee shop we like to argue good-naturedly over who has the least success. 'It's me!' one will say. And the next guy says, 'No, it's me!' We are skeptical of success, and if someone does well there's a suspicion."

May/June 1996

SALE DAY AT ST. ONGE

Bernie Hunhoff

WEST RIVER RANCHERS get one respectable paycheck a year. It comes in winter when spring calves are sold at livestock auctions to buyers from cornbelt feedlots. St. Onge, a little community of about 100 people in the northern Black Hills, grew to become one of western South Dakota's most colorful auction markets in the 1990s. Hundreds of sellers and spectators, a dozen buyers and thousands of cattle converged for weekly sales that transcended ranch country commerce.

Sale day at a livestock auction barn is like lunch at Rotary, the bank board meeting, golf in the afternoon and Thanksgiving Day — all at once. Add a dash of Wall Street or the Chicago Mercantile, overshoes and kerchiefs, and you get the picture. This is business with some socialization mixed in. Yuppies might call it networking, but nobody pushes anything but cattle at St. Onge. When ranchers bring their cattle to town, they are often accompanied by family. Sometimes three generations sit together on wooden bleachers and wait their herd's turn before the buyers. Ranch hands also come. The rancher usually buys supper for everybody after the sale. A celebration is expected.

St. Onge is not one of South Dakota's oldest sale barns. It was started in the 1960s by Jim Madden, a popular Sturgis cattleman who convinced local ranchers to invest money to build a modern stockyards. Madden's dream was an 80-acre facility with room for big yards, easy loading routes, and a bunkline along the pens so the cattle could easily be fed ground hay with a tractor and feedwagon. In the spirit of West River conservatism, Madden and his backers agreed that if the sale barn failed, they could turn the yards into a feedlot and fatten their own cattle.

Plan B wasn't necessary. With Madden as boss man, the new barn flourished. The number of cattle sold at St. Onge grew steadily to a high of 265,000 in 1977, making this tiny town the biggest feeder cattle market in the region. But Madden died in 1979, and his son Mike assumed control. Mike was a good livestockman, but apparently he was not as conservative as his father. For a reason that is still the subject of rumor and gossip in the Northern Hills, Mike badly needed cash in 1986, so he took $400,000 from the seller's trust account. He still wrote checks to the sellers, but they bounced like a healthy week-old calf in the noonday sun.

St. Onge Livestock closed in disgrace. Mike Madden went to prison. Ranchers took their cattle elsewhere. Still, the original owners didn't turn

St. Onge into a feedlot. Ted Thompson reopened the facility in 1987. A year later, Gail Sohler of Yankton purchased the business. Fridays at St. Onge gradually got noisier and busier again. In the 1990s, when we visited, auction posters and business cards were once again tacked to the bulletin board. Harold and Bunnie Draine advertised their Big Sky border collies, "bred to work." Steve Simpson was touting Trout Haven Ranch at Buffalo Gap, where you can buy dressed trout or fingerlings for a stock dam.

But the main attraction is always the cattle. Pictures of every breed decorated the walls. In the sales ring, the head mount of a longhorn steer presided high above padded bleacher seats. In the lounge, near a big framed picture of Ronald Reagan in cowboy garb, were dozens of livestock magazines.

Cattle are a mainstay of the South Dakota economy. Three to four million head live here, about five cows to every human. Markets like the one at St. Onge turn those critters into cash. To a rancher, winning the lottery would be a boondoggle. Getting $1.10 a pound at St. Onge — now that would be real excitement.

Jan/Feb 1992

SCOOPER WAS A SQUATTER

GRASSHOPPER JIM Fredrick was a German squatter who lived near Bear Butte before the Black Hills were opened to white settlement. An unsavory character in some ways, he acquired his nickname because he made grasshoppers part of his diet when they infested the land. He made shady business deals and was known to fire shots at people crossing his land. But he was also a proponent of making Bear Butte an Indian shrine, and he was among the founders of Sturgis.

He also initiated the tradition of "scooping" cash from soldiers at Fort Meade in exchange for Deadwood liquor and women and other necessities. Fort Meade was built from August of 1878 to August of 1879 with a $100,000 federal appropriation. Sturgis developed a mile away with scooped cash, mostly of course, scooped by legitimate businesses like barbershops, clothiers and grocers. Today the Sturgis High School athletic teams are called The Scoopers.

Jan/Feb 1993

RAISE PRICES OR THE BUILDING

Bernie Hunhoff

MABEL AND Charlie Almos bought the Buffalo Lake Restaurant in 1970, when it sat on the shore of Buffalo Lake, west of Sisseton. When their lot rent was increased in 1988, they didn't want to raise the price of a hamburger steak so they raised the building onto a truck and moved a mile north.

Sept / Oct 2001

FREE STEERS

HOW BAD ARE cattle prices these days? So bad that one farmer returned home from town and found six cows in his yard which had been stolen three years earlier. A note attached to his front door read, "Here, you feed them for awhile. I can't afford it anymore!"

Another rancher hauled four young steers into the livestock auction barn and asked the auctioneer what he thought he could get for them. "Nothing," answered the auctioneer. "Nobody wants to buy cattle right now." So the rancher, who was out of feed, posted a sign on the side of his truck that said, "Free steers. Take what you want." Then he went inside to watch the auction for a few minutes. When he returned, he looked in the back of the truck and discovered he now had eight steers.

July / August 1996

REGULATION IN THE GOOD OLD DAYS

DEADWOOD GAMBLING establishment owners looking to differentiate themselves from the casinos springing up from coast-to-coast might consider resurrecting a custom from the past. Gambling wasn't uncommon in the town's saloons, according to old-timers, and it operated under a gentleman's agreement: if a man was unlucky enough to lose his paycheck gambling, his wife could go to the bar owner the next day to retrieve the money. A gambling overseer, called the Czar, would then put the man's name on a blacklist and he wouldn't be allowed to gamble again. The system worked for the most part, except when someone didn't honor the gentleman's agreement. Then the law would be obliged to notice what was going on and shut everybody down.

May / June 1988

How About Some Really Great Faces

WHEN THE S.D. Department of Tourism first coined its "Great Faces, Great Places" slogan in 1990, not everyone was pleased. One caller to *South Dakota Magazine* complained that Gutzon Borglum and the DOT got it all wrong to begin with. He suggested Cheryl Ladd of Huron, Catherine Bach of Faith and Mary Hart of Sioux Falls — South Dakota beauties who found success in Hollywood — would be better choices than the four stone heads of Rushmore. "None of THOSE GUYS were born in South Dakota," he huffed, "and three of them never even set foot here."

March/April 1990

Quotables

"Labor trouble is practically unknown in the relations between sheepman and herder ... the fact that one herder would have to walk several miles at night in order to organize with the next one may have something to do with that."

— Archie Gilfillan

"It didn't take long to realize the water wasn't going anyplace, so we thought we might as well work with it."

— Mary Pollock, explaining why she and and her husband decided to open a marina after Lake Thompson flooded their farm.

"There are a lot of people who are damned mad and don't have the slightest idea why."

— Homer Ayres, agricultural activist of Perkins County, on why he spent years trying to educate his fellow ranchers about the consequences of monopolies in the meatpacking industry.

"The plan was to get in and get out quickly, but I fooled around and fell in love."

— Tom Didier, on his plan to buy and sell Rapid City's Alex Johnson Hotel

"If time were really money, the sheepherders would soon exchange places with the multimillionaires, for the latter never have any time at all and the former have all there is."

—Archie Gilfillan

"People often ask if I ever get tired of ice cream. I don't. It's usually what I have for breakfast."

— Wendy Hyatt, owner/operator of Fjord's Ice Cream Plant in Rapid City

"We even kicked two governors out of here for lighting up. They took it very well."

— Oscar Austad, on how he enforced the "no smoking" policy at Austad's Sporting Goods

Challenge

WE TITLED THIS *chapter in deference to and respect for one of my favorite authors, Bob Karolevitz. Among his several dozen books is* Challenge: The South Dakota Story, *one of the very best histories ever done on our state.*

In the foreword, Karolevitz pays tribute to how South Dakotans meet their tests. "Other states may possess greater wealth, have more natural attractions, boast of teeming populations and beckon job-seekers with massive, depersonalizing industries," he wrote. "But South Dakota's uniqueness comes from less definable characteristics relating mostly to her people. If there are any general traits which seem to epitomize a majority of South Dakotans ... they include a fierce but quiet pride in an independent spirit, an intense insistence on "elbow room," and a sense of personal conquest...."

Karolevitz even made a pitch, in his book, for a new state nickname. He says The Coyote State, Sunshine State, and Land of Infinite Variety are all more promotional than descriptive. (He'd say the same about our newest slogan, The Rushmore State.) He suggested The Challenge State. "Unlike the previous nicknames, the challenge concept is appropriate to both the land and the people," he argued.

So far, the State Legislature has ignored the recommendation of the scribe from Mission Hill. Read these stories — again, they are excerpts and quips from our larger articles — and I think you'll side with Bob Karolevitz.

— Bernie Hunhoff

DAY COUNTY'S GOVERNOR

DAY COUNTY HAS had more than its share of politicians. It is one of only two counties in the state that can boast of being the home of two governors (Minnehaha is the other). Charles Sheldon was the first and Sigurd Anderson the second.

Anderson grew up in Canton, where he had two favorite haunts — the corner drug store, where he read everything but prescription labels, and the Lincoln County courthouse, where he sat enchanted by verbal battles between country lawyers. His love of language seems a little surprising, since he was born in Norway in 1904, and came to South Dakota at age three not knowing a word of English. He and his brother, George, were singled out in school for dressing and talking differently. Their words came out with a distinctively Scandinavian brogue. The other kids teased, "Oh, the Norwegian and the Dutch, they don't amount to much!"

Despite the teasing, the Anderson boys adjusted to American life. Their father, Karl, loved life in Canton and he took his children to the local political debates, where Sig received even more exposure to fine oratory. He got a law degree from USD, served as a legal officer in the Navy, became attorney general of South Dakotan and beat Joe Foss, who downed 26 enemy planes in World War II, in the 1950 Republican primary for governor. Running against the famous pilot was tough, he said. "Every time a plane would fly over, a little kid would say, 'Hey, that's Joe Foss up there!'" laughed Anderson. "No one had any battleships for Anderson." That fall he beat Joe Robbie, a young Sisseton attorney who went on to become owner of the Miami Dolphins. The boy who couldn't speak English was governor of South Dakota.

May/June 1988

CRAZY HORSE: MAN & MYTH

Roger Holtzmann

TASUNKE WITCO (Crazy Horse) had very fair skin and hair for a Lakota, so much so that he was known as Curly, and sometimes Light Hair, in his youth. He was a physically unremarkable man at maturity, neither tall or short, broad or thin. Up close, his most distinguishing features were eyes that, "looked through things...[as if he was always] thinking hard about something," remembered Nicholas Black Elk, who was a generation younger. A contemporary, Short Buffalo, put it another way:

Continued on page 135

Elsie Meeks sought to create a business tradition on Pine Ridge as leader of the Lakota Fund. Story, page 200.

Native American art found a bearded booster when Brother Simon came to Pine Ridge's Red Cloud Mission.

Once advertised as "The Wonder Hotel of the West," Rapid City's landmark Hotel Alex Johnson was struggling when young Tom Didier fell in love with its history and architecture in the 1980s. He guided it back to more glory days.

George and Alice Stroppel's hotel and hot baths business in Midland celebrated its 60th anniversary in 2000. The peacefulness of Midland is almost as restful as the 119-degree geothermal waters. Story, page 98.

Gladys Pyle of Huron nearly became South Dakota's first woman governor in 1930 but the "good old boys" blocked her nomination. No matter, she was still an amazing woman and a U.S. senator to boot. Pictured with her is Katie Hunhoff, who grew up to write for *South Dakota Magazine*. The Pyle family home (below) became a museum. Story, page 144.

Casey Tibbs of Fort Pierre became an international rodeo star by riding ornery broncs like Nugget (above). He won ten world championships and legions of fans before retiring in 1964 for movie and television roles. Story, page 64.

In 1989, *South Dakota Magazine* reconnected Ethel Roberts with the Verendrye Plate. Story, page 178.

Hooky Jack Leary constantly fought adversity, even losing both hands in a dynamite accident. Story, page 229.

South Dakota Magazine's 1997 photographs and story on Beryle Seaman drew as much reader reaction as anything published in 20 years. Seaman was living in a tiny wood shack on the Bad River, southwest of Pierre — a solitary man surviving one of the snowiest and coldest winters of modern times. His stark lifestyle, plain talk and yearning for companionship were cause for reflection.
Story, page 225.

Ruth Ziolkowski emerged from the shadows of her late husband, Korczak, to preside over the world's largest sculpture. The likeness of Crazy Horse will be 563 feet high and 641 feet long. Story, page 186.

Ed Yost left the corporate world to attempt a record-setting trans-Atlantic balloon flight. Story, page 191.

Oscar Howe became South Dakota's best-known Indian artist. He also excelled as an art educator.

Michael Ziegler of Lower Brule traveled the world to show the traditional dance of his ancestors.

Wall Drug's Ted Hustead collaborated with *South Dakota Magazine*'s editors to publish a brochure for tourists.

Can a South Dakota bison beat a Spanish fighting bull? Scotty Philips, well known for saving the buffalo from extinction, sent his nephew and two bulls to Juaraz, Mexico to solve the argument. Inset: South Dakotans in native attire. Story, page 51.

Audrae Visser, Elkton's poet laureate, loved writing both prose and poetry on the whimsy of rural life. Story, page 24.

Dave Ploof, South Dakota's most successful Legion baseball coach, always helped other teams. Story, page 159.

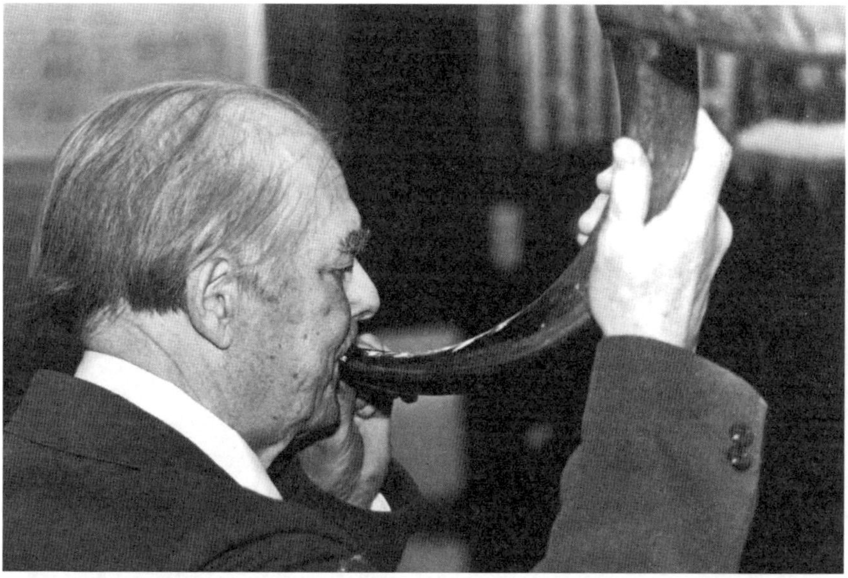

Arne Larson started to collect musical instruments as a teenager. Eventually, they filled his Brookings home. In 1973 he moved everything to Vermillion where the world-class Shrine to Music was established. Story, page 183.

Martin Collins raised a family of seven kids by penning wild creatures on his tiny ranch. Story, page 146.

Nellie Willhite, South Dakota's first female pilot, formed a flyer's club with Amelia Earhart.

A.M. Jackley became South Dakota's official rattlesnake exterminator in 1937. The colorful, story-telling hunter once captured 300 rattlers in three days. Small crowds sometimes gathered to watch him work. Story, page 28.

Jim Korkow (center), with the help of his parents, LaFola and Erv, was "superintendent" of the Korkow Rodeo School at Blunt in 1990. The three Rs? Roping, Riding and Rolling (as in roll away from the hooves!)

Mary Groth's paintings inspired South Dakotans to remember the spirit of the pioneers. Story, page 180.

Dona Brown of Huron championed art and historic preservation in several *South Dakota Magazine* stories.

Tipperary, foaled in 1905 near Camp Crook, grew to be a beautiful bay that was all but unrideable in his rodeo prime. From 1916 to 1926 he bucked off 91 men. Only champion Yakima Canutt (pictured far right) stayed in the saddle. Story, page 57.

Clyde Ice traded two used cars for an airplane after World War I and helped to pioneer air travel in South Dakota. Thousands of people took their first plane ride with the barnstormer. A few owed their lives to him. Story, page 16.

Poet Laureate Badger Clark, wrote "The Cowboy's Prayer" — a rodeo favorite. Story, page 192.

Artist Alice New Holy joked that her toughest task is pulling the quills from the porcupines. Story, page 101.

A *South Dakota Magazine* photographer arrived at Lawrence Brown's ranch near Buffalo in 1993 just as the well known rural activist's grandsons Nathan, Joseph and Justin, were preparing to milk their goat, Eugenia Blue Flower.

“God wants us to reach,” said Kevin Locke, hoop dancer, “reach for more light, feed our roots and blossom.” He took a message of harmony to 70 countries but the kid from Wakpala always came home to South Dakota. Story, page 156.

South Dakota Magazine readers want to learn about interesting out-of-the-way places. An example is Frank Day’s Bar at Dallas, east of Winner on Highway 18. Old West history, hamburgers, hats and boots create a rare ambiance.

"He had black eyes that hardly ever looked straight at a man," which was a telling observation.

Crazy Horse was honored by his people as a man of uncommon spiritual power, a great warrior and selfless leader, but he was a distant, almost unapproachable character in some ways. "[I was] a little afraid of him," said Black Elk. "Not afraid that he would hurt me. I was just afraid. Everybody felt that way about him, for he was a queer man and would go about the village without noticing people or saying anything. In his own teepee he would joke, and when he was on the warpath with a small party he would joke to make his warriors feel good. But around the village he hardly ever noticed anybody, except little children. All the Lakotas like to dance and sing, but he never joined a dance, and they say nobody ever heard him sing."

Or even speak much more than was necessary. There was more to his reticence than a mere quirk of personality. Crazy Horse was a mystic: He lived in the physical world, but at times he seemed more attuned to, "the world where there is nothing but the spirits of all things," Black Elk said. Many have referred to Crazy Horse as a holy man, but he was not so in the same way as his father. He did not act as a teacher or guide for others. His was a solitary spiritual journey, one that often carried him away from people, and unconventional from the first step.

There was no set year for a young Lakota's first vision quest, but when the time came, there were formalities to be observed. "It was very important for a person who wished to [cry out for a vision] to receive aid and advice from a "wichasha wakan" so that everything was done correctly," said Black Elk. "If things were not done in the right way, something very bad could happen." Crazy Horse sought his first vision while in his middle teens, and at some point well after the fact he related what he'd experienced to his father. Apparently he had not consulted with him or anyone else beforehand. Crazy Horse the elder could not have been pleased with his son for disregarding convention in such an important matter, but he helped him interpret his encounter with the spirit world.

Crazy Horse was not the type to speak openly of such things, so accounts of his vision must be looked at with some suspicion. We can only say for certain what he did in response, especially regarding his conduct as a warrior. Unlike many Lakota, he painted sparsely for battle — a few spots and a jagged streak of white on his face, signifying hail and lightning and the power of summer storms. He wore but a single feather in his hair, and always carried a small stone tied in a leather thong. All these were sacramental symbols, outward signs of the sheltering power that came to him through his visions. In Christian cultures, soldiers sometimes wear crosses or medals as symbols of their trust and hope that God will safeguard them in war. The actuality of divine or spiritual providence can be accepted or dismissed as wishful thinking, but one fact pertains here: Through more than two decades of close combat, when he was in the vanguard of countless charges, Crazy Horse suffered only minor injuries. He was either very lucky, or protected in some way that does not lend itself to rational explanation.

What was imparted in each man's vision became a guide and source of power for him, but a select few received the great visions, "which gave strength and health to [the] nation," in Black Elk's words. That was Crazy Horse's distinction and his burden, for much is asked of those to whom much is given. He was bound to a selfless, almost ascetic life by the dictates of his vision. His prowess at war, rooted in the spirit world, was for the protection of the people, not a means to win personal glory or wealth. He never sang of his deeds, as most warriors did, and he gave away all that he won as the spoils of war. When the responsibilities of leadership were laid upon him, he would return again and again to the spirit world, always seeking help for the people with an anguish that grew more acute as their condition worsened.

May/June 2003

THE MAN WHO MOVED A TOWN

Marcia Hill

ALVIN CARLSON ONCE moved the old mining town of Trojan to save some of its history, but there comes a time when you have to let go. Carlson had lived his entire life in Trojan. He was married there. He raised a family in the house he built in 1937. So he wasn't happy when Wharf Mining Company bought the land to expand its surface gold mine in 1998. Wharf would bury Trojan under a mountain of earth removed to get the gold.

What could a man do? Carlson had already moved the town once, and at age 74, he wasn't up to the task again. It wasn't much of a town, to be sure. In fact, it had officially ceased to exist in 1959, and some in Lead had taken to promoting it as a "ghost town." That's when Carlson visited the Chamber of Commerce. "I told those people if they didn't stop tellin' folks this was a ghost town that this old ghost was gonna start shooting a few people. They'd come here with out-of-state license plates, walk in, snoop through my stuff and just take it. I come unglued when people take my stuff and that's when I decided to move it back down the road a ways."

In the 1970s, with the help of his brother-in-law and a heavy truck, Carlson moved most of the remaining buildings onto some newly purchased land about three-quarters of a mile away. "We laid 16 x 16 timbers across the back of a fifth wheel, jacked up the buildings, and with a cable and dollies moved them onto the truck. We took them off the same way," said Carlson. Now the relocated buildings would fall to a new version of progress. Only the old red schoolhouse building would remain as an office. As for Carlson, he had no choice but to leave Trojan at last.

"I could go to Florida or Alabama where I have family, but it's too hot down there," he said. "I'm only satisfied here. As soon as I get to Boulder Canyon I start to feel better. The closer I come to Trojan the better I feel. I'll find a place in the hills not too far away."

Nov / Dec 1998

FROM BRIDGEWATER TO COOPERSTOWN

Paul Higbee

SPARKY ANDERSON was inducted into the National Baseball Hall of Fame at Cooperstown, N.Y,. in 2000, the first South Dakotan to reach the sport's most famous shrine. The Bridgewater native certainly belongs there. He ranks third all-time among major league managers in wins (2,194), behind only Connie Mack and John McGraw. For folks who know their baseball history, that's like saying a politician stands behind only Washington and Lincoln. Anderson managed the Cincinnati Reds and then the Detroit Tigers. He won World Series titles with both teams, becoming the only manager to bag world championships in both the National and American leagues. Because there was no question Anderson belonged in Cooperstown, the only debate among sportswriters and commentators was whether he would be enshrined as a Red or a Tiger.

Knowing Anderson's love of his home state, he might not mind being the only Hall of Famer to wear a feed-and-seed cap. "I remember more about South Dakota than any part of my life," Anderson told his biographer, Dan Ewald. "I remember all the sights, the sounds, the smells, the people. Maybe I remember Bridgewater so well because I was so happy there."

Anyone who's met Sparky Anderson remembers two characteristics

— the firm handshake, the kind that seals business deals on the prairies, and the natural warmth directed toward anyone: a marginal player whose time in the big leagues would be short, a sportswriter who needed extra insight so his story wouldn't read like every other, a wayfaring South Dakotan who dropped by the ballpark to say hello. Anderson credits both his handshake and his manner to his father, LeeRoy Anderson, who painted barns, worked for the postal service, and played semi-pro baseball. He was "lead-pipe tough," Sparky told Ewald. He walked with a self-assurance that let him treat everyone with dignity. Powerfully shaped by the Depression in South Dakota, LeeRoy Anderson taught his son that kindness is a valuable gift that doesn't cost anyone a cent.

Anderson was born in 1934, when the Depression and dust storms were ravaging South Dakota. His family had next to nothing in material wealth. That isn't a bad way to start life, Anderson noted, because you expect to work hard for everything, and you never take anything that comes your way for granted. Moving from that humble life to the very pinnacle of pro sports didn't affect Anderson much, either. "He's the same as he was 45 or 50 years ago," said baseball broadcaster Vin Scully. "He hasn't changed. I think the greatest thing about Sparky is that he really does feel that he was blessed. He is as modest as anyone who will ever reach the Hall of Fame."

July/August 2000

SUN DANCE AT GREEN GRASS

Marian Mathews Hersrud

In 1975, Marian Matthews Hersrud attended the annual Sun Dance held at Green Grass, on the Cheyenne River Sioux Reservation. The following is excerpted from her account of that experience.

IT WAS STILL dark as we approached Green Grass. Cars crawled ahead and parked at random under a grove of Russian olive trees. I parked the car and we groped our way to a dimly-lighted area where women stood behind a small counter making coffee, grilling fry bread and stirring "wojapi," the delicious fruit pudding. I bought food for Della and me, and we strolled to the bleachers behind the center of camp. When the first, faint rays of the rising sun glowed on the horizon, we could see a small cottonwood tree, about 35 feet tall, standing in the center of the cleared area. Heavy ropes hung from its top branches, swaying gently in the morning breeze.

"That's the Sun Dance tree," Della explained. "Yesterday four young girls called 'tree choppers' and several men went out to find the perfect tree. When they found it, the girls stood around the tree, and beginning on the west side, made four symbolic cuts for each of the four directions. The men cut the tree down and brought it here." She looked up at the tree. "This one is just perfect."

An old man walked among the dancers, making signs with his hands and touching their shoulders. His face was lined and wrinkled, but the long braid that hung down his back was as black as a young man's, and his walk was erect and firm. "That's Fools Crow, our medicine man," Della said. "He's almost 90."

The men helped each other prepare for the dance. They carefully cut their chests with knives and inserted three-inch chokecherry branches into the cuts. The dancers then tied heavy ropes to the sticks. My God, I thought. They should be screaming in pain and bleeding. But there were no screams and very little blood. At last the dancers were ready. They formed a circle around the tree, and the drumming grew louder. One by one, women came and stood behind their men. Nobody hugged, kissed or touched, but I sensed a oneness and understanding among them, a sharing of anguish. Many would follow a man all day. Some would leave and return. But no matter where the women were, you could hear their keening, a sound like no other. It is the wind wailing a mystery of pain, a lonely calling to someone unheard, unknown. The cry enters your body, your mind, your heart. You are one with the women. You feel their anguish, their togetherness with their men who dance in the August heat.

As the sun appeared on the eastern horizon, the men began to dance. They would dance all day, until the sun had sunk into the western hills. What were their thoughts? Would they see visions, dream dreams? I would feel their pain as they danced, sometimes pulling back on the ropes, increasing the agony. People sat on the bleachers, wandered about, talked together. They shared everything — cigarettes, sodas, fry bread. Sounds of the Sun Dance blend — eagle bone whistles, keening, drums. They would linger long after the sun dips below the horizon and the dance is finished.

What is the meaning of the dance? Is it a search for absolution? A need to look beyond the ordinary, the drudgery, the seeming uselessness of life? Does the dance transport the dancer into realms of fantasy and faith? Does he find a new level of reality? What are his thoughts as he circles the tree, pulling back with wrenches of pain, blowing his whistle harder now. Does he look up at the sky and ask Tunkashila to remember him in his hours of torture? "See me, Wakan Tanka, feel my hurt, answer my prayer."

Small children dart among the trees away from the center of camp. Their shouts blend with the keening, the whistling, the drumming — a cacophony of Indian sound.

At sunset, the dance ends, and dancers are relieved of their ropes. Everyone helps to untie, stroke, hug, murmur. Dancers smile, shake hands, embrace. It is over. They've survived, and they are strong. The dancers form a line, and each participant shakes the hand of each onlooker. I follow Della down the line.

"They prayed today," Della says, "so that the people may live."

July/August 2003

INDEPENDENT LIVES IN AVON

Bernie Hunhoff

NEIGHBORS NEVER saw Abe and George Voigt and their sister Esther as extraordinary. Abe sold farm machinery over cafe coffee and a phone in nearby Avon. George, a homebody, kept a cow herd and maintained a 240-acre farm. Esther kept house, milked cows and socialized in town. There was nothing unusual about them, other than the fact that all three became blind in their youths. Abe lost his sight at about age ten. Esther lost hers at nine. George's world gradually went dark in his twenties.

Emit and Katie Voigt had nine children in all; the three who lost their sight were treated like the rest. They were expected to help earn their way, and when it came time to divide the family farm, each of the nine received 80 acres. George, Esther and Abe pooled their land and lived in the farmhouse. That's where we met George and Esther on a sunny spring day. George looked the stereotypical elderly farmer as he welcomed us at the front door of the well-painted white-frame farmhouse. He was dressed in a red plaid shirt and blue striped overalls. A dog called Pumpkin was at his knee. His handshake is strong, his smile disarming. His face is gently wrinkled. He sat in a chair near a woodstove and grinned at the absurdity of answering personal questions.

Maybe the questions are absurd. After all, George's friends and relatives seem little surprised that he has built several buildings, or that he splits wood, or cares for a cow herd, gardens, or does dozens of odd jobs.

Not long ago, he went to a hearing aid specialist to complain that his hearing aid buzzes.

"When does it buzz?" asked the specialist.

"Mostly when I'm running my chain saw," he replied.

George doesn't act impressed or unimpressed with his ability to work. "I always liked to be doing something. I never liked to sit around," he said. "I'm getting older, though. You can't do things like you do when you were young. Everything gets a little harder to do." At age 78, George instantly recalls dates, names and events. He doesn't care to dwell on details or the meanings of things. George was more reclusive than his sightless siblings, Abe and Esther. He likes the quiet of the farm. Seldom seen in town, his accomplishments are less visible except to immediate friends and family. That makes them no less remarkable.

"If something is broke we holler 'George!' and he can fix it most of the time," Esther said. He seldom drives a tractor, but he is skilled at repairing them. With pointers from a brother, John, who farmed nearby and was a good mechanic, George began to overhaul M and H Farmalls, red icons of farm country. Ask how he does it and he gets a quizzical look, as if to say, "How would you do it?"

"We farmed with horses when I was a kid. I never did drive tractors but I found I could fix them," he said. "I can remember pretty well where everything is on the tractor." He doesn't have to see the spark of the ignition. He can hear it jump. He didn't have enough tractors to fix in the 1950s, apparently, because that's when he constructed his first building, a 24 by 30-foot storage barn. He admits to having help with the rafters. Ask how he could run a level or square the corners and you get another quizzical look. "How would you do it?"

"Well, how would you know where to cut a board since you could not see a pencil mark," we asked?

"I made a notch with a jackknife."

He kept a square handy at all times, and had a level with a ball that could be felt instead of the customary air bubble. His brothers helped with the rafters, not because George was blind but because a man always needs help with rafters. The rest he did on his own — the frame, the siding, the doors. He handcrafted steel door handles. Over the years, he built a granary, a machine shed and a garage. All three are sturdy, straight and used today. The pattern of the shingles is near-perfect, both horizontally and vertically.

Most of the 240-acre farm is pasture, so George kept a beef cow herd. He clipped each cow's ear so he could identify her. We asked another stupid question. How could you identify her if you couldn't see the notches? "I tame them when they're calves so I can walk up and feel their ears," he said.

At age 78, George remains an early-riser. He gets up about 6:30 and has tea and cereal before going outside to feed the cows and the few chickens that remain on the farm. In nice weather, he spends most of the day outdoors with the dog, Pumpkin, at his heels. He works in his garden and fixes fences. He checks the tautness of each wire between each post. Occasionally, he backs a tractor from a shed, lines it up with a grinder, connects the two with a belt, and grinds grain for the livestock. He knows the home farm so well that, for years, he could cross a fence at one point, walk diagonally across a pasture, and know exactly where he was when he reached the next fence or gate.

George Voigt's way has a simple nobility. He moves around his farmyard, with purpose but never in a hurry. He raises cattle and cares for the farm with a joy reminiscent of the days when agriculture was less about money than about a way of life. Smelling the roses, breathing the fresh air of Bon Homme County, hearing the meadowlarks, feeling the difference between a tomato plant and pigeon grass — those senses are more than most of us get to enjoy all day every day.

July/August 2002

The Father of South Dakota

Ried Holien

ARTHUR CALVIN Mellette sacrificed much by moving to Dakota Territory. He said good-bye to his mother and father and his lifelong home in Indiana. He gave up the sterling reputation he had earned working as a lawyer, politician and newspaper publisher. His reason was simple: Nothing was as important to Mellette as his family. When a doctor said Arthur's wife, Maggie, needed a change in climate to preserve her failing health, he never considered staying put. They looked throughout the country before selecting Springfield, Dakota Territory, as their new home. When they arrived by train that morning in January, 1879, they must have thought they had made a terrible mistake: The skies were pouring snow, and it was 35 degrees below zero.

In Springfield, Arthur worked as registrar of the public land office, a post he secured by political appointment before leaving Indiana. A year after he arrived the office moved to Watertown, and the Mellettes followed. Arthur prospered through buying and selling land, but he found no housing he deemed adequate in the two-year-old town, so in 1883 he built a fine home in his new housing development.

Over the next decade, Mellette was active in pushing statehood for Dakota Territory, and spent over $16,000 of his own money traveling to Washington, D.C., lobbying congressmen. He was appointed territorial governor in 1887, and he would be the last. Late in 1889, Mellette got his wish when President Benjamin Harrison signed legislation creating two new states. Mellette was elected governor of the newly-minted state, and recognized for his efforts by having the title Father of South Dakota bestowed upon him.

Any grand plans Mellette may have had for South Dakota were quickly forgotten as the state was crippled by a terrible drought that hung on for years. Mellette appealed to charities in Eastern cities, making trips at his own expense to seek help in person. On one trip he raised $39,637, and to keep his promise that all donations would go directly to the poor without any being siphoned off for administration, he spent $3,600 of his own money to manage the funds. When his second two-year term ended in 1893, Mellette did not run again. His health was failing, and he was further devastated when Wylie, his eldest son, committed suicide in a fit of delirium from typhoid fever. The final tragedy came in 1895. Mellette's good friend, state treasurer William Walter Taylor, stole $300,000 from South Dakota's treasury and fled to South America. Because Mellette served as bondsman for Taylor, he was legally required to help pay for Taylor's thievery. Worse, Mellette felt betrayed and personally responsible. He immediately handed over all his money and property to state officials. Taylor was later apprehended and returned to South Dakota, and most of the stolen money was recovered, but Mellette never regained his property.

Broke, homeless, and embarrassed, the Mellette family moved to Pittsburg, Kansas. Arthur tried practicing law, but poor health limited his working. He died on May 25, 1896. Maggie fulfilled her husband's dying wish, returning him to South Dakota for burial. Thousands paid respect when Arthur lay in state at Watertown's Arcade Hotel, and at his burial in Watertown's Mount Hope Cemetery. At his funeral, Arthur's final statement as governor was remembered: "May God bless the people of South Dakota and their children forever and make them all worthy representatives of a great and grand state."

March / April 1999

GLADYS PYLE: NEARLY THE FIRST LADY GOVERNOR

Margaret Moxon

SHE WAS THE first woman elected to the South Dakota Legislature. She was the first woman elected to statewide office. She was the first woman in the nation's history elected to the United States Senate without a previous appointment. She also came closer to being elected governor than any other South Dakota woman in the 20th century.

She was Gladys Pyle, born the year after South Dakota was admitted to the Union. When she was elected to the state legislature in 1922, three years after women got the right to vote, her arrival wasn't the cataclysm hyperventilating opponents of suffrage had predicted. Pyle was a staunch Republican, and quietly went about the business of representing her Huron constituents without rocking the ship of state or disturbing the good old boys. Much. One legislator told her she made him quit smoking, though she protested she'd never said a word about his habit. "I know," he told her. "I was determined to smoke you out, and I smoked my pipe so much I got sick of it."

Pyle was elected Secretary of State in 1926. In 1930 she took a historic step by announcing her candidacy for governor. She garnered almost a third of the Republican primary vote, and the *Watertown Public Opinion* heralded her, "unattached candidacy, garbed in the political novelty of skirts." No candidate attained the 35 percent required to secure the nomination, so the final decision was left to the state convention. Delegates voted 11 times, and Gladys received the most votes on seven ballots. Between the eleventh and twelfth ballots there was frantic behind the scenes maneuvering, causing the announcement of the results to be delayed for a half-hour. In the end, another candidate, Brook Howell, threw his support to Warren Green, putting Green over the top. South Dakota, it seems, was not yet ready for a woman governor.

"Miss Pyle didn't weep and wail and scatter hair pins and tears about the convention hall," wrote Will A. Wells of the *Webster Journal*. "She thanked her friends, smiled at the jubilant guys who had played the scurvy trick and returned to her home as a good sport."

Gladys Pyle wasn't through trailblazing. She was elected to finish out U.S. Senator Peter Norbeck's term after he died in office in 1936, a milestone even though she served while Congress was in recess and never cast a vote. In 1940 Pyle was the first woman to deliver a presidential nominating speech at a national convention, doing the honors for Harlan J.

Bushfield at the Republican gathering that eventually selected Wendel Wilkie.

Gladys Pyle wasn't through yet. After two decades of trying, legislation allowing women to serve on juries in South Dakota was finally passed in 1947. She and five other women were seated at a Deadwood grand jury in September. "This jury duty has been a valuable experience and a real lesson in good citizenship," she said later. "One can not help being a better citizen as a result."

"Do not surround yourself only with those who supported you," Pyle replied when asked what advice she had for officeholders. "You need the views of those who opposed you." Good advice in any era.

Sept / Oct 1986

SMOKEY JOE, WORLD'S FASTEST HUMAN

Colin Kapitan

"I FELT LIKE running," said "Smokey" Joe Mendel. Did he ever! The day was May 23, 1931, at the S.D. Intercollegiate Conference track meet at Huron College. Mendel, competing for the Yankton College Greyhounds, had run well in the morning's preliminary heats, qualifying for the 100 and 220 yard finals, plus the broad jump. He and the other 100-yard finalists were called to the blocks shortly before two o'clock. Mendel was pleased — he'd drawn a fast lane.

Although he was normally a slow starter, Mendel leaped out of the blocks and flashed down the track. Three watches at the finish line were trained on him. Two clocked him at 9.5 seconds, the third a tenth of a second slower. By the rules of the day, that made Mendel's official time 9.5 — equal to the world record then held by Eddie Tolan of the University of Michigan. Officials checked and rechecked the distance, and verified with the weather bureau that his race had not been aided by a tail wind. Mendel's time was verified, and for a time he shared the record with Tolan. They both lost that distinction when Frank Wykoff ran a 9.4 a few weeks after Mendel's effort.

As a high school senior, Mendel had single-handedly carried Onida to the state track title. His four first-place finishes earned the team 20 points, besting Sioux Falls Washington's 19 points. Not a bad memory to carry through life — many a man's later years have been warmed by less — but nothing compared to that glorious spring day when a South Dakota farm kid won the title of World's Fastest Human.

July / August 1990

HIGHWAY 385'S MAN OF ADVENTURE

Bernie Hunhoff

MARTIN COLLINS WAS 98 years-old, and cautiously feeding a caged bear when we first met. The bear had recently bitten off part of his finger. We hoped to determine the secret to Collins' longevity, but soon discovered it was luck. He could have been killed many times, what with getting stomped, gored, kicked, and bitten by critters five to ten times his size.

His troubles began with rodeoing, and grew with his choice of livestock — buffalo and bear, for example. "One time I got between an old cow (buffalo) and her calf and she poked a hole in my stomach," he reminisced. He also survived a tangle with a tractor's power take-off and 20 years on the county commission, equally perilous activities in South Dakota.

Collins stood straight and lean as he closed in on the century mark, a throwback to simpler days when a man and wife could raise seven children on a rough piece of land, some imagination and a lot of sweat. For much of his life, he kept bread on the table by hanging a "donations accepted" box on a wooden fence at his ranch and encouraging motorists to stop and see his buffalo collection. His tourist attraction on Highway 385 between Hill City and Deadwood became known as Collins Buffalo Home. But savvy travelers realized that the most interesting inhabitant of the Collins ranch had two legs, not four — old Mr. Collins himself.

He traveled by covered wagon at age two with his parents to Lyman County. One of his earliest memories is of he and his father visiting Scotty Philip, one of several men credited with saving buffalo from extinction. "Right then, I got the idea that someday I was going to get some buffalo of my own," said Collins. As a young man, he hit the rodeo circuit — first as a saddle bronc rider, later as a clown. He won $1,200 at the big Wynot, Neb., rodeo by riding a terror named Graveyard. In 1942, he and his wife, Leonida, bought a ranch north of Pactola in the Black Hills, and Martin went back to the Philip ranch to buy buffalo. He fenced the buffalo along the road and hung the donations box. He never charged admission.

When buffalo became commonplace, Collins expanded to goats, horse rides and a tame, wide-horned Scottish Highlander steer. He bought the black bear cub a few years ago. The story behind Martin Collins wasn't that he lived so long (he died in 2003 at age 102), but that he packed in so much adventure. A horn one inch longer, a goring just a bit deeper, a kick just a littler harder, a disgruntled and manic taxpayer, and a lot of family, friends and passers-by on Highway 385 would have been the poorer.

July/August 1999

BUILDING THE "NEEDLESS" HIGHWAY

Roger Holtzmann

FIRST NATIVE-BORN governor. United States senator. Man of the people. Impractical dreamer. Progressive politician. Peter Norbeck was all this and more. But his most enduring contributions to South Dakota had little to do with his progressive ventures. In 1912, five years before he became governor, he was instrumental in establishing a Black Hills game preserve; as governor he expanded upon that work, creating a legacy for generations to come. In 1919 Norbeck proposed the creation of a state park board to develop Custer State Park.

The new state park was one of the largest in the nation, but Norbeck was not satisfied. He longed to include the Sylvan Lake/Needles/Harney Peak area, which was part of the Harney National Forest, within the park. At Norbeck's suggestion, Representative Harry Gandy of Rapid City introduced a bill in Congress to transfer the land from federal to state control. With that the park size nearly doubled, to over 70,000 acres.

Establishing the park was only part of Norbeck's vision. He and highway engineers C.C. Gideon and Scovell Johnson spent several days on horseback and afoot, tramping through the rugged area, seeking a route from the game preserve, through the Needles, to Harney Peak. His trousers torn and his legs scratched and bleeding, the 240-pound governor sat on a log catching his breath. "Can you build a road through there?" he asked Scovell Johnson.

"If you can furnish me enough dynamite," the engineer said.

Norbeck supplied the dynamite — 150,000 pounds of war-surplus blast, with which Johnson created 14 miles of breathtakingly beautiful road, the Needles Highway. Johnson's completed work almost came to naught, wrote Jessie Sundstrom in her history of Custer State Park, when signs ordered to show motorists the way to the highway read "Needless Highway." Whether that was somebody's opinion or bad spelling is not known, but, "Johnson lost no time in scraping off the offending last "S" with his pocket knife." Travelers have been finding the highway ever since, enjoying the Hills just as Norbeck hoped they would.

Nov / Dec 1998

NOBODY YELLED "KILL THE UMPIRE!"

Colin Kapitan

AMANDA CLEMENT'S story began in Hudson. Her father died while she was young, leaving her and her brother Hank to be raised by their mother, Harriet. The Clement house was next door to the ballpark, so the children spent a lot of time with baseball in hand. Amanda was attracted to the game, and had enough ability not to be embarrassed when a shortage of players forced the boys to let her play, but mostly she was relegated to umpire duty. If only the boys could have known! By giving Clement that often-thankless task they set her on a path toward the S.D. Sports Hall of Fame, the first umpire inducted, and the Baseball Hall of Fame at Cooperstown, N.Y.

Mandy, as she was called, got her first taste of umpiring for pay at the age of 16. She and her mother had traveled across the Big Sioux to Iowa to watch Hank pitch for Renville against Hawarden. Two local lodge teams were scheduled for a preliminary game, and when the umpire failed to show, Mandy was drafted from the crowd. The players were impressed by her work in the first game and begged her to umpire the second; mother took more persuading than daughter, but finally Mrs. Clement relented and allowed Amanda to take to the field. That Renville-Hawarden game of 1904 is the first on record of a woman umpiring a baseball game for money.

Every town and hamlet had a team in those days, and spectator interest ran high; from April to October, Saturday and Sunday afternoons were set aside for baseball. As the action heated up and local pride grew, larger towns like Sioux Falls and Sioux City hired the best players they could find. That took money, which meant attracting paying spectators, and promoters quickly realized what the novelty of a good-looking young lady calling balls and strikes could do for them. Soon every baseball team in the area was vying for Amanda Clement's services. She was billed as the "World Champion Woman Umpire," a true statement since she was the only one.

Mandy made quite an appearance on the baseball diamond. Standing 5'10" in a full-length blue skirt, black necktie and white blouse with UMP stenciled across the front, she was described as an "inspiring sight" and "more than just a pretty face" by local newspapers. "She is death on balls and strikes," one reporter wrote. A no-nonsense Congregationalist, she often lodged with local ministers when working away from home. She refused to umpire on Sundays, and once left a game after two innings because a player swore. A longtime friend, Janet Mills, recalled that Amanda always marveled at the players' uncharacteristic politeness when she was behind home plate. Instead of "Kill the Ump!" they said, "Beg your pardon, Miss Umpire, but wasn't that one a bit high?"

Amanda Clement called games throughout the upper Midwest, and was always the first person contacted to umpire a game of any importance. Baseball earnings paid her way through college, and after her graduation from the University of Nebraska in 1909, she gave up the life of an umpire — but not her love of baseball. She remained a fan until her death in 1971.

July / August 1985

HARDY AND THE LAZY NEIGHBOR

Peter Carrels

WHEN HIS butter tub manufacturing business in New England went under, Hardy Webster Campbell headed west, lured by free homestead land in Dakota Territory. He settled a claim in what is now Brown County and managed to eke out a living. Besides the usual homesteading difficulties, Campbell had a lazy neighbor who'd gotten in the habit of cutting across his land, leading a team of four mules through his plowed field. The following year, when the wheat planted in the rest of the field was withering in the July heat, Campbell was intrigued to see that that the wheat planted where the mules had trampled the earth was thriving.

Though a newcomer to farming, Campbell was a studious, perceptive man. He began a series of experiments to try and understand what had happened, a path that led eventually to a variety of dry land farming techniques that emphasized the then-novel idea of adapting farming methods to conditions on the plains rather than trying to farm with techniques that had worked back east, where rainfall was consistent and plentiful. His efforts were met with skepticism at first, of course, but when his yields began to consistently outpace those of his neighbors people began to notice. With the financial backing of railroads, which had a vested interest in seeing farming succeed on the plains, Campbell began publishing "Campbell's Soil Culture Manual." Eventually he came to manage a string of 43 model farms in five states, pioneering dry-land farming techniques that helped agriculture thrive across the Midwest — all because of an inconsiderate neighbor.

March / April 1987

THE MAN WHO WOULD FEED THE WORLD

Jerry Wilson

IN THE EYES OF the world's hungry, the handful of heroes that include Gandhi and Mother Theresa would also include George McGovern. Few people — perhaps nobody in human history — has worked longer or harder to provide food to the poor than the minister's son from Mitchell.

As a World War II bomber pilot in Italy, McGovern found himself surrounded by hungry children begging for food, mothers scratching through the soldiers' garbage for something to take home to their kids. "It sensitized me to what that meant in the life of a family," he said. "The streets were full of young women selling themselves, not because they were immoral, but because that was the only way they could scrape together enough to take care of their children. That made a lasting impression on me." McGovern flew 35 bombing missions over Nazi Germany. When the war was over, his final run was to fly surplus food to former enemies. "I was very eager to get home at the end of the war," he said, "but I'm glad we were asked to fly one last mission, to take food to the hungry."

Back home, McGovern couldn't put what he'd seen behind him. He saw that the world had two surpluses: farm commodities and empty stomachs. He realized that until we get the two surpluses together, we won't solve either problem. The up side was that farm surpluses could be a blessing instead of a curse. McGovern's eye has been steadily trained on those conclusions ever since. Elected to Congress in 1956, he served two terms in the House of Representatives and three in the U.S. Senate. Between his house and senate careers, McGovern headed the Food for Peace program when John F. Kennedy was president. Campaigning for president in 1972 opened McGovern's eyes wider. "I discovered pockets of hunger in the United States," he said, "millions of children without adequate diet, poor people all over the country, skimping to get by."

From the beginning McGovern saw that appealing to the interests of farmers, food processors, packers and shippers was half the battle. "If we can get this program moving it's going to drive up prices and lower surpluses, and farmers will have the satisfaction, not only of increased income, but of seeing what they've produced used for constructive purposes," he said. "Everybody in the food or agriculture or shipping business will profit."

How much would McGovern's international feeding plan cost? "About the cost of one B-2 bomber," said the former bomber pilot. "But feeding the hungry would enhance our national security a lot more than one more bomber. This is something we can do. I wouldn't argue that mankind yet has the faculty to put an end to war and killing. Those things are probably going to be around as long as there are human beings. But I would argue that we can end hunger on this planet, and we should be able to do it in the next couple of decades."

Nov/Dec 2001

Postcard to the Future

Paul Higbee

FOR AN ORDINARY man, the carving of Mount Rushmore as it is would have been accomplishment enough. But Gutzon Borglum was no ordinary man. Speaking at the site in 1936, before an audience that included President Franklin Roosevelt, the sculptor outlined his soaring vision of the carving as more than just four presidential heads: "There should be a great stairway of stone cut from the local rock on the east facade, easy to ascend, and back of the sculpture into the mountain itself a great room, at least 90 by 110 feet, should be cut. Into this room the records of what our people aspired to and what they have accomplished should be collected and preserved, and on the walls of this room should be cut the literal record of the conception of our republic." Half a century later there was no great stairway, just a steep path winding between boulders and then metal, ladder-like stairs for the ascent's last stage. The Hall of Records, cut 70 feet into the mountain wall, contained not records of the republic's conception, but compressed-air pipes, left from the carving years ago.

If anything epitomized the unfinished nature of Gutzon Borglum's great dream, this tunnel did. But Borglum's descendants hadn't given up on completing the Hall of Record. The Borglum family found an ally in Rushmore Superintendent Dan Wenk, who suggested using part of the $56 million dollars raised for redeveloping visitor facilities to make a start on completing the Hall. Finally, on August 9, 1998 — 62 years after Gutzon Borglum's speech — 16 porcelain enamel panels were fitted into a special box in the Hall's floor. Pictures and text are intended for future civilizations that may be awed by the great heads, yet clueless as to who or what the figures represent. "You might as well drop a letter into the world's postal service without an address or signature, as to send that carved mountain into history without identification," Borglum had said.

Not many people will ever see the Hall. There are no plans for bringing the great stairway to fruition. But future explorers may find the description of Rushmore's creation, the memorial's meaning, and the lives of the four presidents and Gutzon Borglum. The U.S. Constitution with all amendments is reproduced, as is the Declaration of Independence and the Gettysburg Address. Architect Ron Mason designed the excavation and everything placed inside, as well as the 1,200 pound capstone used to seal the crypt. Inscribed on the capstone is Gutzon Borglum's hope that the sculpted figures will survive "until the wind and rain alone shall wash them away."

Nov / Dec 1998

BLACK ELK'S RETURN TO HARNEY PEAK

Hilda Neihardt

IN 1931, LAKOTA Holy Man Black Elk described his youthful vision on Harney Peak to John Neihardt and his daughters, Enid and Hilda. Then, with Black Elk's son, Ben, they climbed the mountain. Hilda Neihardt tells the story in this excerpt from Black Elk and Flaming Rainbow.

THE MORNING OF May 30, 1931, we breakfasted at Sylvan Lodge, then started the long walk to the top of the rocky peak called Harney. Isn't it ironic that the peak bears the name of an army general who was no friend to the Indians? The path up the mountain is said to be four miles, but what a long four miles it is! The altitude at Sylvan Lake is approximately 6,000 feet, and the top of Harney Peak is 7,240.

Black Elk had carefully planned what would happen on the peak. Before leaving Manderson, he had purchased a set of red flannel underwear. In his vision his whole body had been painted red, and to reenact the scene on this day, he really should have been naked, his body painted red, wearing only a breechclout. But Enid and I were there and he did not wish to embarrass us. Thus the red underwear. Black Elk went behind a large rock, and after a few minutes he came out wearing the red underwear with a breechclout over it. Then, with his sacred pipe, he was ready to stand on the highest part of the rocky peak and send forth a voice to the six grandfathers of the universe.

Looking about the rough surface of the peak, Black Elk immediately recognized and pointed out to my father the particular high, jutting rock on which he had stood in his vision. Because that point was not easily reached, however, Black Elk chose a lower portion of rock that was as near as possible to the sacred spot. Now he stood on that flat rock, offering the pipe with its mouthpiece upward in one hand and reaching skyward with the other. As the holy man sent forth his voice to Wakan Tanka, the Great Mysterious, offering the stem of his pipe to the One Above, my father took the picture of Black Elk that more than one photographer has praised. The camera he used was a Kodak 3A, with a pull-out bellows for focusing, and it took a postcard-sized picture. Black Elk holds the pipe in his left hand, with his right hand uplifted, palm forward to the emptiness in front of him. I mention this because Black Elk had stated more than once that the pipe should always be held in the right hand. Was there a sacred reason he held it differently on that day?

Looking up into the bright, brassy, cloudless sky, the holy man faced the west, whence his power came, held his pipe with its buffalo hide-covered mouthpiece toward the sky, reached up and out with his other hand, and spoke words that have touched the hearts of many. Let me recall some of those words:

"Tunkashila, Wakan Tanka [Grandfather, Great Mysterious], you have been always, and before you nothing has been.... There is nothing to pray to but you. You yourself, everything that you see, everything has been made by you. The four quarters of the earth you have finished; the day, and in that day, everything you have finished.

"Grandfather, lean close to the earth, that you may hear the voice I send.

"Grandfather, Great Mysterious, all over the world the faces of living things are alike. In tenderness they have come up out of the ground. Look upon your children, with children in their arms, that they may face the winds and walk the good road to the day of quiet.

"In sending up my voice I pray that you may cause the tree to bloom again so that my people may see happy days. My grandfathers, you have sent me to the center of the earth and showed me the good things that were to be. Hear me now, that my people may live.

"Again, and probably for the last time, I recall my vision and call upon you for help. I send a voice again so that you may hear me and bring my people back into the sacred hoop. At the center of the hoop there should be a tree, a tree that was to bloom and help us.

"Hear me, 0 Great Mysterious One, that my people may live and that the tree may bloom, and that the people may see happy days and the happy land that you have promised.

"Tunkashila, Grandfather, behold this pipe. In behalf of my children and also my nephew's children, I offer this pipe, that we may see happy days!"

As Black Elk prayed, a little black cloud had come overhead, and a scant, cool rain began to fall. As the drops of rain mingled with the tears running down his face, the holy man cried out: "Oh, make my people live!"

The little black cloud went back the way it had come, and the rain stopped.

March/April 2001

IPSWICH'S PROMOTER: PONIES AND YELLOW PAINT

Bernie Hunhoff

A PHOTOGRAPH IN the Edmunds County museum shows Joe Parmley's big herd of Shetland ponies. Why did he own so many? "He loaned them out to the country kids so they could ride them to school in the winter," explained Phyllis Herrick, an Ipswich woman who lobbied the town to move the museum into Parmley's brick and concrete house. Parmley bought his first Shetlands to provide outdoor exercise for his son, Loren, who suffered from asthma. As the herd grew, Parmley "farmed them out" to kids who needed transportation.

The Shetlands are just one reminder of Parmley's beneficence to the town he helped found in 1884. He was superintendent of schools, a state legislator and county judge. He was so busy with public service that friends wondered how he managed to eke out a living in his abstract business. He spent years promoting the Yellowstone Trail as the preferred route "from Plymouth Rock to Puget Sound." Local jokesters said he spent all his money on yellow paint. It may have been true. He personally helped paint yellow signs with a black arrow on utility poles, rocks and anything else seen by motorists.

He arranged for an arch to be built over Highway 12 as a memorial to a dozen Ipswich area men who died in World War I. The first, a wood structure, blew down in 1922. It was replaced by a sturdy arch of steel and stone. State officials demanded that it be removed in 1973, so it was moved to a nearby park where it still stands.

Parmley bought his own grader to improve the roads in northeast South Dakota. He helped new settlers get a start in farming. In the 1930s, he joined the effort to build the International Peace Garden on the U.S.-Canadian border. Parmley also promoted soil conservation, hydro-electric power, construction of bridges and dams on the Missouri, and dams to create artificial lakes. When Snake Creek east of Ipswich was dammed, the impoundment was called Parmley Lake in his honor. When he died in 1940, many of his dreams for South Dakota had come to fruition. Others happened in the years to come, but nobody's passing out ponies anymore.

That's a shame.

Nov / Dec 1995

THE LITTLE TOWN WITH THE BIG CHURCH

Jerry Wilson

THEY ARE THE highest work of God or man for many miles of prairie. More elevated than the Equity Exchange grain elevators, towering above the water tower, they loom on the Potter County horizon, taller than the tallest trees. They dwarf the modest homes of Hoven and the one-story businesses that flank two blocks of Main. They are the twin towers of the Cathedral of the Prairie.

It isn't really a cathedral, just a prairie church. But Monsignor Anthony Helmbrecht, who presided over the Catholic parish for half a century, harbored hope that one day Hoven might be a bishop's home. Bishops have visited, and in the Jubilee Year of 2000, Bishop Robert Carlson declared St. Anthony's Church a destination for Catholic pilgrims. But no bishop has resided in Hoven, and the Cathedral of the Prairies remains a small-town church — a church of beauty and grandeur.

Perhaps Father Helmbrecht thought the church would grow the town — economic development with a spiritual twist. But just as Hoven failed to gain ecclesiastical might, it never achieved worldly power, either. On the Potter-Walworth county line, it was not well-situated to become the seat of either county. And 118 years after its founding, the town faces the same struggles as its neighbors. Fewer farmers. Fewer stores. Fewer jobs. Fewer people. But if Hoven's residents hold their heads a little higher than people in neighboring towns, perhaps they have a right. Their ancestors built, and then maintained, the church of the monsignor's dreams.

Hoven's pioneer Catholics worshipped in small frame churches that fit their humble needs. But in 1908 Father Anthony Helmbrecht arrived from Bavaria. He brought a romantic bond to the medieval churches of the old world — and a dauntless vision that a great cathedral could be built upon the plains. He wanted to build a church like the 1,000-year-old churches in his birth area of Ruhmannsfelden. He believed his flock of hard-working townsmen and farmers could build such a church, and in time, he convinced them to pursue that dream. The men of Hoven excavated a huge hole, 64 feet wide and 161 feet long, and each time the farmers came to town, they brought a wagon load of gravel, sand or stone — more than a thousand loads in all. In a couple of years the foundation and the basement were complete, covered with a temporary roof. For a decade the church was underground. Urged on by Father Helmbrecht, little by little the congregation planned and saved, and at last they began building up. To celebrate Easter in 1921, they moved into the finest house of worship most of them had ever seen. Their towering Romanesque church stood seven stories tall to the peak of the roof, 130 feet to the crosses atop the towers. Sixty long oak pews could seat at least a thousand people.

No expense or detail was spared. The church is entered through massive oak doors, guarded by glaring gargoyles. Bas-relief stations of the cross grace the side walls. Twelve tall Bavarian-painted windows depict the life of Christ, from birth to ascension. Three huge bells, weighing a total of two tons, still gong from the spires, though for everyday use they've given way to recorded sound. The north tower displays the face of a clock whose gigantic machinery ticks and purrs in the garret. In 1930 a superb organ was added, 1,127 pipes in 17 ranks. The woodwork is tooled and polished oak — all the way to the attic.

Not even the strongest of men, or the best-built edifice, can last forever. Father Helmbrecht died in 1956, and by 1980 the church needed major repairs. The roof was leaking, and 60-year-old art that graced the church from crown to sole was stained and crumbling. Now the priest was Father Ed Burian. Renovating the huge structure was a forbidding task, which once again called for leadership. The congregation began restoration which, though not as ambitious as the building project of their grandparents, was none-the-less a daunting task that consumed the extra energy and resources of many people for five years. After 20,000 hours of donated labor, they were finished — at least for a time.

March/April 2000

DANCING IN THE SACRED HOOP

Jerry Wilson

KEVIN LOCKE enters the powwow circle, and like a magnet draws all eyes. He is vigor and smile, a muscular man in long black braids. He wears an aqua ribbon shirt, beaded moccasins, a breechclout over shorts. A duffel bag balances on his shoulder. He strides to the center and slides his load to the floor. He opens his bag, extracts a traditional Lakota cedar wood flute and begins to play. The song is a courtship melody Locke inherited from a generation of elders. The tune comes to its end and he lays the flute aside. From the duffel bag he draws a handful of four-colored hoops — red, white, yellow and black. Four men around a hide-topped drum begin to play. Locke picks up the beat, and the dance begins.

If the wistful notes of the flute had calmed the soul, the dance could boil the blood. A whirling dervish, the soul of a whirlwind, Locke scoops up the hoops, one by one, with his toe. They spin about his ankles, rise to his knees, then to his hips to meet his hands. Clockwise he spins, but in the blink of an eye his motion reverses. Around and around he whirls, the throbbing nucleus of the circle of humanity of which he has assumed the center. Above his shoulders a delicate flower blooms, metamorphoses into a fluttering butterfly, then stars and moon and sun. As the dance goes on a madly spiraling eagle spreads its wings. Long past normal bounds of human endurance, the final movement of Locke's dance begins. In a final symphony, a fabulous interlinked structure evolves, an orbiting globe of human diversity, 28 interlocked hoops, a picture of the unity of humankind.

The dance at its end, Locke bows low to the audience, extracts his body from the structure he has built and tells with words the tale his dance has spun. The four-colored hoops represent completeness and unity — the four human races, four directions, four seasons, four winds. "God wants us to reach," he explains, "reach for more light, feed our roots and blossom. We are all branches of the great human family tree. We can soar like the eagles, give off fragrance like the flowers." But we can realize our beauty and our potential only as we set aside our divisions, our distrust, our prejudice and fear of one another, he says.

Firmly rooted in Lakota culture, Kevin Locke has become a missionary for human harmony and global unity. Though South Dakotan by birth and by choice, he is also a cosmopolitan citizen of the world, having performed in 70 countries. Locke didn't plan to spend his life dancing around the globe. He grew up near Wakpala on the Standing Rock reservation; his formative years were passed in close communion with an elderly traditional uncle, Abraham End of Horn, who spoke Lakota and trained the boy in the traditions of his culture.

A friend named Arlo Good Bear offered to teach him the hoop dance. Kevin would travel many places, meet many people, be an emissary from the Lakota people, his friend told him. Good Bear taught Locke one lesson, and a week later he was dead. Locke was among the men who carried him to his grave. But then the dreams began. Again and again, he met his friend in his dreams. And there were others too, people from across generations, from around the globe, from many tribes, Europeans, Asians, Africans. In the dreams, Good Bear danced designs — designs of nature, of birds and flowers and rainbows. Locke saw that he must carry this thing forward, create patterns of beauty that would unite peoples around the Earth.

Locke grew up under the influence of both Christian and Lakota spiritual traditions, but his personal vision coalesced when he found the teachings of Bahá'u'lláh, a Persian nobleman in Iran who in the middle of the 19th century gave up the comfort and security of his princely life to seek and teach a vision of worldwide unity. Kevin Locke felt compelled to be a global wanderer, a Lakota ambassador, an international envoy for peace.

Jan/Feb 2000

SCHEMING FRANK LEAHY

Paul Higbee

NO UNIVERSITY IN the land has a richer football tradition than Notre Dame, and no single individual, not even the legendary Knute Rockne, contributed more than Frank Leahy. He was head football coach at Notre Dame from 1941 to 1953, interrupted by two years in the navy during World War II, during which time his teams went 87-11-9. He won three national championships, coached four Heisman Trophy winners, and became famous — or infamous — as a schemer who would do anything to win, a trait he first exhibited as an eighth-grader in Winner, S.D.

Young Leahy had not gotten off the bench all season, and it didn't look like Coach Arthur Neff was going to give him a chance in the final game of 1922 against Gregory, who was on its way to a 108-0 victory, scoring touchdown after touchdown. Just when it seemed things could get no worse, the referee ejected a Winner player, for some unspecified offense, and Neff had no choice but to put Leahy in the game. Later it came out that the referee was dating Leahy's sister, and Frank had convinced the man it would make no difference, in a lopsided game, if a Winner player got ejected. When it was over, only one Winner player left the field with a big smile on his face.

Leahy's career as a player at Notre Dame was undistinguished, but Knute Rockne loved him for his win-at-all-costs ways. When he went on to become a coach Leahy carried that attitude with him — carried it to extremes, on occasion, as when he told a player who fumbled on a key play that the error would result in eternal damnation. Success, in Leahy's mind at least, only increased the pressure for more success. As the years went by he became more and more obsessed, which contributed to health problems that eventually forced his retirement. Losing was never again as fun as it was that long-ago day in Winner.

Nov / Dec 1987

NELLIE WILHITE: OUR FIRST LADY OF THE AIR

Dorene Weinstein

SHE WAS THE 13th student to sign up for Harold Tennant's class, and after 13 hours of instruction, she took off for her first solo flight on Friday, the 13th of January, 1927. So much for omens. Nellie Wilhite did just fine, and when she landed on the soggy grass of Renner airfield that day she became South Dakota's first licensed female pilot. Nellie was 34 years old at the time, and went on to fly in air shows across the country, doing acrobatics and puncturing stereotypes. Wilhite later obtained her transport license, became a flight instructor, and flew with Amelia Earhart — with whom she was a charter member of Club 99, an organization of female aviators. Nellie Wilhite's accomplishment would have been noteworthy in any event. What made them all the more remarkable was that she had been deaf since childhood.

May / June 1989

NO SECRET TO SUCCESS

Bernie Hunhoff

DAVE PLOOF, WHO founded Rapid City's American Legion baseball dynasty, regularly got calls from other coaches asking about the program, and wondering whether they might come to town and observe. "We welcome them to come in here, because we're really all in the same business. We're developing young men, and if we can help show them some of the things we are doing then that's great." But visiting coaches who expected to find a secret curveball or a better way to hold the bat went home disappointed. "It's like the game of golf," said Ploof. "Everybody is looking for that unique toy that'll cut five strokes off their game. It doesn't exist. Intelligence and hard work, that's what'll get you success."

Sept / Oct 1988

QUOTABLES

A young state like South Dakota, with its fulfillment still in the future, may be the proving ground for the ideas and resolutions of the next century.

— John Milton

Success against odds is always more gratifying than unearned reward, and in that regard South Dakotans can stand tall ...

— Bob Karolevitz

South Dakota, where men are men and steaks are three inches thick.

— Time Magazine, 1945

Mysteries

*L*ife itself is a mystery, but that's a bigger issue than we've tackled in* South Dakota Magazine. *We have covered smaller mysteries that have become legends throughout the land.*

Why are footprints embedded in a boulder at Gettysburg? Is the Thoen Stone a fake or a message from a tormented gold miner? Were the petrified men at Hot Springs for real? Where is the world's largest painting? What species of fish pulled a boat up the Missouri? Is there a bandit's cave somewhere on the Pine Ridge? Are ghosts for real? Why would a lawman switch sides to be a gangster?

For some odd reason, South Dakota mysteries often involve stones. We have not figured out what that means. If we do, we might set our writers to work on the meaning of life. Meanwhile, here are some of our more mysterious excerpts, rocks and all.

— Bernie Hunhoff

MISSOURI RIVER MONSTER MYSTERY

Marilyn Kratz

ON THE WARM Sunday afternoon of May 31, 1992, Lynn Wysuph and his wife Dawn floated lazily down the Missouri River near Yankton. At about 3:30, they turned off the motor of their 16-foot boat to enjoy the peace and quiet. Suddenly, they heard a splash.

"What's that?" asked Dawn, pointing to an object heading upstream. It appeared to be a marker of some sort, about ten inches across and two feet long. One end was pointed. On top was a little yellow flag. The object was being pulled by a nylon rope about a half-inch in diameter. Another piece of rope about six to eight feet long trailed behind the object.

"It must be a marker that got loose somewhere," said Lynn. "But I wonder what's pulling it upstream. Let's follow it."

Lynn started the motor and began to follow the mysterious object. Suddenly, it disappeared below the surface and reappeared behind them.

"There it is!" shouted Dawn.

But, before Lynn could turn the boat around, the object surfaced ahead of them again. After repeating that maneuver three more times, the object surfaced close to the boat. "I'm going to try to catch it," said Lynn. He dipped their fishing net towards the object. But it was pulled away too quickly for him to get it.

"Where is it now?" asked Dawn, searching for the elusive object. She did not have long to wait for her answer.

The motor on their boat stopped abruptly. It had become entangled in the piece of rope dangling behind the marker. The young couple's excitement with the chase turned to cold fear as their boat was hauled around and began to be pulled upstream — backwards. "Hold on!" shouted Lynn. He grabbed his fillet knife and tried to cut the rope, but whatever was pulling their boat along had decided to go down in the water and pulled the end of the boat down with it.

"Get to the front of the boat!" Lynn shouted to Dawn. The transom of their boat was only inches above the surface of the water now. Lynn hung on with one hand and leaned out of the boat as far as he dared. He slashed blindly in the water, trying to connect with the rope.

At that moment, Dawn spotted a boat upstream. She waved and shouted for help. The man in the boat turned his craft around and raced to their aid. "Motor trouble?" he called, pulling up beside them.

"Something is pulling us under," shouted Lynn. Just then, his knife slashed through the rope entangled in their motor. Whatever was attached to the other rope on the marker headed upstream.

"What is that?" asked the man, staring.

"We don't know," gasped Lynn, catching his breath. "But whatever it is, it's mighty powerful."

"I'm going to follow it," said the man, and he sped off after it.

Lynn cut the rope out of the propellers of his motor and went after the other boat. But the marker disappeared under the water about 300 yards upstream.

"I wonder which way it went now," said the man, steering his boat near the Wysuphs.

"I don't think we want to know," said Lynn. "We've had enough excitement for one day!"

Dawn nodded in agreement, still too stunned to speak.

They were at least a mile upstream from where their adventure had begun. Lynn estimated they had been pulled by the mysterious object the last 200 yards.

A few days later, their story was published in a local newspaper. People began to speculate about what could have been pulling the marker — and the 16-foot boat — upstream in the river. It must have been something large and powerful. But what?

The muddy Missouri is home to many species of fish, some of which can grow to enormous size. The 50 million year old species of paddlefish can grow to 250 pounds and river catfish can grow to about 100 pounds, but neither of those would be large enough to pull a 16-foot boat upstream backwards.

When dams were built along the Missouri River, stories were told of divers seeing fish up to 15 feet long near the bottom of the river. These may have been lake sturgeon, which can live to 100 years and attain the weight of more than 1,000 pounds. Their slender body and long snout, covered with bony plates, would be a terrifying sight at that size. They certainly would be large and powerful enough to pull a boat about their same size.

The muddy Missouri continues to flow lazily through the heart of South Dakota. Every year, millions of people enjoy swimming, fishing, and boating in its tranquil waters without giving a thought to what lurks in its murky depths.

March/April 1994

Boss Cowman's Secret Cave

HIDDEN TREASURE in secret caves is the thing of legend. If this story had been told by most cowboys it would have seemed unbelievable, but it was told by Ed Lemmon, known as "Boss" Cowman in the town that bears his name, and his credibility was never questioned.

Lemmon was raised in Nebraska, the son of a pioneer railroader. He began to ride with trail herds while still a boy, and arrived in South Dakota in the summer of 1880 to work for the Sheidley Cattle Company in West River. He soon became a partner in several big ranches. Widely respected in the cattle industry, he helped to found state cattleman organizations.

In an autobiography, *The Recollections of Ed Lemmon*, he wrote of a secret cave on the Pine Ridge Reservation. Some of his cattle had strayed onto the Pine Ridge and he was hunting for them along the White River. He worked his way down a gully that opened into a large canyon opposite the mouth of Grass Creek.

Lemmon came upon a large cave opening and decided to explore. With a torch in one hand and his revolver in the other, he walked deep into the cave and came upon a treasure room. He later wrote, "The walls were covered with hangings and with other relics of all kinds. I didn't see any white robes there, but there were lots of others. I just stood there and gazed as far as I could see in the light of my torch. It was about all the same for 40 or 50 feet, to where the cave widened to about 25 feet across by 15 or 20 feet high, and all of it was covered with relics."

Lemmon thought it was a bandit's hide-out and he departed quickly. Later that same year he returned to look for the cave but couldn't find it. He concluded that landslides along the river had covered the opening.

July/August 1994

Sioux Falls Ghost Buster

Ann Grauvogl

IT IS 8:30 p.m. on a green, spring night in May. The cafe in Canton has just closed. A few stragglers who may have had one of the specials — grilled cheese, an Indian taco or chef's salad — are paying their bills. A compact car from Sioux Falls arrives in the setting sun. Donna O'Dea wears thick-soled sneakers, loose jeans and a windbreaker. She looks like a favorite teacher ready for a field trip. She's down to earth, looks you straight in the eye. She didn't drive to Canton for a piece of homemade strawberry-rhubarb pie.

Ghost busting is on the psychic's menu for the night, and she's ready to get to work. "I've done quite a few," O'Dea says. She means ghost busts. Every few months, someone calls. "I get people who are just hysterical," she says. "They don't all have ghosts when they think they do. You know how that goes. People hear something, then their imaginations get going, and they don't have anything more than the wind blowing."

After cafe owner Jan Vandekieft called a week ago, O'Dea made a preliminary trip to the 125 year-old main street building to make sure ghosts, not pranksters or imaginations, were at work. Tonight, she'll ask the ghosts to leave. She expects four. She'll find five. Before she's done, ghost busting will seem more like shooing chickens than the serious business of letting spirits know they're dead, and liberating them from their earthly ties. "OK, you guys need to quit," she'll tell the ghosts of a U.S. cavalry soldier killed at Little Big Horn and that of a Lakota warrior killed at Wounded Knee. "Custer lost," she says, patiently but firmly. "It's the year 2001. It's over."

O'Dea wields no cross, carries no Bible, hasn't invented a ghost vacuum. She trusts she'll be able to reason with these earthbound ghosts, because she's been seeing and communicating with spirits since she was a kid. "They're not evil," she says. "They're just lost."

The Canton ghost bust takes O'Dea to a dark, stone wall basement storage room. O'Dea says two of the ghosts, a soldier and an Indian, have been in a constant fight. The warrior scalps the soldier again and again. "The fight is over. The fight is over," O'Dea says, stepping between them in the chilly room. "See, you can't punch me. You can't hurt me," says the ghost buster, although she will later admit that her scalp tingles. "My body is alive."

Her voice is urgent. "The blood is over. The pain is over. The war is over. Work for peace on the other side." O'Dea calls on angels and White Buffalo Calf Woman to lead the men to the light. "There are drums in heaven," she says, answering one more ghostly question. "Go."

And they do, perhaps. The most noticeable difference to the cafe workers who have followed O'Dea into the basement is that the smell in the room, a nasty smell that's lingered for years, is not so strong anymore.

Ghosts, if you listen to O'Dea, are all around us. They're in public buildings and private homes. They're in the country and in the city. O'Dea estimates as many as a third of the people who die don't go to heaven right away. Humans are mind, spirit and soul, says O'Dea, who believes in a benevolent universe and a God who gives people chance after chance after chance. "We're taught the spirit lives on," she says. "It's hard to comprehend, but it actually does." She sees ghosts as earthbound souls. "The body died, but for whatever reason they don't go to God, go home, go to the light, whatever you call it.... They have a life to get onto on the other side. They should do it."

While some ghosts don't know they're dead, some are willfully stuck, she said. "Denial is a strong force. They can be in denial for quite a long time."

Jan/Feb 2002

WHY DID A COP BECOME A CROOK?

Brad Smith

IN 1920 THE *EVENING HURONITE*, promoted a Huron man for Beadle County sheriff by editorializing that with his election "crooks and licentious characters will have no protection and the safety of our wives and children and the future well-being of our families will be fully guaranteed." Thirteen years later the U.S. Justice Department announced a manhunt for "the most dangerous criminal in the country." Both referred to the same man. Verne Miller has been described as "the most contradictory and mysterious figure of the 1930's Public Enemy community." A handsome blue-eyed redhead, he did not drink, gamble or swear. However, he was a suspect in up to 12 murders and may have participated in more.

His path from lawman to lawlessness is puzzling. In 1922 Sheriff Miller seemed assured of re-election. Then his wife, Mildred, was admitted to a Rochester, Minn., hospital. Miller told his deputies he was taking a leave to visit his wife. From Rochester they would go to a Washington, D.C., sanitarium to take treatments for his lungs. After weeks with no contact from the sheriff, his deputies became worried. Then they discovered Miller had withdrawn $4,000 from accounts — money apparently from tax collections. The career of Sheriff Miller came to a startling end. The career of Verne Miller, gangster, was just beginning. For three months there was no sign of him, then South Dakota officers received a call from a St. Paul hotel operator wondering if they were still looking for Miller.

In the 1920s there were several places outlaws could "cool off." The most popular was St. Paul. As one criminal noted, "In those days if you hadn't seen a friend for a few months you looked two places — prison or

St. Paul." Before the hotel owner notified South Dakota officials, he had called the St. Paul chief of detectives and was assured that Miller was no longer wanted. The deputy who arrested Miller reported that Miller's first phone call while in custody was to that same chief of detectives.

In the Beadle County jail, Miller displayed his resolute self-reliance. He turned down offers from friends to raise the $10,000 bond, pled guilty to embezzlement of $2,600 and was sentenced to two years. He entered the state penitentiary April 4, 1923, and landed the cushy job of warden's chauffeur. Paroled in 1924, he found work as a farm laborer near Doland. But within a year he was indicted for bootlegging, paid a $200 fine and disappeared. In 1928 he was indicted for his part in a Minneapolis speakeasy shootout. Charges were dropped for lack of evidence.

In 1929 Miller was running Canadian gambling interests for Lepke Buchalter, one of the most powerful figures in East Coast organized crime. In 1930 Miller held up the Wilmar, Minn., bank with Machine Gun Kelly and the dean of bank robbers, Harvey Bailey. In 1931 with Bailey and Oklahoma outlaw Frank Nash, Miller robbed a bank in Sherman, Texas.

In 1932 Miller paid his last visit to his father's White Lake farm. Friends and relatives said the gangster's shiny car and expensive clothes made quite an impression. In December of that year Miller drove a get-away car for the Barker gang when they held up a Minneapolis bank. Two police officers happened on the scene and were slain in a hail of machine-gun fire. The Barker gang split up after that; Miller moved to Kansas City.

A few months later Miller received a frantic call from the wife of his old friend, Frank Nash. Her husband had been arrested by federal agents. The call touched off events that culminated the next day in the bloody outrage that will forever be known as the Kansas City Massacre. On the morning of June 17, 1933, the parking lot of the Kansas City Union Railroad Station was crowded with passengers, their family and friends. Few paid notice to the seven nervous lawmen surrounding a handcuffed prisoner, Frank Nash. The lawmen had reason to be nervous. Nash had strong underworld ties. They feared his friends might attempt a rescue. As they loaded Nash into a car, their fears were realized. Three men jumped from a nearby car and one, brandishing a Tommy gun, commanded the officers to "Hold it!" Time froze as the two armed camps regarded each other. Then an officer went for his pistol and all hell broke loose. Within seconds it was over. Four officers were dead and two were seriously wounded. Nash was also dead. The bandits escaped unscathed.

The FBI identified Miller as leader of the Kansas City gang. No stone would go unturned in their search. In October of 1933, the FBI traced Miller to Chicago. They surrounded his apartment and Miller escaped in a flurry of bullets. Still, Miller's days were numbered. On the evening of November 29, 1933, a motorist on the outskirts of Detroit discovered a naked mutilated body alongside the road. Fingerprints taken by the FBI confirmed that the search for Verne Miller was over.

His grief-stricken father made plans for the funeral; plans that, like most of Verne's life, were plagued with controversy. As a veteran, he was entitled to full military rites. However, the national Legion commander forbade the local post from participating. National proclamation notwithstanding, Miller's flag-draped casket was escorted from White Lake to Huron by uniformed ex-servicemen, Miller's friends. In a simple ceremony before an overflow crowd, his journey ended.

In a final twist, the erstwhile lawman contributed greatly to the future of law enforcement. FBI Director J. Edgar Hoover used the outrage generated by Miller and the Kansas City Massacre to lobby for a national crime-fighting force. Prior to the massacre, FBI agents could not carry weapons and were not authorized to make arrests. Within months of the Kansas City killings, Congress passed a comprehensive crime bill giving the FBI all the powers they sought.

Verne Miller squandered what seemed a promising life. The reason why he turned from lawman to lawlessness remains a mystery.

May/June 1996

PETRIFIED MEN

Katherine Twomey

When stories about petrified men surfaced in the Hot Springs area more than a century ago, disbelief and curiosity filled the air. Was it real? Or was it merely a hoax designed to lure tourists to that part of the state?

THE FIRST PETRIFIED man was found a few miles north of Wind Cave in the summer of 1892. But townspeople were skeptical. Memories of the Cardiff giant fraud two decades earlier were fresh. That giant, a 10-foot tall figure found near the small town of Cardiff, N.Y., created a sensation. Eventually it was revealed to be a hoax. The so-called giant had been carved from a block of gypsum from Fort Dodge, Iowa, buried and later "found" by men digging a well in 1869. It was retired to a museum at Cooperstown, N.Y., where it presumably resides to this day.

So, more than 20 years after the New York fraud, Hot Springs residents were understandably cautious. The editor of the *Hot Springs Star* drove out to Wind Cave to see for himself. He described what he saw in this July 15, 1892, account: "When it was reported a few days ago that a petrified man had been found out near Wind Cave people smiled and called it a fake to draw crowds to the cave. But there's no fake to it. They have this most wonderful piece of petrifaction out at the cave where it is on exhibition at 25 cents an exhibit. The *Star* man went out Tuesday night to view what many were free to term 'a Cardiff giant fake.' We were fully repaid for the trip, for it is a curious sight to see a petrified human being. The form is perfect in every way, and one feels, when viewing it, that they are in the presence of a corpse. The features are all perfect and distinct, even the eyebrows being plainly discernable.... Three of four physicians have examined the form and pronounce it a genuine petrifaction of humanity."

The unnamed discoverers found the specimen while crossing the bank of a creek, according to accounts by Arthur Vagg. They came across what looked like a fossil, similar to those found in the Badlands. But, after taking a second look, they said it looked like the shoulder of a man.

For $2,000, they sold the petrified man to a Mr. Bronte, who eventually put it on display on Chicago Avenue in Hot Springs. It wasn't long, however, before the petrified man departed for a tour to Grand Island, Neb., to be shown at the G.A.R. encampment. The next stop was the state fair in Lincoln. After about a month of traveling as far as Topeka, Kan., John Stabler and Mr. Bronte were ready to sell their interest in the petrified man to a gentleman named Miller, who started showing it throughout the country.

Although the petrified man seemed to have disappeared, another one "surfaced" about a month later. The Oct. 28, 1892, edition of the *Star* said this new find from the Badlands was almost perfect. It was missing the point of its nose and parts of its ears. Nothing else was known about it, other than it was already on tour. No one was sure if it was the same petrified man whose story came to life in the fall of 1924, when one of the old Petty livery stables was being razed, the figure of a man, constructed out of some kind of bones, was found in the loft of the building. No one knew who built the man or even who found it.

"For months and months," said the Nov. 17, 1924, issue of the *Star*, "that exhibit was displayed, at ten cents a head, in the back room of a Hot Springs store. It was purchased, so the story goes, by John Stabler for $1,000. He traveled with it through several states and probably got his thousand dollars back and a good deal more." Finally he took it to the New Orleans exposition, where the Badlands' relic was revealed to be a fake.

When a huge tusk, thought to be that of a prehistoric animal, was found in the Hot Springs area, skeptics were fewer. The first six-foot tusk, possibly that of a mastodon, was uncovered by graders working on River Avenue. A newspaper account from June of 1892 didn't mention claims that it was a fake. On the contrary, as the specimen began to decompose when exposed to air, some who came to view it carried the tusk away piece by piece. Since then, bones of creatures other than mammoths have been found. They range from short-faced bears to tiny mouse-like animals, but so far, no more humans have surfaced. And residents of Hot Springs no longer pack the specimens up for traveling tours. Now they just keep them at the Mammoth Site, designated a national natural landmark in 1980, and let the crowds come to them.

Nov/Dec 1995

Footprint Mystery of Medicine Rock

A HUGE BOULDER at Gettysburg has fascinated people for centuries. The rock is millions of years old, but the mystique isn't longevity. It's the five imbedded footprints visible on the surface.

Sioux Indians believed the prints belonged to the Great Spirit. Some tribes made sacrifices at the rock and held pow wows there to ask for help before they went to war. Others put garments or herbs on poles around the rock, seeking better health or virtue.

In addition to the human footprints are two other depressions that resemble the claws of a large animal. According to one Indian legend, when the rock was still soft mud an Indian girl was chased across it by a bear. Petroglyphs of the legend picture the body of the girl in the animal.

The 10-foot rock is a limestone substance. Scientists think it was formed somewhere far to the north, maybe in southern Manitoba. A glacier probably carried it here a million years ago.

All we know for certain is that it was across the Missouri at the mouth of the Cheyenne River when Lewis and Clark explored the area in 1804. They mentioned it in their journals. General Alfred Sully also made note of the rock when he camped nearby in 1863. General Custer saw the rock in 1873. Smithsonian investigators came as early as 1899.

In 1925, Shield Eagle of the Two Kettle Tribe of the Dakotas gave an Indian interpretation of the stone markings during a peace expedition held at the site. He said in ancient times a wise man inspired by the Great Spirit engraved the footprints to remind Indians that they were in the care of God. His tribe looked on the rock as an oracle and thought when proper prayers were offered it would guide them to good hunting grounds or to victory in battle. Indian women came to pray for the safety of their children.

When white families settled in the Missouri valley, many planned outings around the rock, including rodeos and big picnics. A half-century later, when the Oahe Dam was constructed at Pierre, many historic buildings and farms in the area were inundated by water. But not the rock. Local people hired Ernest Eggers, a house mover, to transport the rock to Gettysburg in 1954 before the water reached that height. He trucked it to Medicine Rock Cafe, where it became an attraction to travelers on U.S. Highway 212. The mover estimated its weight at six to eight tons.

Kids of every age matched their feet to the prints on the rock. All the attention, combined with wind and rain, began to erase the depressions, so local Jaycees built a roof overhead to provide some protection.

In 1989, when a new museum was completed in Gettysburg, the sacred rock was moved again to an indoor room near the entrance. The rock's origin remains a mystery. Scientists say it is possible that the footprints were actually imbedded by pre-glacial men when the limestone was still soft. Or were they carved later by Indian artists? Or did a bear really chase a girl?

May / June 1995

TURTLE AND SNAKE MOSIACS

Bernie Hunhoff

MYSTERIES ARE RARE in the hill country of central South Dakota. Nearly every square foot of grass has now been walked by farmers, cattlemen, sportsmen, historians, and archeologists. When something of interest is discovered — perhaps an ancient bone or a shard of poetry — testing, research and analysis follows. Almost everything has been identified, but a few finds remain unexplained, like the stone mosaics of snakes and turtles on hilltops above the Missouri and James rivers. The snake effigies stretch several hundred feet and are made of boulders the size of footballs and bowling balls. The turtles are smaller; their rock outlines are the size of a single car garage.

Medicine Butte, just west of Blunt in Hughes County, holds special significance to Vine Deloria Jr., a respected scholar and author who retired from a teaching career at the University of Colorado in Boulder. His great-grandfather, Saswe, survived a surreal experience there with rattlesnakes while on a vision quest in 1831.

He had been praying night and day for two days without food or water. On the afternoon of the third day, he was no longer visible on the hill. His mother became frightened and asked a cousin, Brown Bear, to see if Saswe had fainted. As Brown Bear rode to the top of Medicine Butte, his horse became nervous and tried to turn back. Suddenly the horse and rider found themselves surrounded by hundreds of snakes.

Determined to find Saswe, Brown Bear swung his rope at the snakes to open a path. He found a large bundle of snakes writhing back and forth over Saswe's prostrate body. He figured Saswe had fainted earlier and the snakes, finding his warm body, had swarmed over him and killed him.

Brown Bear returned to camp and told what he had seen. Saswe's loss devastated the family and great mourning began. But suddenly Saswe walked back into the camp, and when asked about the snakes he seemed perplexed. He remembered nothing about them. The account was among the 19th century stories passed down within Deloria's family. Saswe grew to be a respected Yanktonai chief, so his vision quest added even more mystery to the snake mosaics on Medicine Butte.

The rattlesnake effigy was in place on the butte in 1831 when Saswe did his vision quest, according to family history. Deloria says to the best of his knowledge, the origins of the mosaics are a mystery. "Nobody I know in the scholarly world or the Indian world can say for certain how old they are or who made them or even why they made them."

Jan / Feb 2003

WHERE'S THE WORLD'S LARGEST PAINTING?

Ried Holien

WHEN JOHN BANVARD died in Watertown in 1891, newspapers throughout America and Europe ran his obituary — though it was hardly the kind of attention the town fathers might welcome. Most wondered how it came to pass that one of the 19th century's wealthiest and most renowned artists could die penniless in an American frontier town. John Banvard achieved international success by fulfilling a boyhood dream of creating the largest painting ever. When completed, his "Mississippi Panorama" stood 12 feet high and stretched three miles in length. It depicted nearly 3,000 miles of riverbank, from the mouth of the Yellowstone River on the upper Missouri all the way to New Orleans.

As a young man, Banvard traveled the Mississippi and Missouri river valleys, seeking jobs as an itinerant artist. He painted portraits, decorated public buildings and for a short time worked as a scene painter on the first Mississippi showboat. Some think he tackled the mammoth canvas because of a foreign critic, who wrote, "America has not the artists commensurate with the grandeur and extent of her scenery." Banvard resolved to prove him wrong. Once the painting was completed, he invented a mechanical device consisting of two tall cylinders attached to either end. By hand-cranking the cylinders, the panorama scrolled from one side to the other. He rented a hall and showed it to full houses in Louisville and Boston. He gradually perfected the presentation with narration on stage as the panorama passed behind him. He lectured on science, explained the scenes and told amusing anecdotes.

One performance stopped completely when a St. Louis businessman jumped up and shouted, "That's my store! Halloa there, captain! Stop the boat — I want to go ashore and see my wife and family!" The merchant later admitted he believed, at that instant, he was sailing through St. Louis. Banvard took the show to England, Egypt and the Holy Land in the early 1850s. He made a fortune, but when he returned to America he lost it all in several other entertainment endeavors. Finally he lost everything in the Panic of 1877. In 1880, he moved to Watertown where his son, Eugene, was an attorney, and became active in the city. He penned a poetic plea to spare the life of a Native American activist, befriended Territorial Gov. Arthur Mellette and other leaders, lectured on his travels, and supervised construction of an armory near Lake Kampeska. He also painted another panorama, "The Burning of Columbia," which depicted the South Carolina capital's destruction in the Civil War. In 1943, the U.S. Navy commissioned a Liberty Ship called the USS Banvard. During the dedication, he was proclaimed "the first motion picture producer."

The fate of the "Three Mile Painting" is a mystery. In 1948, Edith Banvard said, "As to what became of the panorama which my father painted, I cannot say with any certainty. I always understood that part of it was used for scenery in the Watertown opera house." Local legend says it was shredded for use as insulation in Watertown area houses. If that is true, then the largest painting in the world, like its creator, still resides in South Dakota.

Sept / Oct 1997

THERE'S GOLD IN THE BADLANDS

Philip S. Hall

"THERE'S GOLD in the Badlands!" Tell that to a crusty old geologist and he'll call you loco. "Gold," the geologist will tell you, "forms when chemically suitable magna, as it cools, hovers between the critical temperatures of 400 and 12 degrees Celsius. Gold is found in precambrian igneous rocks — granite. The Badlands is 500 feet of sediment laid down at the bottom of an ancient, inland sea. It's dried mud. Only a romantic would search the Badlands for gold."

Louie Blummer, who homesteaded along Sage Creek in 1907, probably never read a book on geology. He was too busy trying to eke out a living on 160 acres of Badlands gumbo. One of his first improvements was to dig a well. Clive Wyant, the son of Charley Wyant who had located a ranch in Sage Creek Basin in 1890, was helping Louie. They dug down 12 feet, the last two in wet sand. Clive was handing down flat stones so Louie, who was down in the bottom of the hole, could build a curb. As Louie worked, water trickled in at his feet. The sand walls slowly crumbled. While fitting a rock, Louie noticed a bright flash. He reached for it and picked up a bright, pea-sized rock. It looked like a gold nugget!

"Watch out! It's coming in!" Clive suddenly shouted. Louie scrambled to get out of the well. As he did, he dropped the supposed nugget. The cave-in was minimal. Louie was soon back down in the bottom of the hole. He tried to find the nugget, but couldn't. That was the last time Louie Blummer thought about gold in the Badlands for the next 25 years. Then came the "Dirty Thirties." There was no grass, no money, no work. Louie had time on his hands. He recalled the remnants of a prospector's crude rocker made out of a cottonwood log and other signs of excavation he had previously seen along the middle fork of Sage Creek. Having nothing but idle time to lose, Louie decided to search for gold.

Years later, I learned through word of mouth about Louie Blummer's prospecting efforts in the Badlands. Some people swore he had found gold. Others said he hadn't. I looked Louie Blummer up in the summer of 1973. He was then retired, living in Wall, and graciously told me the story. He described the remnants of prospecting he had discovered on Sage Creek. He related that he had set out to search for gold during the drought, when there was little water. He told about digging up the dirt from the top of the sod to just below the grass roots. He described shoveling the dirt into gunny sacks. He recounted loading the sacks on a pack horse. He lamented about how far it was to water. He bemoaned the heat. He cursed the hot winds.

I could not stand the suspense. "Just tell me," I interrupted him, "did you find any gold?" Louie's eyes twinkled. Without saying a word, he got up and went to another room. He came back carrying a small, glass vial tightly capped with a cork. In the bottom of the vial was an inch of yellow flakes that glittered in the sunlight. It was Badlands gold. Sometimes the romantics are right.

May / June 1993

LOOKOUT MOUNTAIN MYSTERY

Paul Higbee

The legend on Lookout Mountain began in March of 1887 when brothers Louis and Ivan Thoen, Norwegian born farmers, found a sandstone slab. It was ten inches by eight inches, and three inches thick. Carved in cursive script, an inscription read:

Came to these hills in 1833
Seven of us DeLacompt Ezra
Kind G W Wood T Brown R Kent
Wm King Indian Crow all ded but
Me Ezra Kind killed by Ind
Beyond the high hill got our gold
June 1834 Got all of the gold we
Could carry our ponys all got by
The Indians I have lost my gun and
Nothing to eat and Indians hunting
Me

WITHIN A DAY the slab — soon to be called the Thoen Stone — sat prominently displayed at John Cashner's store in Spearfish, and the Thoens and Cashner printed photos and sold them. The next year Cashner traveled to Michigan and impressed a Detroit *Free Press* reporter with the tale and the slab became minor national news.

Back in Spearfish a debate was under way. Had the stone been created by a gold seeker who, had he survived, might have started a gold rush 15 years before California's? Or had Thoen and Cashner created a scheme for drawing the curious to Cashner's store and moving photo inventory?

Today the debate continues. The Thoen Stone itself is displayed at Deadwood's Adams House museum, and an X marks the spot on Lookout Mountain where the Thoen brothers said they found the slab.

March / April 1998

Roberts County Rock Riddle

Amy Dunkle

THEY LIE EMBEDDED in valleys and hills of Roberts County. No doubt, somebody in each passing generation has pondered their meaning, but few have pursued the riddle of their origin. They are rocks so big you can't put your arms around them. What distinguishes them from other glacial debris scattered across the region is a small, triangular hole — the source of intriguing mystery.

Somebody, or something, somehow gouged, drilled or pounded deep holes in granite boulders. Wilmot businesswoman Judi Rudebusch has catalogued 57 such boulders in the valleys and hills near her home. One has been found on the Missouri River bluff in Clay County. Many more, we are told, are strewn across the upper Midwest and Canada to New England.

Tramping across fields and deftly crossing barbed wire fences, Rudebusch ticks off guesses as to why the holes were made, then discards them one by one. Clearing fields? Possible, but all the rocks are on hillsides rather than on flat land. Blasting the rocks to break them apart and make them easier to move? Plausible, but early dynamite sticks were too large for these holes. Anyway, she says, farmers typically packed dynamite on the rocks with mud. Making foundation stones? Rudebusch chased that theory down, looking up plats of homestead sites. Nothing. Survey markers? The boulders don't fall on mile lines, and anyway, markers were generally driven into the ground and surrounded with smaller rocks.

That leads to consideration of a long-standing theory that Rudebusch isn't ready to accept: Medieval Scandinavian explorers bored the holes. It might have been possible for explorers to get to Roberts County by boat from Hudson Bay to Lake Winnipeg, up the Red River to the continental divide east of Sisseton, then down the Minnesota and up the north fork of the Whetstone River. Some have speculated that the holey rocks could have been mooring rocks for Viking ships sailing waterways of the upper Midwest.

Rudebusch isn't sure where or how the mystery will be solved — or if it ever will.

March/April 2003

TERMESPHERES

Roger Holtzmann

IF SOMEBODY TELLS you they understand a Termesphere, don't believe them. Nobody understands a Termesphere. Don't listen to Dick Termes explain one, either. That just makes things worse.

Spearfish artist Dick Termes has been baffling his public for years, though they don't seem to appreciate him any less for it. His unique artistic creations begin with a large polycarbonate sphere, rescued from what might have been a mundane, boring existence as a lighting fixture. After filling and sanding it to a globular smoothness, he begins to paint upon its surface. That's where it gets complicated. Those who seek to plumb the mystery of a Termesphere should try to imagine themselves inside a transparent globe, Termes suggests. "You could then paint what you see from that vantage point inside the sphere," he says. "If you could then move outside the sphere, and see what you had painted, you would be viewing a Termesphere."

Sounds simple enough. Those who would like to test their understanding of the concept can check out Saloon No. 10, the Termesphere which hangs in the historic Deadwood bar and gaming house of that name. When Termes first started displaying his spheres they were stationary, requiring the viewer to move around them to view the entire work. Then he hit upon the idea of suspending them from a chain attached to a small electric motor. In the case of Saloon No. 10, this allows the viewer to remain stationary as images of the establishment's interior float serenely by, presenting aspects of the room such as you might see if you stood in the center and turned slowly around. Two patrons seated at a table are close by, then they recede into the background and the bar comes around.

"Very cool," says the viewer. "Look how it ..." Silence.

"I think I understand," he says a trifle uncertainly. "I'm inside the sphere." Silence. "Looking out." More silence. "But I'm in the bar. How can I be out here ... when I'm in there shouldn't it be ... reversed ... or something. If that table is over there and the bar is there and I'm inside the sphere ... looking at ... oh, never mind!"

July/August 1991

THE MISSING VERENDRYE PLATES

Bernie Hunhoff

WHERE ARE THE missing Verendrye plates? That's not a mystery most South Dakotans ponder, but it deserves some thought because the plate discovered by Ethel Roberts and two friends while at play in 1913 on a Fort Pierre hilltop is considered the oldest written record of the visit of white men to the region now known as the Dakotas.

King Louis XV of France sent three such plates with the Verendrye brothers and the men of their expedition in 1743. Their journals indicate that one of the plates was given to an Indian chief and another was placed at a site easily identified as modern-day Fort Pierre. The explorers made no mention of where they left the third.

The Verendryes came into the Missouri River valley from Canada. Their exact route has long been a topic of debate among historians. Some think the explorers roamed as far west as the Rockies while others believe they never left the Dakotas. Not much new evidence surfaced until May of 1985 when Max Rittgers, a Madison native who operates a winery in Florida called Dakotah Vineyards, found what appeared to be a second Verendrye plate.

Rittgers was canoeing the Cheyenne River with his black lab, Ben. They stopped at the juncture of the Cheyenne and Belle Fourche rivers. As Rittgers made camp, he noticed that something had caught the eye of the lab. Eventually, he walked up the hill to see if the dog was alright. When he got close, the dog urinated on a flat plate.

Rittgers' friends at Augustana College, his alma mater, identified the find as a likely companion to the Verendrye plate on exhibit in Pierre. However, Rittgers grew weary of being in the middle of a controversy over who owned the plate and where it should be displayed. In 1998, the dispute ended when he announced that he had flown over the Cheyenne in a small plane and dropped the plate in the vicinity where Ben had found it.

Did he really throw away one of the oldest artifacts of white civilization in the Dakotas? Will it be found again? Where is the third plate? Do black labs have a nose for history?

Dreamers & Builders

Nearly all the stories in this book are about dreams, some lost and some gained. While we consider ourselves a practical people, how could we not also be big dreamers considering, as centennial artist Mary Groth noted (in the selection immediately following) that many of us are descendants of homesteaders, the ultimate dreamers and doers?

Some South Dakota dreamers have been so unique, however, that we felt they deserved a chapter all their own. The stories are otherwise unrelated. They happened in various parts of the state and in different decades. Taken together, they stand as clear evidence that the "big dreams" genes of the homesteaders have not gone dormant.

— Bernie Hunhoff

AN ARTIST'S CENTENNIAL VISION

Mary Groth

Mary Groth was a young artist in Aberdeen when South Dakota celebrated its centennial. She was chosen to do a poster for the occasion. Her illustration showed a confident young homesteading couple. Here is her explanation.

IN THEIR FACES and in their stance, I wanted to express the strength and hope and determination to make their dream a reality. With all their possessions in a covered wagon, they have chosen a place to begin a partnership of building a home and raising a family. One hundred years later, we South Dakotans are still firmly rooted in these same traditions of independence, hard work and a love of the wide open prairie land and sky. We are the descendants of a diverse people who came to the heartland of the plains with a vision of the lives they could build on this vast, often unpredictable frontier land called South Dakota.

May/June 1989

THE GUTZON BORGLUM SHOW

Roger Holtzmann

CRITICS OF THE Rushmore project, of which there were a considerable number during its early days, used to say they were surprised any carving ever got done on the Shrine to Democracy — workmen seemed to spend all their time dedicating it. There was a kernel of truth in the jest. John Gutzon de la Mothe Borglum liked nothing better than a grand event. He orchestrated dramatic ceremonies, with a starring role for himself, whenever the opportunity presented itself. Actors in colonial garb and Indians in finery, along with Sen. Peter Norbeck and assorted local dignitaries, made their way to the top of the mountain in 1925 for its initial dedication. Caught up in the moment, Borglum promised that the first figure, Washington, would be done in 12 months. Carving didn't even start until two years later, but that was of no concern to Borglum. The first stone actually removed from the mountain was reason for another ceremony.

President Calvin "Silent Cal" Coolidge established his summer White House in the Black Hills in 1927, and Borglum wasn't about to let such an opportunity pass. He invited Coolidge to the mountain for another dedication. On the appointed day Borglum hired Clyde Ice, South Dakota aviation pioneer, to fly him over the State Game Lodge where Coolidge was staying so he could drop a bouquet of flowers to Mrs. Coolidge. They flew so low Ice thought it might be his last flight, but Borglum hardly noticed. Silent Cal showed up and allowed himself to be talked into donning a white, ten-gallon hat, which made for one of his presidency's more ridiculous moments.

When Washington's likeness was complete, Mary Borglum and friends sewed a giant American flag to cover the face during another ceremony. At the climactic moment, to the accompaniment of a 21-gun salute and martial music from the Fort Meade band, Gutzon unveiled the face. During his speech he promised Jefferson would be finished within a year. True to form, it was six more years — a long time to go without a ceremony. So Gutzon dedicated it twice. President Franklin Roosevelt was in South Dakota for the event, but he decided to go to church on the day Borglum scheduled the ceremony. Borglum went ahead without him, and obligingly staged a second dedication when the president could attend.

Lincoln's dedication in 1937 was a gala event, with fireworks, Indian dancing and 5,000 people. Borglum used the occasion to honor Peter Norbeck, who had died the previous year. South Dakota celebrated its golden anniversary of statehood in 1939, which coincided with the formal unveiling of Teddy Roosevelt. Cowboy star William Hart was on hand, and the event was broadcast over radio. There was no tape delay in those days. Whatever was said went straight into the mike and out over the airwaves from sea to shining sea. Timing was critical, and Hart's allotted time in front of the microphone was up long before he'd run out of things to say. He was abruptly shunted to one side, which didn't sit well with the hot-tempered actor. He vented his feelings, at the top of his voice, on a radio technician. Listeners across the country were treated to an earful of Hart's colorful language until Lincoln Borglum's pretty young wife, Louella, managed to coax him off the stage.

Ironically, there was no ceremony upon the carving's completion. Lincoln Borglum turned the monument over to the National Park Service on October 31, 1941, eight months after his father died, without so much as a drum roll. Who can say what Gutzon Borglum might have done. Trumpet fanfares. Fireworks. Dancers. Dignitaries, perhaps. A speech by the sculptor certainly, for he loved to hear himself speak. "I know a man my age should learn to keep his mouth shut," he said once, paraphrasing a quote from Teddy Roosevelt. "But I can't. I have too much to say."

May / June 1991

DOANE ROBINSON, the longtime state historian, gets the credit for inspiring Mount Rushmore for it was he who looked upon the granite spires of the Needles and imagined statues of the larger-than-life figures of Western history — Red Cloud, Lewis and Clark, Jedediah Smith. But if it was ever going to be more than a pipe dream, Robinson knew that it had to speak, "a language [his fellow South Dakotans] understood. Debt-ridden farmers and hard-bitten businessmen would hardly be interested in gigantic sculpture for its own sake or for the sake of history," wrote Gilbert Fite in his history of the mountain carving. When he broached the idea publicly, Robinson told a newspaper reporter that, "hundreds of visitors would be drawn into the state to view such a landmark," and some of them, he figured, might be persuaded to leave a few dollars behind.

Even so, not everybody was convinced. One anonymous poet, writing in the style of Badger Clark, thought Robinson and Borglum ought to leave the Black Hills just as they were.

O Gutzon Borglum, have a heart,
Spare just one mountain top;
Leave one, I beg, just one at least,
That you won't chop and chop.

You cruise around with dynamite
And drills and tools and gears;
And carve up some grand mountain
That has stood ten thousand years.

PRESIDENT CALVIN Coolidge attended a Mount Rushmore ceremony in 1927 to mark carving commencement. It's not surprising, given Mary Borglum's head for finances, that she later recalled a conversation about dollars between her husband and the president. Gutzon told Coolidge he expected money for the Rushmore carving would be raised locally.

"The people of South Dakota can't even pay the interest on their farm mortgages," said the president. Well, Borglum responded, maybe the state's economy would improve if it rained the next year.

"Nonsense," said Coolidge. "They never get water out there. When I get back to Washington, I want you to come to the White House. I know great governments do things like this."

May/June 2001

NEARLY 400 MEN worked on Mount Rushmore at various times during its carving. When Howdy Peterson died in 1998 one of the great storytellers among that fraternity passed from the scene. Over the years, those who were lucky enough to know him were treated to many amusing, sometimes mildly ribald, accounts of pranks the Rushmore workers pulled.

"Sometimes," he remembered, "a man would go over the side of the mountain in a swing seat, and from up top we'd pull the cables back up a little, real slow so he didn't notice. Then we'd let go and for about two feet he'd think he was falling off the mountain." Or when blasting presidents from granite began to feel like just another day at the office, the men would occasionally goose one another with high-powered compressed air hoses. As for Rushmore sculptor Gutzon Borglum, the best strategy many days for staying in the man's good graces was to steer clear of him. But watching Borglum work inspired awe. Howdy recalled the sculptor studying the sunlight on the faces for hours, "and then he'd come up top, swing over the side, and with red paint he'd mark to take off three inches here, five inches there. It amazed me how he could do that. I guess you call that ability."

Nov / Dec 1998

ARNE LARSON: A CALLING TO COLLECT

Bernie Hunhoff

ARNE LARSON might have ended up a farmer if not for a story as old as time. He was young and impatient, eager to try new methods, new machinery, new seeds. His father thought the old ways were just fine.

To keep peace in the family, Arne chose a path that could scarcely have been more unlike farm life. He enrolled in the Minneapolis College of Music in 1922 — he'd been playing various instruments since he was six, entertaining folks in his hometown of Hanska, Minn., — and eventually earned his Masters in music from Northwestern University. After graduation, Arne worked as a music teacher, first in Little Falls, then Brookings. His students consistently earned high honors in band competitions, but it was through his hobby that Arne Larson would make his most lasting mark on the world.

Arne caught the collecting bug at age 16, and the disease only got worse as time went by. From barrel cellos to Tibetan serpentine horns, violins to keyboards, it didn't matter. He loved them all. His collection got a jumpstart in 1920 when the United States adopted the A-440 standard, which at one swoop made many of the existing band instruments obsolete. Such a bounty could never be repeated, but Arne wasn't deterred. He couldn't afford to buy instruments on a teacher's pay, so he earned money to feed his collecting habit by tuning pianos. As he moved around he kept an eye out for collectible instruments; over time, he also built up contacts across the country, and with missionaries in the Orient, Africa and India, who did the same. Gradually he accumulated a collection that filled the family's Brookings home to overflowing. Larson rarely paid more than $5 for an instrument. After World War II, there were bargains to be had in Europe, where desperate people were willing to trade musical instruments for food. "We used to think he was just telling stories, because my father loved to tell stories, but after he died we had a chance to look through some of his letters," recalled Arne's son, Andre. "We found that he had literally paid for some of his instruments with SPAM and tea."

Once his children were grown, Arne Larson decided a career change was in order. He put out feelers, seeking a place for himself and his collection, which had grown to more than 2,500 instruments. A number of major institutions were interested, but I.D. Weeks, president of the University of South Dakota in Vermillion, prevailed upon him to accept a position at the school and keep the collection in-state. A parade of grain trucks backed up to the Larson home and hauled away the fruits of his hobby.

No one knew what to do with the instruments once they arrived — for years they were scattered around the campus in nooks and crannies. When a new library was constructed in 1966, the old Carnegie building was made available, and the collection finally found a permanent home. The Shrine to Music (now the National Music Museum) was established as an independent entity in 1973. Six years later, Arne officially donated his collection to the museum. At that point it was valued at over $1 million, but such a measure was meaningless. The collection, from 17th century Stradavari stringed instruments to a rare, four-valve sousaphone to an African kudu horn, could not have been duplicated for any amount of money.

Arne was a natural entertainer, giving tours, telling stories, and spontaneously picking up instruments to play a tune. Museum officials, who rarely touch a piece without gloves these days, would be aghast at such behavior. "[My father] was the personality of the place," said Andre, "but being a collector is not always the same as being a museum person. The collection became a part of his personality. It was a private part of him, and all of a sudden there was me and a staff working with the collection and cataloging it." Still, he was proud of the institution. When questioned about the wisdom of having a world-class museum so far off the beaten path, Arne would invariably answer, "It's no further from New York to Vermillion than it is from Vermillion to New York."

May / June 1986

PETER NORBECK: WELL-DRILLER

Roger Holtzmann

FEW MEN COULD lay claim to a more brilliant public life than Thomas Jefferson: Author of the Declaration of Independence, founder of the University of Virginia, two-term president of the United States, visionary advocate of the Louisiana Purchase. Yet when Jefferson took stock of his own achievements, it was his work as an agriculturist that he considered most significant. "There is no greater service a man can perform for his country than to introduce a useful plant into its cultivation," he wrote. Putting those words into practice, he turned his Monticello plantation into a laboratory for experimenting with crops from cotton to tomatoes, enriching the nation for generations to come.

Jefferson's example comes to mind while considering the life of one of South Dakota's most accomplished public men, Peter Norbeck. Born in 1870, Norbeck rose from a Clay County dugout to become the state's first native-born governor, then moved on to a seat in the U.S. Senate. Proud as he was of that, Norbeck himself likely would have approved of the plaque dedicated to his memory that stands beside Iron Mountain Road in Custer State Park. Listed first on the roster of achievement for this governor, senator, founder, builder, patriot and gentleman is well driller.

Using rigs that he designed himself, Norbeck's well-drilling company bored more than 10,000 water wells. To dig a well might not, at first glance, seem like much of an accomplishment in comparison to becoming governor. Yet it would be difficult to overstate the significance of that humble hole in the ground. On many farms and ranches where he worked, the abundant water from one of Norbeck's deep artesian wells was literally the difference between prosperity and just getting by — between moving on and staying put to build lives and families and communities.

PETER NORBECK was an idealist. A dreamer, even, who did more than any other single individual to help preserve South Dakota's natural beauty for generations to come. But above all else he was a simple, utterly unpretentious man. Ken Way, publisher emeritus of the *Watertown Public Opinion*, met Peter Norbeck in the 1920s. He and his father, S.X. Way, had breakfast with the politician. "Governor Norbeck double-ordered everything," he said. "He ordered a cantaloupe and told the waitress to bring both halves." Though the weather was rainy, Norbeck insisted that S.X. and young Ken accompany him deep into the Black Hills to see a grand cabin he was building near Sylvan Lake. (The cabin, called Valhalla, is used by South Dakota governors for special events to this very day.)

They were driving along a narrow guage railroad in the rain when their open touring car became mired in gumbo. They could not go forward or backward. Ken's father was worried because they were far from any towns. But Norbeck wasn't concerned. "Eventually, the governor saw a train coming down the track," Ken remembered. "So he stood right in the middle of the track and waved it to a stop." Norbeck convinced the engineer to hook a long rope to their car, and the train pulled the governor and his guests to dry land.

Anyone who knew Norbeck, or who has researched the man, can picture his portly frame on the track, arms extended with a Teddy Roosevelt authority that even a steam-powered locomotive wouldn't ignore.

Nov/Dec 1998 and Jan/Feb 2001

THE WOMAN BEHIND THE MOUNTAIN

Paul Higbee

RUTH ZIOLKOWSKI emerged from the shadow of her late husband, Korczak, to become one of South Dakota's best-known women, superintending work on Crazy Horse Monument near Custer. She presides over the carving of the world's largest sculpture, and a large extended family, with a gentleness that belies her toughness.

I drove down to meet Ruth and learn about her work. Although it was a raw spring day, I first went to Thunderhead Mountain to see the carving. There were more mountain goats than carvers on the rocks. Crew members were warming themselves in an equipment building and passing around a new *Weekly Reader* which described their work. Through such articles, Korczak Ziolkowski's sculptural design — Crazy Horse astride a great horse, pointing southeast where his people's dead lie buried — became well-known to many Americans long before any features were discernible on the granite outcrop. These days the design is increasingly recognized worldwide. Journalists from everywhere document the crew's progress; the day before my visit, a French TV team had wrapped up a shoot. For years it was standard practice to photograph the mountain with a model of the finished sculpture in the foreground. Not anymore. By the mid 1990s, the mountain carving was speaking for itself. No longer is it a generic mask, but a Lakota face, with cheekbones, strong nose, and furrowed brow. The head is cocked slightly to the left. Korczak noted that people usually tilt their heads when they point.

The crew went back to their tasks and I to mine, talking with Ruth while she fixed lunch and answered telephone calls. She described herself as the project's chairman of the board, "but I do the dishes, too," she said, displaying the self-effacing humor and gentle manner that have always marked Ruth's interaction with her crew. But make no mistake, long-time acquaintances say. She is in charge.

"When Korczak died in 1982, Ruth was an unknown quantity to the public," said Robb DeWall, the project's communications director. "Some people wondered what would happen to the sculpture, though people who knew Ruth were completely confident she'd continue her husband's work. But the public didn't know her then, and we didn't know the skills of the children."

Seven of Ruth and Korczak' s ten grown children are part of the Crazy Horse project. On this day, three — Mark, Anne, and Monique — stopped in for lunch, along with her ten-year-old grandaughter, Heidi. "I'm lucky," Ruth said. "My children are working with me. Every one of them went off and did something else for awhile, but seven came back here. We've all grown in our jobs."

Korczak was nearly 40 when he began Crazy Horse, and early on he drew up plans for continuing the work after his lifetime. But when you're sculpting a mountain, even detailed plans don't mean you simply check off completed tasks and move on to the next. "There's lots to learn as you go, and that's the challenge, the fun," Ruth said. "For everything you finish, about three more jobs come along."

Beyond the carving itself, there are always management decisions to make: how much revenue should go into the sculpture, and how much should support visitor services. The project is also committed to a scholarship program that's the forerunner to the university and medical center

Korczak envisioned. Even occasional revenue windfalls mean hard choices. Additional money might allow for more mountain carvers, but more workers mean more equipment, and that equipment will need maintenance in the future. Where that maintenance money will come from in the future has to be considered in the present. By far the most difficult decision Ruth made was when she determined, in 1987, to make Crazy Horse's head the focus of work, rather than the horse's head. It was the right call, gaining the project greater credibility as the facial features emerged. Fewer and fewer comments are heard along the lines of one that former CBS newsman Charles Kuralt heard in Rapid City several years ago. A rental car clerk told Kuralt that Korczak Ziolkowski was perpetrating a scam, living well off admissions, and blasting a little rock now and then for effect. Kuralt didn't buy it, and ended up staying several days with the Ziolkowskis that trip, as well as reporting on the carving's development several times over the years.

Confront people who said Crazy Horse was a scam a few years ago, and they'll say that thinking was understandable if you compared Mount Rushmore's progress to Crazy Horse's. Rushmore, even with chronic funding problems and crew layoffs, was brought to its present state in 14 years. The Crazy Horse folks, after four decades, could claim more than eight million tons had been blasted away, but could point to nothing resembling a chief on a horse. Supporters were quick to respond that work on Thunderhead Mountain was a privately-funded, one-man show, while Rushmore had benefited from federal funding that employed over 300 carvers during the course of its creation. And then there's the size. The four Rushmore heads combined could fit into the area planned for Crazy Horse's head.

"Korczak never liked those comparisons, because that' s not what this carving is about, and it's not what Mount Rushmore is about," Ruth said. Rushmore sculptor Gutzon Borglum was among Korczak's three personal heroes, along with Michelangelo and da Vinci. Her husband knew it would have been easier to sculpt a mountain away from the object of comparison — Rushmore is 17 miles up the highway — but that was never a possibility, said Ruth. The Black Hills were Crazy Horse's native land.

Korczak worked part of the 1939 season as a Rushmore carver, the same year his marble "Paderewski: Study of an Immortal" won first prize for sculpture at the New York World's Fair. That publicity, combined with the fact that Korczak knew something of mountain carving, led Lakota chief Henry Standing Bear to approach him about Crazy Horse. About this same time a teenage girl showed up at Korczak's West Hartford, Conn., home, hoping to get an autograph from movie star Richard Bennett, who was visiting. The girl was Ruth, and she later volunteered to help Korczak as he sculpted a Noah Webster statue in Connecticut. As a college student she came to South Dakota, in 1947, to assist with the very first work at Crazy Horse. "Back in those first years here, he never said if the sculpture is completed," Ruth recalled. "It was when the sculpture is completed. So people around him, and visitors, talked that way, too. That was the power of his personality."

Ruth and Korczak were married in 1950. In a way, Ruth also found herself married to the mountain and surrounding Hills. She receives many invitations, but has no desire to leave home even for brief trips. Ruth hasn't been back to her native Connecticut since 1962. "I like being surrounded by evergreens year-round," she said. "Besides, like Korczak always said, wait and eventually everyone you'd ever want to meet will come here." It proved a prophetic statement. Artists, politicians, reservation school kids, and vacationers from around the globe all make the trek to Crazy Horse.

Ruth doesn't get up on the mountain often. She has complete confidence in her children, and in foremen and crew who work on Thunderhead Mountain. "I told Korczak I'd keep Crazy Horse together as an organization, but I can't carve a mountain," she said. "So when I go up, it's just to see. I'm not about to tell anyone where to drill, or blast, or anything else. It's absolutely amazing to see, but I'm like Korczak. There's never been a time I didn't think it would happen."

May / June 1995

WELCOMING THE WORLD TO SOUTH DAKOTA

Dan A. Johnson

NOBODY EVER accused Rapid City businessman Paul Bellamy of thinking small. When he heard the nascent United Nations was looking for a home, Bellamy thought: Why not South Dakota? It seems safe to say the state hadn't occurred to any world leaders, but that hardly mattered. If anybody could make such an improbable thing happen, it was Bellamy.

With a breezy disregard for geographic logic, Bellamy coined the term 'Switzerland of America.' Elaborate, leather-bound promotional packets were prepared for the delegates to the San Francisco conference where the treaty establishing the United Nations was signed. Mitchell architect

Luvine Berg prepared a map which proved conclusively that the Black Hills were the most convenient spot for all the nations of the world. A comprehensive plan for the World Peace Capital, a city laid out along spiral streets, was also developed. Governor M.Q. Sharpe lobbied for the plan, and President Roosevelt made favorable noises about the Hills, mentioning the area's healthful climate and natural beauty. Then again, FDR was notorious for publicly encouraging everybody and everything, never closing the door on any option.

When the United States dropped the atomic bomb on Hiroshima, Governor Sharpe put out a news release stating that the Black Hills were, "in a region best suited to atomic bomb defense and adaptable to atomic bomb maintenance of world peace." He never fully explained what the last meant. Berg contributed an "Atomic Bomb Map" which showed that the Hills region, because of its low population, would never be a target in an atomic attack. Bellamy, armed with his maps and brochures, attended a site selection conference in London. More than 50 other cities, from Atlantic City to San Francisco, made presentations, but even in that company, Bellamy garnered three paragraphs in *Time* magazine's account.

"The star performer was Paul Bellamy, a bull-necked businessman who represents no city, but the bleak Black Hills of South Dakota, where men are men and steaks are three inches thick," reported the magazine. "Yugoslavia's gaunt, gray Stoyan Gavrilovic was visibly affected [by the presentation]. Bellamy's best argument had a pessimistic undertone: Boston, Philadelphia and coastal cities were within easy reach of atomic bombings. 'In the Black Hills there are no military objectives, and the gentlemen who are striving for the peace of the world can live at peace while the atomic bombs are falling.' It is not part of Bellamy's job, or of the booster tradition, to ask what the gentlemen would be doing at that point."

Edward R. Murrow, the pioneer CBS radio newsman, thought the Black Hills location was a fine idea. Greece thought so, too, but in the end, John D. Rockefeller trumped all other proposals by offering the United Nations $8.5 million to purchase a 13-acre site along the East River in New York City. "Unwise, almost tragic," mourned the Sioux Falls *Argus Leader* of the choice to locate amidst, "the sham, the tinsel, the glitter, the cocktail lounges, the synthetic glamour and the fleshpots of the nation's metropolis."

Nov/Dec 1986

ED YOST AND THE USEFULNESS OF HOT AIR

Bernie Hunhoff

OF ALL THE WAYS there are to move through the wild blue yonder, none quite compare to the silent majesty of a hot air balloon. Although the first hot air balloon to carry a man ascended in 1793, the art of building such craft languished for many years until it was revived by the efforts of Paul Edward "Ed" Yost.

Flying had long been part of Yost's life. After high school, he attended Boeing School of Aeronautics at Oakland, Calif., where he learned aviation engineering. He took a cadet pilot training course in the U.S. Army Air Corps, graduating as a pilot in 1945. After his service years, he piloted for Alaska Airlines. In 1949, he was hired as General Mills as senior engineer and tracking pilot in Minneapolis. There, he was introduced to helium balloons.

In 1956, he and three friends sold their Minneapolis homes and used the money to start Raven Industries in Sioux Falls. "We started out in an old, wooden hospital building on the old airbase grounds," Yost said. "I think we bought the building for $3,000 and we were allowed to use it rent-free on the land for two years. Raven quickly grew into a major Sioux Falls manufacturer. During the Vietnam War, Raven workers built 87,000 cargo parachutes. From 1968 to 1975, Yost served as corporate president, overseeing 800 employees at six factories. Then he opted for a less-structured lifestyle. He left Raven for Tea, where he insulated an old metal quonset, installed a single-line black telephone and posted a small, red and white wood sign that reads Universal Systems, Inc. He and a small staff specialized in custom-made helium balloons.

He also planned for the first successful trans-Atlantic balloon flight. He didn't seek publicity or commercial sponsors. "Everybody is reluctant to put a sponsorship on a deal like this because chances are it's going to be a miserable flop," he said. Yet, he devoted a year of his life and $70,000 to a flight for history. Yost and his crew constructed an 80-foot high balloon that contained 60,000 cubic feet of helium. The gondola was built like a catamaran. If it went down at sea, Yost planned to sail to safety.

The balloon was dubbed the Silver Fox because of its silver top and black bottom. Yost chose to fly without oxygen because he wanted no advantage over the 1913 German balloonists whose distance and duration records he was challenging. All Atlantic flights since have had oxygen on them.

The Silver Fox traveled 589 miles the first day and 741 on the second, thanks to a 31 mile per hour wind. On the third and fourth days he flew 514 and 627 miles, but by mid-ocean he realized his major goal of crossing the Atlantic would be impossible because of adverse winds that carried him on a northeasterly course. His ballast and expendable gear were nearly exhausted when he landed in the ocean. He had traveled 2,740 miles and set time and distance records. He was pulled aboard a West German freighter and delivered to a hero's welcome in Gibraltar. President Gerald Ford telegrammed congratulations; the South Dakotan was the cover story for *National Geographic*.

Yost returned to Tea, where he was hardly known, to build balloons and other products, like an inflatable dome to replace the original dome on Germany's old capital building, the Reichstag. The building was damaged in World War II and Berliners wanted the landmark to temporarily look like it did. Yost also built the balloon that finally managed to cross the Atlantic.

With rawhide from St. Paul and wicker from the Philipines and nylon fabric from North Carolina, Tea's adventurer was busy as ever. Dressed in denim, with a yellow-stemmed pipe close at hand and a red bag of Prince Albert on the desk, he always looked the part of the daring adventurer who challenged the Atlantic. He enjoyed the pace of life in Tea.

"Everybody finds us," he said of his customers. "We don't want any more work. The main thing is to enjoy life. The bigger you get, the more problems you got … and what the hell!" Then, the black, one-line phone rang.

May / June 1987

The Old Romantic

Roger Holtzmann

WITH HIS HIGH polished boots, meticulously trimmed beard and perfectly knotted tie, he could have been cast as a handsome plantation patriarch. Combined with his quick wit and natural gallantry, he might have made quite a lady's man. The only problem was he didn't care much for romance. As a working poet, he knew that every so often he was required "to grind out something on the subject of love." He could do it when he had to, he used to say, but only after reading up on the subject.

That romantic requirement was but one of several conventions Badger Clark, South Dakota's first poet laureate, decided didn't apply to him. By choosing to be a professional poet, in a state where that wasn't considered much of a career, he marked himself as a man who would follow his own path, not society's. Once on that course, Badger Clark used his talent not to distance himself from ordinary people, but to celebrate them. His heroes and those who became his most loyal fans were one and the same — both created from the clay of South Dakota and the west.

Charles Badger Clark arrived in Dakota Territory in 1883, at the age of three months. His father, on sabbatical from his duties as a Methodist minister because of ill health, homesteaded in Aurora County, just south of Plankinton. (Though most readers assume the name Badger was linked to the animal, it was in fact an old family name from his father's maternal side. Father and son shared the name Charles Badger Clark.) The elder Clark eventually returned to the pulpit, and in 1898 he accepted a pastorate in Deadwood. His wife, Mary Ellen, had contracted tuberculosis; it was hoped that the mountain air would help her condition.

Deadwood was still full of the "spontaneous and exuberant cussedness of a frontier mining camp," recalled Badger later. It was also a town of nearly 10,000 souls, at least some of whom, the Reverend Clark hoped, were ready to be nudged toward respectability. That task, noted Badger, was made considerably more difficult by the fact that services were held just two hours a week, while the competing bawdy houses and saloons ran 24 hours a day.

Badger finished a "very undistinguished" high school career in 1902, following it with "an even less distinguished one year at Dakota Wesleyan" in Mitchell. Uncertain about his future but eager for adventure, he joined a colonizing expedition to Cuba, setting sail just before Christmas in 1903. Those grand plans came to an ignominious end less than four months later. Badger returned to Deadwood flat broke. He caught on with a surveying crew, and loved the strenuous, outdoor work, but, "I well knew that knocking about in outlandish places at low wages and having a perfectly gorgeous time was something less than respectability demanded." Badger still wasn't sure what he wanted out of life, but he knew what society wanted of him, and it sounded mighty dull. "I must establish myself in a respectable line, make a respectable amount of money, marry a respectable bride and in due time, die with a respectable circle of grandchildren around my bed."

He was spared that respectable, deathly pale existence by two experiences that proved watersheds in his life. For one, he landed a job as a reporter for the Lead Daily Call, and sensed that in writing he had "struck his line" at last. The other came when he visited a doctor about a persistent cold and was diagnosed as having tuberculosis. He wasn't seriously ill, but with his family history, a move to the hot, dry climate of the Southwest was advised. There he discovered the poet inside.

Badger found himself a job in Arizona, though not much of one. He tended a small herd of cattle on an isolated ranch while the absentee landlords were away, earning only room and board. His only visitors were cowboys from surrounding spreads, and he found them to be kindred spirits. He absorbed their stories and began to write about them. In letters home to Deadwood Badger began including poems about his experiences. Without his knowledge, Badger's stepmother, Rachel Anna Morris, submitted one of his verses to *Pacific Monthly* magazine. When Badger received a $10 check in the mail for the poem, "I saw that I had the ideal job cinched right then," he later wrote. "If they'll pay me for stuff such as that, I'm fixed."

Before he moved back to South Dakota in 1910, Badger had written much of what would later become two volumes of poetry, as well as his most famous individual work, "A Cowboy's Prayer." Rachel asked him to write it, and Badger recalled that he, "laughed at the idea at first. I told her I never heard a cowboy pray in my life; I had heard them use language that had kind of a religious flavor but it was decidedly not in a religious spirit."

Though his ranch experiences were among the richest of his life, and he had grown to love the harshly beautiful landscape, Arizona was not home. Badger returned to the Black Hills in 1910. By day he helped care for his increasingly feeble father; by night, he studied and wrote. During this period Badger came as close as he ever did to conventional romance. "To tell the plain horrible truth," he wrote a friend, "I am once more engaged to be married. No dates set yet, of course, but I don't see how anything short of death will prevent this arrangement from coming to its logical. conclusion ..."

His unquenchable passion was directed at Helen Fowler, a Deadwood beauty he'd known since before his days in Cuba. There was a "restful, inevitable quality" in their relationship, wrote Badger, but their engagement quietly ended little more than a year after his return. "He enjoyed their [women's] company but didn't care to become involved to the point where he would have to support one," remembered Edwin Clark, Badger's nephew. "He used to say he could easily ward off any matrimonially inclined woman by merely mentioning the sad state of his bank account, his poor financial prospects and his suspended case of TB."

His literary career was more successful. "Sun and Saddle Leather," first published in 1912, went through three editions. "Grass Grown Trails" followed in 1917. Their success was a springboard for Badger's second career as a public speaker. From 1920-24 he criss-crossed the country as part of the Redpath Chautaqua. His out-of-state "hot-air raids" became less frequent after that, but he remained a popular attraction at South Dakota's colleges, high schools and civic events for many years.

Badger lived in Hot Springs until his father's death in 1921. Then, craving solitude and a natural environment, Badger asked for permission to build a small cabin in Custer State Park, near Legion Lake. Badger Hole, as he called it, was home for his remaining years. Life there was one of Spartan simplicity: wood heat, kerosene light, no telephones, no automobile and no radio. He did, however, have "runnin' water," but only because he ran it up from the creek himself. Badger Hole, almost as much as his poetry, accounted for the Badger Clark legend. His work and his way of life were so perfectly mated it was difficult to tell where one ended and the other began.

Badger had been sending poems to the *Custer Chronicle* and other magazines all along, and in 1935 he gathered these together into "Skylines and Wood Smoke," which proved to be his most popular book of poetry. His reputation was well established, but as one story goes, his elevation to the status of poet laureate of South Dakota came about almost as a joke. It was Christmas Eve, 1937, and Governor Leslie Jensen was holding his regular news conference. "News was short that day," recalled Governor Jensen some years later. So when he spotted Badger, on a whim he announced, "Here comes the poet lariat of South Dakota." The title stuck, and in 1939, the legislature made it official.

By the time of his death in 1957, from lung cancer, Badger Clark had published over 200 poems, along with countless other works he had written for special occasions. Though he never got rich he died wealthy, owning that which a man accumulates when he finds what he wants to do and spends a lifetime doing it. Badger Clark didn't believe in romance of the marrying kind, but he was able to see the romance in sunsets, sagebrush and a cowpoke's weathered face. His job was to make us see it too. And he did it well.

Sept / Oct 1992

DOC LEE'S ADVENTURE IN THE ARTS

Roger Holtzmann

MEMORIAL DAY, 1946, was a time for looking back. With less than a year gone by since the end of World War II, many families were still keenly aware of absent brothers, fathers and husbands. But it was also a time for looking ahead. Everyone, it seemed, had something they wanted to do that the war had put on hold. Dr. Warren M. Lee was one such. A professor of dramatic arts at the University of South Dakota, Lee had been involved in every facet of theater life during his career, from stage hand to actor to playwright. Running a professional theater company had been a dream of his for years, and on that Memorial Day he took the first steps toward making it happen.

Doc Lee, as he was affectionately known by all, had the then-novel idea that tourism in the Black Hills would take off in the postwar years. He was convinced the traffic could support a theater company. When the spring term ended, Lee headed west with his wife Margaret and their infant son Byron. They barely made it to Chamberlain that first day — Lee's old car wasn't up to pulling an overloaded trailer filled with scavenged bits of scenery. More problems awaited when they finally reached their destination. Homer Myers, operator of the Coolidge Inn in Custer State Park, had promised to house the cast and crew in exchange for performances at the Inn. When that offer fell through Lee and company ended up at the old Civilian Conservation Corps camp — luxurious accommodations with wood heat and cooking facilities, a central bathhouse and electricity for about an hour a day.

Despite all that, "Claudia" was staged on June 19 at the Coolidge Inn, as well as five other productions that summer. Besides the Inn, plays were staged in Lead, Rapid City, Hot Springs, Sturgis, and even Igloo. Every night was a different production, but every night was the same story. Put up the set. Perform the play. Take down the set. Move on. Such a schedule wore exceedingly on the troupe, and high transportation costs put them in the red for the season. Doc Lee was convinced the company needed its own theater to survive, so the following year he approached the Game, Fish & Parks Department. They loaned him lumber, Lee scrounged up some war surplus tarps, and a theater was built near Legion Lake.

Opening night in the cobbled together house was a disaster. It poured rain, there were no lights due to electrical problems, and one customer showed up — with a complimentary ticket. Doc Lee and his merry band survived their rocky start, and were encouraged by the enthusiasm of their audiences, but the company lost twice as much money as they had the previous year. Lee forged ahead, but decided the company would no longer tour. They would live or die in their canvas home, now known as the Frontier Theater. That third season was notable for two other developments. I.D. Weeks, president of the University of South Dakota, agreed to grant academic credit for work at the theater, creating a link to the university which persists to this day. 1949 also witnessed the premiere performance of "The Legend of Devil's Gulch," Doc Lee's original play about the gold rush days, which has been an audience favorite ever since.

By the fourth season, living conditions at the CCC camp were getting a little better. The company's canvas theater, on the other hand, was beginning to show its age. Despite some misgivings, Lee felt confident enough in the drawing power of his shows to move the theater from Legion Lake to the camp grounds, thus eliminating all but occasional travel for the company. He decided to convert the old CCC mess hall into a theater, but it burned down before the first performance. Next on the list was the post exchange building. Several seasons of overflowing crowds there convinced Lee a proper theater should be built. He designed one and began looking for financing. In what was then a somewhat controversial decision, the Game, Fish & Parks Department agreed to put up a shell if the company would pay for the interior fittings and equipment. That investment has been repaid many times over. By 1960, the Black Hills Playhouse had entertained its 100,000th patron, and established a standard for excellence in South Dakota theater that stands to this day

May/June 1991

CALLIHAN'S INFERNAL MACHINE

Roger Holtzmann

EDWARD SCOTT Callihan was a herald of the Machine Age, and like the prophets of old, he was not always the most welcome of men in his hometown of Woonsocket. He was constantly tinkering with all things mechanical, an eccentric, overflowing font of ideas — a man who didn't have time to get along with his neighbors. His more outlandish ideas were an ongoing source of amusement around town, but even the locals were surprised when Callihan clattered into Woonsocket aboard a steam-powered, kerosene-fueled horseless carriage.

The year was 1884, 12 years before Henry Ford built his first automobile. With the exception of a few tinkering types here and there, few had ever seen such a thing. Callihan's vehicle was a tricycle design, with a single, spoked wheel in front and two in the rear; he sat behind the steam boiler on a seat borrowed from a reaper with the steering levers firmly in hand. His two-cylinder contraption had a top speed of 15 miles per hour. The run from Callihan's home near Artesian to Woonsocket, a distance of about 20 miles, took two hours. With a whistle and water gauge mounted on the dashboard, Callihan can even be credited with inventing options.

Callihan never went past fifth grade. His mechanical aptitudes were inborn, his inventions created through trial and error and gifted insight. He considered himself primarily a farmer, and most of his tinkering was devoted to finding ways to lessen the toil of farming. Callihan produced well-drilling rigs and threshing machines, even a wind-powered turning lathe, but nothing stirred the imagination like his horseless carriage. Horses reared and children charged about, enjoying the racket as Callihan pulled up to the general store. Among those who could do very well, thank you, without a revolution in transportation was the local constable, who ordered Callihan and his infernal machine off Main Street.

Shortly after the turn of the century Callihan produced his first gasoline-powered automobile. A group of neighbors, by that time accustomed to seeing him astride all manner of strange contraptions, gathered to watch his first test run. Callihan set off down the road, and upon his return the crowd began waving and clamoring for a ride. He waved back and yelled something, pointing at the machine, but he couldn't be heard over the roar of the engine. For almost two hours he continued to circle the mystified group. Finally the machine sputtered to a stop. As he dismounted, Callihan sheepishly explained that he had mounted the shut-off switch out of reach from his position in the driver's seat.

Callihan's original steam vehicle didn't survive to take its rightful place in a museum as the first horseless vehicle in South Dakota. He took the wheels off and used them for a drag cart — which was very much in character, though it was a loss to history. Edward Scott Callihan lived to see ideas he pioneered become commonplace, the seeds of great fortunes by men in the automotive industry. He died on March 6, 1937, in Woonsocket.

May / June 1990

THE HONEST POACHER

Adapted from "Black Horse Butte" by Elizabeth Johnson

THE LATE JUDGE Archie Moore of McIntosh loved three things in life — his family, the law and the outdoors of South Dakota. There were few conflicts between the three even though childhood polio left him with paralyzed legs. Archie embraced life with a rare passion.

His father refused to treat him any differently than his other children. When Archie was still young, his father brought home an old truck and said it would be Archie's when he could climb into the cab. It took the boy many days; one afternoon Mrs. Moore heard a loud "whoop" and looked out the window to see Archie behind the steering wheel. His father adapted the foot controls to fit Archie's hands and the lad had wheels.

He completed law school in 1942 and was promptly elected states attorney because the voters knew he had grit. He married Dorothea Hutton of Egan in 1951 and they immersed themselves in the social, business and political life of northwest South Dakota. For four years, he served in the South Dakota Senate but he quit because of the difficulty of maneuvering his wheelchair up and down the marble capital stairs. It was one of the few concessions he made to his handicap. In fact, one of his favorite pastimes was hunting, and that presented the one occasion when his love for the outdoors and the law came into humorous conflict.

According to Elizabeth Johnson's book, Archie and Dorothea were enjoying an autumn drive and some target practice when they came upon numerous pheasants. Archie took aim at a few and Dorothea retrieved them. They headed home envisioning a fine dinner of wild pheasant. But the waters of the Grand River had risen over the road and the car's engine became wet and stalled.

Dorothea crawled out the window, waded to dry land and walked for help. Archie was helplessly car bound; river water seeped in to his knees, and up to his lap. The pheasants floated in the back seat. The pheasants? Archie remembered that there was a new-fangled idea called a hunting season and he wasn't sure of the starting date. Would Dorothea return with tough old Sheriff Harry Kittelson? How embarrassing it would look for him to be caught red-handed with ringnecks. So Archie tossed the pheasants out the car window and watched his dinner float downstream.

Archie was too honest to keep a secret, so word of his moral dilemma eventually spread around the small towns of Dewey and Corson counties and no doubt elicited many a laugh about the honest country lawyer who almost got caught. It didn't seem to hurt Archie's reputation. He went on to serve in other elected offices and ended his career as county judge.

Sept/Oct 1996

NEW TRADITIONS FOR PINE RIDGE

Candy Hamilton and Cindy Lange

ROSELYN SPOTTED EAGLE fashioned small pieces of beadwork to eke out a living. Now, thanks to a loan from the Lakota Fund, she does large items like leggings and full-length capes for jingle dress dancers. Joe Merrival wanted to operate a buffalo ranch with 51 head of buffalo he acquired through the National Parks Service. The Lakota Fund loaned him $10,000, which he paid back when he sold his first 22 animals. Dave "Shorty" Janis was able to keep his tire repair business going thanks to the Lakota Fund's Circle Banking Project. They and others say the reason for their success is the Lakota Fund, a non profit in the tiny village of Kyle. For nine years, the Lakota Fund's leader has been Elsie Meeks, a Pine Ridge woman who ranches, rodeos and raises money for loan funds with equal acumen. "I was a cowgirl riding around on my horse all the time. I never planned on being a businesswoman," she said.

Her vision for the Pine Ridge, "is for businesses to start popping up all over the reservation ... for people to be able to walk across the street and buy what they want and need, and not have to drive 40 miles." But she said entrepreneurism depends on tradition. It grows out of parents owning a business, allowing the children to work there and teaching them how it works. That hasn't been the custom on the Pine Ridge. Meeks practices the philosophy she preaches. She opened a grocery store at Wanblee that employs local people and helps to establish the business tradition.

March/April 1996

Elsie Meeks has continued her public service after this story was published. She remained involved with the Lakota Fund, campaigned as a candidate for Lieutenant Governor of South Dakota in 1998, was appointed to the U.S. Civil Rights Commission in 2000 and then accepted an assignment as head of an effort to bolster business development on Indian reservations nationwide.

Loving the Land

I got a hunch back mule, a cow and a tater patch
Eggs that are gonna hatch someday;
I got the Lord above and a good girl to love me,
I'm the richest man I know.

That old country-western song sweetly records how most Americans — especially South Dakotans — view life in a roller-coaster world of regulations, responsibilities and deadlines.

Give us a potato patch and good companions, and we'll have all we ever wanted (except maybe Social Security and a television). But it's the potato patch that has stayed in my mind. Land. A piece of earth. Some dirt where a man and/or woman can have a house, let the dog run, maybe even scratch out a garden. And if you're lucky enough, why not dream bigger? Why not enough land to run 10 cows? A thousand? Or a wheat field that runs to the horizon? Now that's a patch of land!

The immigrants who came to the northern plains in the late 19th century were not attracted by high tech jobs, tourism, import/export opportunities or any of the other reasons people might travel across an ocean today. They came for land, pure and simple.

South Dakotans have had plenty of disagreements over land. We've fought about wetlands, rivers, forests, floodplains, corporate agriculture, surface mining, public access and a host of other issues. Oddly, though, the land is also what ties us all together. Naturally, since it inspires so much attachment and conflict, the land is a frequent subject in South Dakota Magazine. *Here are some favorite excerpts.*

— Bernie Hunhoff

IN THE CENTER OF AMERICA

Daniel Dustin

I LOVE THE FEELING of being in the center of our country. It is the feeling of being connected to the bigness outside myself, a feeling that arises from bearing witness to the larger working of things. Under a star-filled sky, with an unobstructed view, I could see the curvature of the earth. And I felt the opposite of being in the middle of nowhere. I felt like I was in the bosom of the earth. I felt safe and secure, and I wanted to stay put.

March/April 2001

A BADLANDS AUTUMN

Jerry Wilson

IN WET YEARS, short prairie grasses and wild flowers lace the lowlands with color. Antelope, buffalo and prairie dogs grow fat and nurse their young. Then searing summer sun bakes and cracks the haggard soil and scorches foliage brown. By fall the sole relief is purplish streaks of manganese, orange iron oxide, phantom clouds and ragged spires against a dome of blue. The creatures remain, thinner now, facing winter that some will not survive.

Journalist Kim Ode called these jagged peaks the headstones of the Oligocene Epoch. This was once a great sea shore teeming with gargantuan life, ruled by tyrannosaurus rex. Slowly the waters receded, then 30 million years ago volcanic ash from the west rained down on a shrinking salt seabed, choking and burying huge reptiles in the dust. Over eons, Black Hills streams licked through sediment and ash, revealing strata of yellow, purple and orange — and the petrified bones of the beasts of our darkest dreams.

Always arid, the thin topsoil is hostile to most sentient life. Yet the crags are home to creatures toughened by epochs of time. Rattlesnakes coil in stark ravines. Coyotes and buzzards scavenge the weak and the dead. Most humans have found the land unforgiving. Frederick Manfred encountered this moonscaped land in the drought year of 1934. "Painful beauty," he called it in his novel *The Golden Bowl*. "Poignant desolation."

There is no soft season to visit the Badlands, only mornings and moonlit nights. Yet each season, every blinding day, has its own harsh beauty. Perhaps fall is best. In the solitude our souls are bared, and we find ourselves.

Sept/Oct 1999

THE COTEAU DES PRAIRIES

Bernie Hunhoff

A FRENCH MAPMAKER and a Sisseton banker lived a century apart, but they both loved the same piece of prairie in northeast South Dakota, the Coteau des Prairies.

Joseph Nicollet, the mapmaker, saw it first. He was a skilled scientist and astronomer who came from France in the early 1830s to explore the Mississippi River. In 1837, the U.S. government appointed him to lead an expedition to complete his scientific mapping of the Mississippi's watershed, which included the Missouri River valley. That journey led him to modern-day South Dakota.

Nicollet loved the northern plains, and was especially enthralled by a view from a hillside west of present-day Sisseton. In 1839, he gazed at a panoramic view of rivers and hills, and wrote in his journal that he hoped to someday return to the spot to build a cabin and live in communion with Mother Nature and the Native Americans who had befriended him.

"So vast is the extent which the eye takes in," he wrote of the view, "no difficulties of road, a far spreading verdure, relieved by a profusion of variously colored flowers; the azure of the sky above, or the tempest that can be seen from its beginning to its end; the beautiful modifications of the changing clouds; the curious looming of objects between earth and sky." Nicollet never returned to build a cabin. He died just four years later at age 57. However, he and his favorite hillside are permanently linked by a 75-foot tall observation tower and museum built by area residents who share his appreciation for the prairie. They were led by Sisseton banker Harold Torness, a descendant of Dakota Territory fur traders. He and his boyhood friends camped on the hill in the 1930s.

Growing up, Torness knew nothing of Nicollet. But when he read *Joseph Nicollet on the Plains and Prairies* by Edmund and Martha Bray, he felt he'd found a kindred spirit. "Here was a man who thought of northeast South Dakota as I did," he said. "I couldn't sleep until I read it." Torness was especially proud to learn that Nicollet referred to the "magnificent and indescribably beautiful" Coteau des Prairies hills near Sisseton as the highlight of his explorations; on another occasion he called them the Alps, perhaps reminiscent of the French Alps where he spent his youth.

After reading about the French explorer, Torness came upon the idea of memorializing Nicollet on the hillside he had so enjoyed in 1839.

Fortuitously, the land was in the process of being taken by the county due to unpaid taxes. Torness and others raised $265,000 to build a 96-step wood observation tower and visitors center that opened in 1991. The banker, who died several years after the tower was finished, hoped the site would help both tourists and local people appreciate the region's history and beauty. Nicollet would have loved the wood tower. Even without that elevated view, he wrote in his journal, "I pity the man whose soul could remain unmoved under such a scene of excitement."

May/June 1992

CUSTER STATE PARK: SPLENDID ISOLATION

Paul Higbee

CUSTER STATE Park has been described as a place of "splendid isolation." Splendid? Hiking a rocky trail along Stockade Lake, I wonder if anyone could deny the adjective, especially today. It's early spring; a day where aspen leaves are half-formed and snow still lies in the shadows of great granite outcrops. The lake surface is perfectly calm, but I can hear wind in the dark pines up a steep slope before me. Isolated? Sure, in the most obvious sense. I can hike all day and most likely meet no one. Yet Custer State Park, for me, will always seem crowded with ghosts: Calvin Coolidge mulling over whether to seek another term as president; Badger Clark writing poetry in his rustic Badger Hole cabin; Doc Lee leading his merry little acting troupe through the park in a 1936 Ford.

Located in the southern Black Hills, Custer State Park's 114 square miles make it not only South Dakota's largest, but one of the nation's largest state parks. About two-thirds of the area is timber, the rest rangeland that supports a bison population that provided the seed stock for herds across the continent. The park's scenery and wildlife have lured movie producers in the past. *How the West Was Won* and *The Last Buffalo Hunt* were both filmed there, and German TV producer Ernst Arendt recently completed a project in the park. Upon returning home he wrote back to park officials: "Quite often we are missing the Black Hills, the prairie, the endless grasslands, the buffalo. Everything is so small, so narrow, and so hectic in Germany, so often we feel homesick for Custer State Park."

May/June 1994

Sioux Falls and its Falls

Ann Grauvogl

TO UNDERSTAND THE Big Sioux in Sioux Falls, it may be easiest to start at the falls. Without the falls, the city wouldn't be here. Without the city ... well, without the city, the falls would still be the rippling, shimmering cascade early explorers discovered. Listen to an early tourist who wrote home about the falls: "There were many waterfalls, arrested for a moment, and then the many cascades finally meet to go laughing, foaming and bounding into the chasm below. From every waterfall and rock, nature with a thousand tongues proclaims 'omnipotence.'"

French explorer Joseph Nicollet saw a "stream of clear, swift running water" and a "beautiful and picturesque falls." He saw the bends in the river and called it Riviere Croche. The Lakota called the Big Sioux Watpaipakshan, "where the river bends," and Tahan-kusundata, "thickly wooded river."

Capt. James Allen, after visiting in 1844, raved about the falls in *The States and Territories of the Great West*, "The rock of these falls is massive quartz," he wrote. "The falls, as near as I could measure it, is 100 feet and 400 yards, and is made up of several perpendicular falls — one 20, one 18 and one 10 feet. The rock in the course and on the borders of the stream is split, broken and piled up in the most irregular and fantastic shapes, and presents deep and frightful chasms, extending from the stream in all directions. There is no timber here on the borders of the bluffs and only a little on the small island at the head of the rapids."

July / August 2002

The Buffalo Commons Theory

Bernie Hunhoff

BEFORE THEY HELD the land sale near Gayville last month — the one where Missouri River bottomland sold for $1,675 an acre — the auctioneer ought to have done the honest thing: he should have told the bidders that soon nobody is going to want that land. Surely, he had read the scholarly prediction that the entire plains region is about to suffer from wide scale abandonment.

The prophet is Professor Frank Popper, chairman of urban studies at Rutger's University in New Jersey. "The rural plains will be virtually deserted," he told our neighbors in North Dakota recently. "A vast, beautiful, characteristically American Plains will go the way of the buffalo that once roamed it." Many of the small towns will die. Over a million people will leave the prairie, from Texas to North Dakota. In the end, Dr. Popper says, the federal government will be asked to "pick up the pieces." He suggests that the region be returned to the buffalo range.

Would the gentleman in Gayville have paid $1,675 an acre if he had known about this latest development? How about the hundreds of other real estate transactions that occur daily throughout South Dakota and nine other doomed states? We have personally witnessed similar auctions and seen a dozen or more misinformed people bid spiritedly for property that will soon be unwanted by anyone.

It is scandalous to think that our country auctioneers and neighborhood realtors are selling property to anxious buyers on the Greater Fool Principle. Then Mr. Popper indicates that the federal government (and you, the taxpayer) may be the final fool. Such blasphemy!

We urge South Dakota lawmakers to consider passage of The Popper Prairie Truth Act, which would require all South Dakotans involved in the sale of real estate to post a disclaimer on the listed property, stating that the entire region may soon be abandoned and the only buyer may be the U.S. Government. Maybe the notices should be placed at every country intersection and convenience store.

Think about it. People are scrimping and saving all across South Dakota (and we would guess in the other nine states) to buy not a piece of that rock on television, but to get a piece of land, whether it be in town or out in the country where they can plant a garden, run a horse, maybe even plant 200 acres of soybeans. Furthermore, most of our present landowners are dreaming of the day when they can buy the lot or the quarter section that adjoins them and tear out the fence.

Jan/Feb 1989

This letter appeared in our next issue:

I read your article and I think Mr. Popper must have rocks in his head. It's amazing how people with that disorder can be kept out of the big house. I have lived in the Dakotas for over 80 years and have enjoyed every day — the beautiful sunshine and clean air, the splendor of the rolling hills and mountains, and the hospitality of the people.

— John Anderson, Bowman, N.D.

And then we received this letter from Dr. Popper of New Jersey:

You have seriously misstated the views of myself and my wife, Deborah Popper. We do not believe that all of South Dakota or any other state will be completely depopulated. Let me explain. Our predictions apply only to the lightly populated, semiarid, more plainsy portions of the states — only for instance, to the parts of South Dakota west of the James River. Even within the plains parts of the states, many places could easily grow or hold steady: middle-sized service center cities (say, Pierre or Rapid City), towns along interstates, areas with persistently strong economies or special amounts of the undoubted plains quality of life you erroneously say we neglect.

— *Dr. Frank Popper, Rutger's University*

WHAT I LEARNED FROM WEST RIVER RANCHING

Wes Jackson

THE SUMMER I WAS 15 going on 16, I abandoned myself to the prairies of South Dakota to work on a ranch belonging to an eccentric and childless first cousin of my mother and her Swedish immigrant husband, Andrew. Ina was Andrew's second wife; his first had been her sister Bertha. Andrew and Bertha homesteaded one half section and Ina another. When Bertha died, Andrew and Ina married and joined their holdings. This was near the Rosebud Reservation, and on Sundays I sometimes rode with Indian kids over those prairies, hearing such stories as how their grandfathers had trapped eagles on this hill or that.

I fell in love that summer at a Saturday night dance in White River. She was a beautiful girl — and the magic was so overwhelming that I swear I failed to sleep the entire night after I met her. Thirty-five years later when I saw her, she was seriously overweight, had lost most of her teeth, her slip was showing, and she neither recognized nor remembered me as she lugged one of her grandchildren into the bar. I think it was the same bar where, as a teenager, I learned more interesting content, at lower tuition than anytime before or since. For it was there that I had scrutinized, with the civilized eye of a Kansas River Valley Methodist, drunk cowboys, married or not, who hugged and smooched young girls and from time to time disappeared into the shadows of the dusty back streets of White River.

The landscape was mostly unplowed then and still is today. The horse, central to that way of life then, is less so now. Out on the ranch, besides the moon and stars, the only lights were of Murdo and Okaton across the river, 12 to 15 miles distant. It was a summer of branding, castrating, fencing, discovering dens of rattlesnakes, catching pond bass. Many evenings on the ranch I'd drive out on "the point" in a Cadillac coup or the pickup to shoot prairie dogs or to see the horses in the bottoms or out on the range. "Junk horses," Ina called them, for in the dry '30s she'd pumped water for hours for the cattle, only to have 50 to 100 head of Andrew's horses show up, run the cattle away, and drink the water. Andrew justified keeping these mostly wild creatures around on the grounds that it was horse trading that had made it possible for him to be so solidly positioned. Now I am amazed to think of the slack Andrew and Ina enjoyed to be able to afford those 100 head of mostly unbroken horses.

I lived in a small wooden hillside shack set up on steel wheels, a shack Andrew had bought from Mellette County, which had used it to house the county road crew. It had been pulled by horses, perhaps the same horses used to pull the grader blade. Andrew and Ina lived in a small two-room house with a large attic that bowed from the weight of such old magazines as Andrew's *Life*, *The Saturday Evening Post*, and Ina's *True Stories*, a magazine devoted to idealized romance. There was no electricity, only cistern water that was used at least twice, the last time always to water a small backyard garden or the chickens. Some evenings Andrew and I would sit on his steps, which overlooked the White River a half mile away, and Andrew would cuss Roosevelt, cuss the Yalta Conference, cuss Indians and neighbors and everybody but Ike the President, who happened to be Ina's first cousin, or I suspect Ike would have caught it, too.

With Ina on her buckskin, Dickey, and me on Bonnie or Violet — names I picked from two of my girlfriends back home — we rode the range from one dam to another, where poles were kept with lures so that we might catch some bass on the way home. Or we might go to the abandoned school on the school section for some cotton seed cake to distribute somewhere across the near 4,000 acres of paradise. I didn't want to go home at the end of summer, and had it not been for high school football in September, I might have stayed. The place became my American dream. And yet, looking back, even though Lewis and Clark's Missouri River was only 50 miles downstream, I now see that little of Jefferson's vision was there beyond the section lines and the system of laws. Here the land determined, for no yeoman farmer could exist here. Even so, I loved everything about it. The Indians, the rodeos, the Danish and Swedish immigrants delighted with their land holdings, the rattlesnakes, even the colorful prejudice and the way the natives got a little bit even with the butchered steer, the grocery bill, and the whiskey.

In the Kansas River Valley it had been another story. We were farmers there. Hoeing was endless during the summer, what with watermelons, sweet potatoes, cantaloupes, strawberries, peonies, phlox, sweet corn, potatoes, tomatoes, rhubarb, asparagus, and more. Kansas was an agriculture, row crop variety, that I knew and, I will say, loved in a certain restricted sense. But it did not compare to the life of the range, with the juxtaposition of natives and grassland, ranchers and rodeos. I made up my mind I would have that South Dakota ranch one day. But Andrew died of prostate cancer and Ina of injuries sustained in a pickup wreck. The ranch was sold and some of the money willed to one of Ina's nephews, who within a year paid it all out in a lawsuit due to being at fault in a car wreck.

Football and love kept me in college in what must have been one of the most misspent youths in history. And what smoldered in me were two experiences with land: the Jeffersonian agrarian, where sod had been busted, and the life of the cattleman. I preferred the latter.

March / April 1995

THE SPRING AT ASTORIA

Katie Hunhoff

THE BETTER YOUR water, the less you ponder water. Nowhere is that more true than in Astoria, where 160 people give little thought to Jorstad Spring, from which flows some of the purest water in the country. Surging up from a shallow aquifer, it's naturally pure due to the spring's glacial origin, and the source has remained relatively unsullied by man or nature ever since. Some ten thousand years ago the glaciers that had gouged the region's valleys and hills began to melt, leaving deposits of gravel, rocks and large boulders. The combination of rocks and hills is not ideal for crop farming, so most of the land remains in grass. Consequently, fewer pesticides and fertilizers are used, which lowers the risk of water contamination.

Jorstad Spring is less than two miles northwest of Astoria. Long before anyone around town can remember, somebody stuck a small sand point pipe into the creek; it has been gushing six gallons of good water every minute since. The pipe is hidden in grass and bushes at the bottom of a ditch along Highway 28, but the visitors from afar who stop to fill jugs know where to find it.

Sept / Oct 2002

Where Wild Horses Roam Free

Paul Higbee

THE BLACK HILLS air feels almost balmy, but the sun reminds us that this is winter. Dusk is approaching at four in the afternoon, and across the Cheyenne River from where Dayton Hyde and I stand, Hell Canyon's rocky cliffs glow orange in the southerly sun's light.

Hyde admires the scene, then glances toward the sun and says, "We've got a lot to see before dark." So we climb into his pickup and rattle off in search of wild horses, over dirt roads, through pine stands, up a stony grade and then along the rim of the Grand Canyon of the Cheyenne. Hyde talks about the 350 horses that roam here, and the 18 books he's written, and how he's lectured internationally about conservation. But as much as anything he talks about these 11,000 acres — the wild horse sanctuary run by the Institute of Range and the American Mustang — and how he finds new treasures every time he explores: wildlife, petroglyphs, rings where Indian lodges once stood. He tells me that a century ago a big outfit grazed 10,000 cattle in a valley that opens before us. And good cavalry horses came out of this country, he says, "because they were sure-footed, raised in rock."

Dayton Hyde's look is as rugged as this terrain. He seems so much a part of the land, in fact, that you have to remind yourself he's been here only eight years. Hyde got his first glimpse of this corner of the Hills, 14 miles south from Hot Springs, during a helicopter flight with Gov. George Mickelson. "I was ready to buy land for a horse sanctuary, and had pretty much decided on Oklahoma," he recalls. "Then Mickelson's people called and told me about this place. I'd been through the Black Hills before and was interested immediately. Honeywell had given up its plans to test munitions in Hell Canyon, and had donated the land to the South Dakota Community Foundation."

The Foundation was eager to convert the land to cash, and Hyde was quick to agree with Mickelson that the site was ideal for horses. At an age where most men are ready to retire, Hyde turned his cattle ranch in Klamath County, Ore., over to his grown children, founded the non-profit institute, and set out to prove what he'd been advocating for years: that wild horse sanctuaries can thrive free of government funding by tapping into tourism. "The winters are so mild here," he says as we step out of the pickup to look at an old sun dance site. "I've got haystacks out for big blizzards, but they don't happen often. Nothing like southern Oregon."

In some ways he's come a long way from Oregon, in other ways not. Here he's a conservationist who's taken it upon himself to see that native short grasses thrive. There, 40 years ago, he took it upon himself to revive an ancient lake on his property. The result was 3,112 miles of shoreline, good fishing, and wetlands for birds. "But I got hit with higher taxes and more regulations because I made the land more valuable," he says. "I'm not against paying taxes, and we certainly pay our share here. But it's like painting your house, which is good for the whole neighborhood, and then you get punished. We would have been better off if, years ago, the federal government had endorsed conservation incentives for land owners, instead of getting into conservation preservation."

There. He's given me something to mull over, and I know he'll elaborate at the right time. These aren't ideas off the top of Dayton Hyde's head. Five minutes later, after driving across a wider meadow, we spot eight sleek horses, grazing a couple hundred yards from us and acting just mildly interested in our presence. "I owe them for a lot of pleasure in my life," Hyde tells me. "To me, they represent freedom."

He knows, though, that wild horses have come to represent something else to some western ranchers, and he understands why. "There are a lot of people out there who consider themselves environmentalists, who have used the wild horse issue to say nasty things about ranchers," he says. "Those people say ranchers are getting rich by grazing cattle on federal Bureau of Land Management lands, and that we should kick them off and turn those lands over to the horses."

It's wonderful to care, he continues, but caring isn't enough. People have to know the facts, and, in this case, people who care but don't understand are not only smearing ranchers, but hurting the horse cause. No, he says, not all ranchers, historically, cared about wild horses. But many did — made sure the animals had access to water, and bred wild mares to keep bloodlines strong. Hyde finds the emotionalism that so often accompanies animal issues distasteful. He's had some outbursts directed his way occasionally, particularly after the publication of his book *Don Coyote*. The American Library Association rated *Don Coyote* one of the best ten books of the 1980s, but detractors, many of them fellow ranchers, didn't like seeing coyotes cast as good guys.

"The thing is, I know by experience what coyotes can do on a ranch," he says. "I never said they aren't problems for ranchers. What I did say was that they need to be considered in terms of an overall land management plan. I've got coyotes here that I hope live to a ripe old age. I'd rather live with old coyotes I know, rather than kill them all off and then have to figure out the ways of new ones that would come in."

Revenue from *Don Coyote* made it easier for Hyde to consider relocating from Oregon when he found the right spot for a sanctuary. He'd been looking for that spot a long while. In 1971 President Nixon signed the Wild Free-Roaming Horses and Burros Act, making the Bureau of Land Management responsible for the animals' wellbeing, and prohibiting private capture or slaughter. Within a decade the population had exploded. Hyde estimates there were about 15,000 wild horses in 1971, and that there are around 65,000 today. Summer range wasn't a problem, but winter range was; lots of horses across the west died of thirst and starvation between fall and spring. Eventually the federal government was paying feedlots $2.64 per day per horse to keep them alive, and Hyde (who believes the Bureau of Land Management did as well as it could with an impossible situation) was spending considerable time in Washington, D.C., pitching his idea about private preserves. President Reagan loved horses, and Hyde and a handful of western senators found Reagan's administration supportive. After Reagan left the White House, though, wild horses weren't trendy in Washington circles anymore.

Hyde had gotten the door open a bit by then, however, and in South Dakota he found a believer in George Mickelson. By the late 1990s, Hyde reported that the sanctuary was working out much as he predicted. "We're paying our bills and taxes," he says. "We're doing fine as far as getting the land paid for, and the horses are leading a quality life."

Jan/Feb 1996

RIVER OF THE WHITE WOODS

Peter Carrels

CARTOGRAPHER AND scientist Joseph Nicollet named it River of the White Woods in 1836. In the 1990s, the name fit the James River again.

It was the trees that drew me to the river 20 years ago. Separated from my hometown of Aberdeen by 10 miles of wheat and cornfields, this river and its corridor of green forests and brushy backwaters became my oasis; I went there for invigoration. The James is a modest watercourse, notable for its near-level gradient. The river's shallow, narrow, winding channel dries up during drought and overflows at the slightest provocation. But the James is the Missouri River's longest tributary, draining 21,000 square miles in North and South Dakota, flowing 740 miles before emptying into the Missouri River near Yankton.

In a recent summer I pulled my canoe down a slippery bank, slid it into the smooth current, and pointed it upriver. I stuck to the main channel, resisting temptation to explore lush riparian marshes half hidden by tall reeds and cattails. The crisp light cast by a setting sun sparkled the land and the water. My boat glided beneath steep dirt banks scoured by high flows, gently sloping hillsides covered with grasses and flowers and muddy beaches jagged with driftwood.

Occasionally I passed a living elm with a sprawling, leafy crown hung over the coffee-colored water, a fortunate and rare survivor, a remnant tree. Three decades ago, rampaging disease nearly wiped out what had been a flourishing forest of magnificent elms shading the James. For three years, from 1981 to 1983, I helped farmers and landowners along 150 miles of the river remove hundreds of logjams and piles of elm tree debris that clogged the channel. I had become intimate with the river by then, and I mourned the demise of the elm forest. But the river's diverse woodlands of ash, oak, box elder, cottonwood and willow began to fill the gaps, tempering the loss, and the wild character of the James remained.

In 1993 the weather turned soggy; snow and rain came in amounts unprecedented in modern times. For five years the wet cycle continued. In 1995 the James was highest in a century, but the record was shattered two years later. Spring floods stretched into summer, then fall, and through winter. Ice encased the trees, and spring thaw tore away at standing timber. Now the dead elms had company. Not even weedy willows escaped drowning, and hundreds of handsome oaks and cottonwoods, some more than 200 years old, perished in the flooded valley.

I paddled toward a cluster of towering cottonwoods that I hoped might have survived high water. I'd launched near the mouth of Mud Creek in northern Spink County, where the curly James creases a broad, flat prairie that 10,000 years ago was the floor of a glacial lake.

I negotiated a sharp bend, and beyond a high bank I glimpsed the cottonwoods I sought. Not a single leaf remained, not a sign of life, just a grove of barkless ghosts. They had been dead a long time; they were startlingly white. In the last moments of sunlight they glowed like glistening ivory. Though they had inhabited and decorated the landscape around them differently when they were alive, their symmetrical, white remains were striking as well. And I found comfort in the fact that the same process of flooding that killed the cottonwoods facilitates their repopulation.

In all likelihood, massive, long-term flooding had happened before. Judging from the age of the most mature cottonwoods and oaks drowned beside the river, the last such high-water years must have been 200 years ago, four decades before Nicollet came. The great flood of the 1990s was only another in a series of climatic events that shaped the James River and the prairie it drains. The James was simply reclaiming its flood plain, recreating its white woods. And I'm still drawn to the river for its trees.

Jan / Feb 1999

HOW WIDE OPEN SPACES AFFECT US

Archie Gilfillan

THOUSANDS OF US hurl ourselves into cities like nuts into a hopper, and there by grinding and rubbing against one another we lose our natural form and acquire a superficial polish and a more or less standardized appearance. In the country, the nuts are not subjected to this grinding process.

Nov / Dec 1996

DISCOVERING THE DAKOTA BADLANDS

Frank Lloyd Wright

Famed architect Frank Lloyd Wright wrote this essay after visiting the Badlands in 1935.

I'VE BEEN ABOUT the world a lot and pretty much over our own country; but was totally unprepared for that revolution called the Dakota Bad Lands. From Mitchell, Paul Bellamy was driving a fair 70 over the brown Dakota prairie to reach the Bad Lands before sunset.

About 4 p.m. something came into view that made me sit up straight and look at Bellamy to see if he saw what I saw. "Oh," said he, "you've seen nothing yet." But I had. What I saw gave me an indescribable sense of mysterious otherwhere — a distant architecture, ethereal, touched, only touched, with a sense of Egyptian, Mayan drift and silhouette.

As we came closer, a templed realm definitely stood ambient in air before my astonished "scene" loving but scene-jaded gaze. The streamline working on a vast plateau of solid cream white clay, something like "calichi," had sculptured this familiar world into one unfamiliar but entrancing. Endless trabeations surmounted by or rising into pyramid (obelisk) and temple, ethereal in color and exquisitely chiseled in endless detail, they began to reach to infinity spreading into the sky on every side; an endless supernatural world more spiritual than earth but created out of it.

As we rode, or seemed to be floating upon a splendid winding road that has seemed to understand it all and just where to go, we rose and fell between its delicate parallels of rose and cream and sublime shapes, chalk white, fretted against a blue sky with high floating clouds; the sky itself seemed only there to cleanse and light the vast harmonious building scheme.

Of course I am an architect and that ride through the land of pure line and evanescent color affected me strangely. Here was the element, architecture, cut of the body of the ground itself, beggaring human imagination, prostrating the simplicities of man before the great cosmic simplicity. Reverence, yes, awe. Deep satisfaction, harmonious like great music drifted over the senses until a new sacred realm was born of light, delicate color and ever changing but immaculate form wherein not even the senses could touch bottom, top, nor sides of its vast repose.

Here, for once, came materiality. Communion calls, "God" is inevitable in this place. It is everywhere around him and when the man emerges to the brown plateau and looks back, as I did, the sun now setting, a pale moon rising in darkening rose and blue sky as rays of last light drifted over, linking drifting water lines of dark rose in pallid creamy walls, gently playing with the sky line, with mingled obelisks, terraces, and temples more beautiful than thought, eternal, who knows, a strange sense of inner experience will come to him of a crisis in his perception of what he has termed beauty. He will leave that place a more humble, seeking soul than when he went in to this pure appeal to his spirit. He will know baptism in its higher than sectarian sense.

Let sculptors come to the Bad Lands. Let painters come. But first of all the true architect should come. He who could interpret this vast gift of nature in terms of human habitation so that Americans on their own continent might glimpse a new and higher civilization certainly, and touch it and feel as they lived in it and deserved to call it their own. Yes, I say the aspects of the Dakota Bad Lands have more spiritual quality to impart to the mind of America that anything else in it made by man's God.

I turned to Bellamy and finally said, "But how is it that I've heard so little of this miracle and we, toward the Atlantic, have heard so much of the Grand Canyon when this is even more miraculous?"

"Oh," said he slyly, "we are not on the through line to the coast."

May / June 1996

Witness to Centuries Past

Jerry Wilson

SOUTH DAKOTA'S oldest tree is thought to be a ponderosa pine that stands in Reno Gulch, south of Hill City. It measures only 20 inches in diameter and stands just 43 feet tall, but forest rangers date it to the late 13th Century. There are a few other ancient pines in the Black Hills but the average lifespan is about 160. In the eastern part of the state, some burr oaks along the Big Sioux River may be 200 to 300 years old, and a stand of oak near Wessington Springs is thought to be over 350 — a mere sapling compared to the grandfather from Reno Gulch.

Nov/Dec 1999

Jeez, They're Scaring the Fish

Ben Hanten

"LOT OF FISH on the screen." Those were typical words of encouragement my father doled out. After hours of failed luck, his "fish finder" would paint new optimism. Growing up in Webster, fishing frustrated me. I'd wake on a Saturday morning with my mind set on nothing but relaxation. Maybe I'd spend all day in front of the computer or television. Dad, however, couldn't wait to get on the lake. Going along wasn't bad. It's just difficult for a kid with a short attention span to sit in a boat all day.

I just couldn't understand why it made sense to spend valuable time and money for only a few fish. Dad's enthusiasm for fishing was hard to figure. He'd work 70-hour weeks, all the time longing to be on the lake. My Uncle Robert was a match for Dad's intensity. He loved to fish. When fishing with them, conversation was often sparse. If Dad felt nibbles on his line, he'd whisper, "Come on you little sucker. Bite it!" It was usually these quiet times when I took a cue to start rocking the boat like we were caught in a hurricane. "Come on, Ben!" Uncle Robert would say. "You're scaring all the fish away!"

I left Webster three years ago, and have returned only a few dozen times for weekend visits. I don't know if it's homesickness or growing up, but now I love to fish. Three years away from home, and I'm hooked. I've bought a few poles and several new lures. Sometimes I'll be fishing from shore next to somebody with their car stereo cranked up, and I catch myself muttering, "Jeez, they're scaring all the fish away."

May/June 2003

BECAUSE OF BUFFALO BERRIES

Linda Hasselstrom

I HAVE OFTEN thought the buffalo berry was designed with greedy humans in mind. You know the ones: they associate size and glitter with quality. It's not love that counts with them, but the size of the diamond. They don't care how a car runs; their eyes shine at spoke wheels, shiny red paint, a large price tag. These folks won't notice the boring buffalo berry, even when it's covered with berries that range from golden to a deep, brownish red.

The flavor of buffalo berries is incomparable. It most closely resembles alum, a cooking ingredient you probably will no longer find in your kitchen if you don't make pickles. One quarter teaspoon of alum, or a handful of buffalo berries, makes your mouth feel like you are eating Death Valley. The secret of buffalo berries is this: it's impossible to eat them from the bush. They are the ideal harvest berry, because you get what you pick. Their other hidden weapon makes buffalo berries the elite among wild fruit. The thorns can be up to six inches long, all scientifically placed so you cannot pick a single berry without puncturing naked hands. Even leather gloves don't save you from injury. The only really effective way to pick buffalo berries is to put on elbow-length leather gloves, a long-sleeved denim jacket over a long-sleeved shirt, and tuck the bottoms of your pants firmly into your boots to keep some of the ticks from crawling up your legs.

Buffalo berry jelly is a tawny peach color, and the flavor is hard to describe. I might compare it to apple pie with lemon: sweet, extra tangy. But another element lurks in the flavor that I can't compare to anything else. I think it's the essence of wildness — clean prairie air made solid. It contains the deer that nibbled the leaves in winter, the beating of grouse wings as they pick berries from the highest branch, the blundering invulnerability of a porcupine living under the ledge. It's the taste of blinding white drifts slowly being built and smoothed into glittering sculpture outside the house as you make morning toast, slathering it with butter and buffalo berry jelly. The jelly brings the flavor of summer heat to your tongue, a sheet of sweat to your shoulders; even as you watch the blizzard, it reminds you of spring fragrance and the cool nights of fall. And there's something more. Buffalo berries are symbolic, to me, of the answer to the question all plains people are eventually asked.

"Why do you stay here? You could he anywhere; you could make more money, have all the advantages. I know it's beautiful, but..." The questioner will shrug, wait a few seconds for an answer that doesn't come. I want to say, "Because of the buffalo berries." Those tart little berries on hidden, thorny bushes are what the modern people of the plains have become. We're not easy to find. And we tend to be a little prickly if we've been here long. Hardship and freedom breed stoicism, and don't leave us with much patience for such questions. But when you get to know us, when you understand a little of our plains habitat, we're rare and tasty.

Though it's difficult to transfer hot jelly from a large pan into a tiny glass, I use my smallest containers for buffalo berry jelly. Almost none of it leaves the ranch. The people I give it to can be counted on the fingers of one hand bloodied with picking berries, and include the best people I know. A few years ago I published in one of my books a map of our ranch; I included specific directions that made my family a bit nervous, and a lot of detail: where the horse stepped on me, where my favorite horse is buried, the dam where the coyotes hunt. I've paid for my candor every time someone uses the map to drive into my yard and ask for a "tour of the ranch." But even while being so naively forthright, I didn't put in the ravines where buffalo berries grow, and it's no use asking me. Find your own. And while you're looking, you might come to understand what we are doing here, and that knowledge will be something else you can savor through a long, cold winter in some sooty, crowded city.

July / August 1991

NOT A LAND OF MILK AND HONEY

Bob Karolevitz

BACK IN 1923, when Doctor J.E. Trierweiler first spanked me into vocal existence at Yankton's Sacred Heart Hospital, South Dakota was just 33 years old. That means I've been around for more than two-thirds of the state's existence; which gives me at least some authority to write about my roots-land as it enters its second century.

I've got to confess that I am one of those South Dakotans who first went away looking for emerald-hued pastures. During that time I experienced a few bright lights — the big city's martini-for-lunch bunch, and a slight touch of Venus. Once I actually pounded my fist on a table and shouted, "Wild horses could never drag me back to South Dakota!" I call that my unenlightened period. I was young, eager, and unappreciative of the advantages of the place of my birth. Fortunately I outgrew that youthful lunacy before it was too late and, like the Prodigal Son, was able to retrace my steps before I was forever disowned. After a 20-year sojourn, I came home to stay. By choice.

I, of course, am a realist about South Dakota. I'm aware that this is not a land forever flowing with milk and honey. The rain doesn't always fall when we need it. Annual temperatures can test both ends of the thermometer. We've got buffalo gnats and leafy spurge; and with our limited population we can't always pay our workers and teachers what they deserve. That's why in one of my books I have labeled South Dakota the "Challenge State." I consider it a highly complimentary title that recognizes the tenacity of tribespeople, pioneering homesteaders, hopeful prospectors in Deadwood Gulch and farmers of the Dirty Thirties who persisted despite adversity.

Along with all that realism, I'm a bit of a romantic, too. I'll gladly put up with our minor drawbacks for a springtime prairie dawn, the song of a meadowlark, the smell of a new-cut alfalfa field and, most of all, for that special geographical boon called elbow room. I like to say that if three cars drive up our country road before noon, I call the sheriff to see if he has issued a parade permit.

Jan/Feb 1990

A PAINTERS' PERSPECTIVE

Harvey Dunn

I REMEMBER WHEN there were no fences and the prairie flowers nodded to each other under the winds to the far horizon, which was broken by the black humps of sod houses and the yellow gleam of pine claim shanties. The creak of an oxbow and the voice of a driver could be heard a long way off on still evenings after a rain, and the air was pungent with the odor of fresh-turned earth.

THE VIEW FROM BEAR BUTTE

Paul Higbee

ONE LAST PUSH through deep snow, along a high ridge with a drop to my right, and I've reached the summit, 4,422 feet above sea level. The view encompasses everything the vision seekers of old knew about their world; mountains, rivers, endless prairie. To the west the Black Hills are impossibly black now, silhouetted against the sinking sun, with wisps of mist rising from deep canyons. To the east the plains stretch toward a fuzzy blue twilight. Studying the prairie I can see the exact course the wind has blown the past couple days, swirling snow around low knolls, filling shallow ravines, blowing flat patches clean.

I shorten my gaze and see Bear Butte's shadow projected with absolute clarity several miles onto the eastern plain. The cone shape reminds me this was a volcano 40 million years ago. Before I begin my descent, the western sky has turned orange. I know that far below, from Highway 34 to the east, the volcano looks active. For a few minutes, there's fire in the sky.

Jan/Feb 1995

Plant Trees for the Unborn Generations

SOUTH DAKOTANS value trees more than most people — scarcity will do that — but few were as eloquent or passionate in praising them as longtime state historian Doane Robinson. He recalled with despair visiting an old settlers association picnic and finding them picnicking in the shade of a grain bin. There wasn't a single tree in sight.

"Few of God's gifts to man serve so diversely and so well as do the trees," he wrote in 1901. "They are the benediction of Heaven, clothing and ornamenting the rough and waste places, healing the man-inflicted scars upon the earth's countenances, modifying the climactic rigors, inviting summer showers and retaining the warm blood of the rain to fatten and ripen the harvest. Blessed be the trees, and blessings upon their sturdy planters. May they live long enough to enjoy the shade and the fruit of their planting. Build for the future, build for your old age, build for the generations yet unborn, but which will bless your name for the good you have done. Plant trees!"

May/June 1989

Brave Little Flower

Jerry Wilson

WHEN LONG winter nights retreat at last and the sun softens the frosted Earth, the roots of spring awake. We know the day has come when pasqueflower's pale lavender petals open.

The Dakota people believed the pasque's appearance awakened other plants from winter sleep and reminded them to emerge from the heart of

Earth — a thought contained within its very name. The Hebrew word *pesah*, meaning Passover, entered English as pasche, or Easter. Like the joyous occasion for which it is named, the pasqueflower signals the resurrection of life.

Some call it the wild crocus, windflower or mayflower; botanists know it as the Anemone patens, a member of the buttercup family. Delicate though they are, pasques bravely blossom in the cool spring air, on barren, exposed hillsides amidst glacial debris and patches of snow. Most wild flowers compete for moisture and sun with prairie grasses, some of which reach six feet tall. By summer only the tallest and toughest of flowers can survive. The smallest, most delicate bloom first, blushing alone before their rivals come.

Pasqueflowers were among the plants whose medicinal uses were known to Native peoples of the Great Plains. Early pioneers learned from Indians that the subterranean portion of this perennial forb is a "headache root." However, for some people, a mere stroll through a pasture of pasques is remedy enough. The floral symbol of rebirth is also the official flower of South Dakota.

March / April 2001

QUOTABLES

I love the dome of the sky and the floor of the land stretching forever, without scale. It is a landscape for dreaming and contemplation.

— Peter Carrels

We don't really regard ourselves as owners of the land, but only as those chosen to keep it in good shape for the future.

— Linda Hasselstrom

It may be that some little root of the sacred tree still lives. Nourish it then, that it may leaf and bloom and fill with singing birds.

— Black Elk

Like liquid gold the wheatfield lies, a marvel of yellow and green, that ripples and runs ...

— Hamlin Garland

We are all Indians here, in as much danger of losing our land as the Sioux of 100 years ago.

— Kathleen Norris

We did not think of the great open plains, the beautiful rolling hills, and winding streams with tangled growth, as wild.

— Standing Bear

O Lord, I've never lived where churches grow. I love creation better as it stood that day you finished it so long ago.

— Badger Clark

IN HEAVEN ON A HORSE

Kyle Evans, centennial troubador (1989)

I'm in heaven on a horse on the wide open prairies of Dakota
Where life sings me a melody and my heart sings in harmony
My troubles never been so few before.

I've tried to live in different ways, where fortune comes and never stays
I'm tired of broken dreams and closing doors
Now nature is my closest friend and I'm content at each day's end,
Alive and free and who can ask for more.

The Hard Road

South Dakotans have weathered many storms, privately and as a community. Some are nature-related, like droughts and tornadoes and blizzards and floods. Others are of our own making. And sometimes, adversity just appears from nowhere. Who can say why?

Many state magazines choose to ignore the "hard road" stories that truly delve into the heart and soul of the human experience. South Dakota Magazine *prints a few because we want to portray a true image of South Dakota. Our troubles and how we deal with them most certainly affect our character. We live in a richly complicated place, and if we don't write about it — and read and think about it — then that part of our South Dakota experience is lost to us.*

So here are the hard times. As in other chapters these are not all of our citizens' hard times. Nor are they necessarily the hardest. They are simply excerpts and condensations of some we've written about. Don't let this chapter leave you sad. Hard times can strengthen people, and over the decades they have done exactly that for our state.

— Bernie Hunhoff

THE BROTHER I NEVER KNEW

Evelyn Brand

I WAS BORN ON the farm southwest of the Bald Mountains in Spink County. I don't remember much about the Great Depression, but I heard about the brother I never knew.

Wesley David was born in October of 1929. He was cherished by his parents and his five sisters and two brothers. Living on the plains was an experience. Drought, dust storms and grasshoppers were enough to make any farmer give up. Many did, but a few determined families held on. In June of 1931, spring fieldwork was in full swing with corn to be planted and hay to be put up. It did not pay to plant a crop, but farmers had to try. Everyone worked hard. But Baby Wesley was a joy to all, like a sunbeam in a very dark time.

One morning that June while bathing Wesley, Mother noticed that his tummy felt hard. She called our dad from the field and they drove my brother to the doctor at Redfield. The doctor made a quick decision to send him to Mayo Clinic at Rochester, Minn. Wesley was examined and put through tests. The diagnosis was liver disease, and there was no cure. He was sent home to die. Our family was devastated but still they had faith. In desperation they took him to other doctors, chiropractors and faith healers. My eldest sister recalls a long ride to Highmore where there was a healer of sorts. It was after dark when they began the trip home. The Model T ran out of gas somewhere along that lonely road and Dad had to walk miles to the nearest farm.

By late summer the heat was unbearable. No air conditioning, no electricity, no fans, no running water. Wesley's condition was critical. Family members were afraid to leave for the fields, thinking he might not be alive when they returned. On Sept. 1, Mother sent one of the girls to pick up her mother, who lived about seven miles away. When they returned, Wesley passed away while being held in another sister's arms. He looked up and smiled just before he died, as if he had seen an angel. Grandma Nuhring, in tears, kneeled beside him and said a prayer in German.

The sadness and grief were hard to endure. The tiny casket in a corner of the living room seemed to scoff at all they called belief. Still their faith grew stronger. By the light of a flickering kerosene lamp they prepared for a funeral. One sister who had a love for wild flowers picked a large bouquet and placed it in a fruit jar. They were displayed with all the other flowers surrounding the casket. The thoughtful funeral director, who understood her love and grief, placed the bouquet next to Wesley in the casket.

Wesley David was laid to rest in the Rockham cemetery near his grandparents' graves. With tired, tear-stained faces the family turned and walked away from the tiny grave. After several days of grieving Dad called the family together. He said, "It's all over now. We did all that we could. God has taken his own. Now, all of you straighten up, hold your heads high. No more self-pity!"

The dry years passed. The rains came; crops were planted and harvested. Life went on.

July / August 1994

OLD MAN IN WINTER

Beryle Seaman, as told to Bernie Hunhoff

Loneliness is everywhere, in big cities and, as we found in the terrible winter of 1996-97, in central South Dakota. Beryle Seaman was living in a tiny house along the Bad River, about 20 miles west of Pierre, when we met him.

IT'S BEEN A long winter. The deer has been here. The antelope. Cattle and horses. They're better than some people, you know. People are busy. They seem like they don't want to come to the house.

If I had it to live over, I wouldn't live the way I did. But you don't know any better. My mother died when I was born. My aunt raised me for a few years. She had 12 children of her own. Dad was an old German. He didn't know any better. I was alone a lot. I have been ever since. That's all I've known.

I went to school. I wish I'd went longer. My teacher advocated all along I should have gone longer. I didn't get graduated from the eighth grade until I was 15 or 16 years old. That's the way it went then because we missed so much school from the weather or working.

No, I can't say it's great to be a bachelor. I can figure this out easily. If you had a wife there's things that would come to this place that she would know about that I've never heard of. "Mrs. So and So told me about so and so the other day," she'd say. They don't tell the bachelor. So the wife would bring in things I never heard of.

I wish I had electricity or a telephone. If I had a phone I could call somebody up. It would probably be a trouble call. I looked into a phone. It's all talk and no do. But of course I don't know how long I'll stay here. I've been here since '47.

Heck, if I've got time I go to Fort Pierre Livestock on Fridays. That's sale day. I go there because you get to see fellas. You can visit with them. You go down to Fort Pierre any other day and the people are all busy. The people will visit with you a little bit but you can't visit like you can at the sale barn.

But that's one thing I miss. The old people are gone. There's very few that are left and I don't see them much.

I was always thinking I should get a place of my own closer to town but I never got around to it.

I'm ready for spring. You bet. I'll enjoy the good weather.

READERS RESPONDED with great interest and empathy to Beryle Seaman's first-person story when it was published in the March/April 1997 issue. It drew more reaction than any article previously published. Some people sent the old fellow cards and gifts. Others wrote letters to the magazine, saying they remembered him from their youth. At age 88, he became a minor celebrity. He died a year later.

THE DEMON WITHIN

Wendy Bell Mendoza

SHE WHISPERS HIS name in her prayers, and his name gives shape to a fear darker than the closet, deeper than the heating vent. Those things, too, are scary for a seven year-old at night. Her prayer is a chant, a charm against drunks, although Ted is the only drunk she knows by name.

He approaches for a couple of dollars when we shop in Faith. Before my husband and I are able to unhook the babies from their car seats, he is there at our elbows, the car door awkwardly, blessedly, between us. Shannon won't look him in the eye; she hangs onto my belt loops, clings to my back, and we shuffle, stagger to the curb. Larry offers to buy him a pack of cigarettes or sometimes snorts, "Hell, no! You want me to give you money to get drunk?!"

He is already drunk. By the time we pull into the mall to do our shopping on Friday afternoons, his eyes are glazed and vacant. Thankfully, he doesn't look me in the eye — he can't focus — but he does ask to hold my youngest baby. My husband gruffly sends him off, but when it's just the kids and me I halfway oblige him by raising my child toward his face, though not close. It is pity I feel.

I have heard such stories about him. He was a star basketball player in the early 50s, an all-stater who led his team to the state B title. He could spin and he could jump. He still calls himself Cougar. His balance is not so good anymore: Booze has staggered his gait, and a harsh cold snap a few years back took his toes. They turned all the muddy, raw colors of frostbite and were amputated.

He is so dark beneath the grimy brim of his cap, so dark below the crude cuffs of his sleeves, that Shannon assumes he must be dark, too, in the hidden recesses of his heart. So she prays each night, a ritualistic chant to protect her, hangs a dream catcher webbed in sinew and beads above her bed, and she cowers when he appears at our elbows in the mall.

I am reminded of the Teds in my childhood and all the stories we told and retold, fabricated, repeated about them. There was perhaps a sliver of truth, a glimpse of character, in all of them: the woman who wandered the aisles of the dime store mumbling of two Vietnamese nieces in a bottle — I'd heard she'd disgraced her family by bearing an illegitimate slant-eyed daughter. The man who walked the streets of Spearfish with a cane and a bag marked with the King of Hearts. He stopped my friend once when we were in junior high and asked if she'd be his assistant in a magic act. Years later, I heard he'd been a vaudevillian. The woman who pulled the three-wheeled cart, sucked on a pacifier, and died in her cabin in the hills outside of town. There was a blizzard, and when someone finally thought to check on her, her body had been partially devoured by her dogs. She was the only one whose name I ever knew: Louella.

But finally, I am reminded of the woman in the black coat, black boots, black scarf knotted under her chin, hands gripping the black umbrella in all seasons of the year. I am the shape her fear takes. I am a disturbing part of her story, part of what is told and retold. Leaving a restaurant once at night with a friend, I came face to face with the Umbrella Woman. Startled, clutching her umbrella like a talisman, she lurched back and flung her arms in front of her face. Her breath caught in her throat, and the squawks she made were birdlike. Her eyes, too, were the round, unblinking eyes of a cornered bird as she crossed her index fingers in front of my face. She made the sign of the cross to ward off what threatened her. I was her demon.

I backed away, embarrassed but strangely frightened at what I somehow had become. As a child, I had crossed to the other side of the street a block ahead of this woman to avoid her gaze. I had peered from behind hedges. For years, I'd known the Umbrella Woman in the shallow way every resident of Spearfish knew her. She was the object of a child's fear, an adult's pity.

She taught me what Ted taught Faith's chief of police and what, no doubt, he will someday teach my daughter. Three years ago, a lawman allegedly took Ted to the sand pit south of town and beat the living daylights out of him. As usual, Ted was drunk and had no charms to ward off the lawman's blows, and so they reduced him to a bloody clump of brokenness. For this lesson, Ted was awarded $70,000 by the community of Faith in a settlement out of court.

Those big bucks are gone, some of them drunk up and some shared with true and fair-weather friends. But Ted keeps a list in his pocket, a grubby list of those who "borrowed" money from him, who for a short while scrambled to be in his good graces, deferred to him. He pulls this list out whenever he needs to remind himself, or the one he's touching, of his humanity.

Shannon's prayers are to a God in heaven, her demons outside her pure, light heart.

I tell you nothing new. It is a rite of passage to realize the demon is within, but tonight Shannon's prayers are to a God in heaven, her demons outside her pure, light heart.

Jan / Feb 1994

A STORY TOO PAINFUL TO SHARE

Paul Higbee, writing on the 25th anniversary of the Rapid City flood

THE DEATH TOLL reached 238 after the names of five people never found were added. About half the dead were American Indians who lived in a neighborhood adjacent to Rapid Creek. In all more than 3,000 were hurt, 1,341 homes destroyed, 5,000 cars lost and damage costs totaled $165 million. It was a rare Black Hills resident who had lived in the area for any extended period and didn't know at least one victim, and lots of people knew whole families of victims. For weeks after the tragedy of June 10, 1972, you could find crowds of people, at stores or at ballgames, and instead of crowd noises there would be numbed silence. For years the stories survivors held — of shivering in the waters all night clinging to trees or rooftops or debris and listening to the cries of neighbors, and knowing what it meant when the cries stopped — were too painful to share.

May / June 1997

MY RATTLESNAKE BITE

Emma Tomsik Streen, writing at age 103

IN 1908 I was nine. We lived on a homestead a mile and a half south of Stamford in Jackson County. On Sept. 2 of my first year there, my brother Otto and I went to the pasture to bring the cows home for milking. I carried my favorite short stick. I had already killed 32 snakes with that stick.

Otto and I spotted one, slithering through the grass. Jumping back, we failed to see the second rattler, coiled. It struck me twice on the lower right leg. Scared as I was, I took time to kill the attacker with my stick. I said to my brother, "If I have to die, it does too." Then I ran home half a mile, carrying the snake. Running spread the venom through my system.

Dr. Winchester sent me to the hospital in Murdo, 20 miles east. That doctor cut flesh away from the bites to make them drain, then stretched a rubber band and wound it below the knee to slow circulation. I was in a coma for many days. The leg turned dark. "Our only hope of saving her is to amputate her leg," the doctor said. Tears in his eyes, my father adamantly refused. He knew I wouldn't want to grow to womanhood with just one leg.

I laid at death's door, but I didn't fall through. After a long struggle, I regained consciousness. Even today, almost a century later, I have two scars from the rattlesnake's fangs and one from the tourniquet. My ankle is stiff and my foot turns out. They didn't have therapy in those days. The rattlesnake — you wonder what happened to the snake after I lugged it home? My sister Helen skinned and tanned it and made herself a snakeskin belt.

Sept / Oct 2002

WALKING A BEAT WITH HOOKY JACK

Enid A. Asheim

JOHN HENRY LEARY got gold fever twice. He left his Newberry, N.Y., home for Nevada at age 16, convinced he was going to strike it rich in Virginia City. That didn't pan out, but hope springs eternal: When news of gold in the Black Hills hit the newspapers in 1874, Leary headed off in that direction. Dakota Territory didn't prove any more hospitable to his dreams than Nevada — quite the opposite. Tragedy would find him again and again, but in finding the strength to overcome adversity, John Henry earned a place in history.

While out prospecting with three other men, Leary returned to camp and found his cohorts murdered, their supplies gone. He gathered scars along the way — one in the shoulder, from an Indian arrow, and another where a falling tree laid open his scalp. John Henry lost an infant daughter to disease, and watched one home burn to the ground. In 1882 he suffered the cruelest blow of all. It was mid-March, and he was hard-rock mining using dynamite. Leary was rolling the sticks between his hands to warm them and one exploded prematurely. Doctors didn't think he would survive the blast, which threw him 40 feet, but survive he did, minus the hearing in one ear, sight in one eye and both his hands.

A friend of the family devised two metal hooks that fit over the stumps of Leary's arms, and Hooky Jack was born. To make a living he got a job as night watchman, patrolling Rapid City's downtown streets with a lantern clutched in his steel hook. He never carried a gun — he had no way to use it — and his only backup was a terrier named Rags. Rapid City was still rough around the edges in those days, with more than its share of murders and rambunctious cowboys, but nobody raised a ruckus on Hooky Jack's beat. He patrolled the streets night after night, year after year, always bidding a cheerful, "Good Morning," to whomever he passed, occasionally asking for help lighting his cigar.

John Henry Leary's end was tragic, but somehow fitting. On Nov. 4, 1926, he started off on patrol as usual and was struck by a passing automobile. Sixty years later a plaque was placed near the Police Department, honoring him as Rapid City's first policeman.

May / June 1989

CENTURY SURVIVOR

Frances Jones, as told to Jerry Wilson when she was 106

A NEIGHBOR by the name of Louis Nickel lived just over the fence line. He'd got tired of life in Chicago, so he came out to South Dakota in 1900 and homesteaded on the river. He was a musician and a tailor, but he couldn't do any tailoring in the country. He brought his violin with him, and sometimes he went to Pierre or Fort Pierre and played for a dance. He was some older than me, but he was tired of being a bachelor and we fell in love and got married in 1912. I was 17.

We got by on practically nothing. We never went to bed hungry, but sometimes we had the same thing over and over and over. We always had hogs and chickens for meat and we tried to have a garden. We didn't have much luck. But we always had potatoes and everybody had beans. We dug a cave, and in winter we cut ice on the Bad River and stored it in the cave, packed in straw. Neighbors would help and we'd all go down to the river and saw big chunks of ice. It usually lasted until sometime in August.

Nov / Dec 2001

TRACY

Wendy Bell Mendoza

I'VE HEARD THAT it was this way: that she loved an older man, a dark, brooding man my age or more, with eyebrows as tangled as his past and a chiseled nose, a reporter for the rival newspaper. He'd been living for some months with an older woman, in her 40s maybe, not much older than he, small and dark, too, with wire rim glasses. He'd been living with her — Debra was her name — and Tracy had visited them on occasion, I guess — listened to 60s music, smoked cigarettes, drunk black coffee.

But some chemistry smoldered — a touch, maybe — his hand on Tracy's elbow when she stumbled over the footstool, sprinkling wine, his breath on her shoulders when they flipped through record albums and then Debra slipped into the kitchen, and there were candles, and incense. He moved out, they say, soon after, and in with Tracy. I don't know.

I know she was pixie-like, truly. Tiny, translucent, sparrow-boned. She loved cats and the sparks she stroked from their fur at night. And even then, when she was young, a student in my English class at high school, she loved the Stones. "We rock to Def Leppard. Tracy rolls to the Stones," her friends teased. Once she wrote a piece about "class," defined it as Mick Jaggar. She wrote another about frustration, the "black sleeping bag that suffocates." There was the one about visiting her grandfather in the hospital — "it was a long hallway, and I was a little girl" — and a tribute to the younger brother she adored.

She was published so many times in *Prairie Winds* that the task force used to joke about the upcoming Tracy edition. I remember she used to beat it home every day after school to catch re-runs of M*A*S*H. She ran cross-country and I can see her still drifting in with the dusk, long after all the others. She ran for discipline, she said, and scenery. She suggested I read *The World According to Garp* and used a word in one of her compositions that I had to look up.

All this I remember, and more, like how it was when I lost my baby. I came home from the hospital more empty than I knew. I stood before my students, chalk in hand, lit book, roll call — turned, and walked out the door. In the hall, I slumped to the floor. It was Tracy who helped me rise. Could she know, could she know how I loved her, my girl?

I've heard it was this way: she wore black, chain smoked, became editor. Time and again, her staff found her at the office in the morning in the same rumpled clothes she'd worn the day before and the ashtrays full. They tell me she fell in love. He moved in. Her father bristled. Her mother raged. He was a brooding man with angry eyebrows. He chiseled her life. She forgot her friends, they say. Something went wrong: he flung her cat against the wall. It had rubbed against his legs one too many times. He stopped by Debra's place and one thing led to another. I don't know.

They say he grew weary of her, shut her out. She clung, like a cat between his legs. He packed his bags. There was a gun in his bundle. The moon rose in the branches. He walked out. She fumbled. There were sparks, I think. A shot, they say. And that fall, one thin, thin morning, we buried her. Leaves fluttered at my feet and life in my womb. Could she know?

Next to my bed, I keep her journal, the one she never picked up that last day of school ten years ago. I guard it. The children know they must not touch it. They have their own paper, I say. Inside are three entries she stapled shut. "I won't read them if you do this, class," I said.

"Promise."

Sept/Oct 1994

ROY'S STORIES

Roy Johnson, as told to Norma Wilson

Roy Johnson was born on Independence Day, 1922, and lived most of his years on a farm near Westreville, just north of Vermillion. When Norma Wilson moved in just across the road from Roy's place in 1982 she became good friends with him, and a fan of his stories.

MY GRANDFATHER came from Norway in 1854 — he was only 12 or 13. He came over with his older brother who must have been 21. They settled first in Wisconsin where there was a Norwegian community. Then they moved to this area, north of Westreville. They lived in a sod house and waited for the Territory to be opened for settlement. While they waited they grew a garden and a few acres of crops. My dad told me that once my grandfather walked all the way to Sioux City for groceries. Vermillion and

Yankton were closer, but my grandfather probably didn't know they were there. He couldn't communicate with anybody because he didn't speak English. Once I asked my father, "Wouldn't that have been an awfully heavy load of groceries to carry all the way from Sioux City?"

And he said, "Well, he probably had a sack of flour and another one of sugar, and 20 pounds of tobacco."

Fifteen years before I was born, my mother lost her first child. She'd been in bed 10 days when she heard my dad's sister was in labor. So she and Dad drove to her house in the buggy. It must have been about 1907. When they got there, the woman had given birth to twins. But she and one of the babies died. When Mama heard about it, she asked, "Where's the other one?" And the father said, "Behind the door in a shoe box." The baby weighed 3 1/2 pounds.

Mama told my dad, "Go and hitch up the buggy. We have to go now." When he got back to the house, she had the baby wrapped up in a quilt. She never liked to ride fast, but that time she told my dad to hurry the whole way. She didn't want the baby to get cold. It was the 15th of December.

My mama raised her. They never adopted her. Her name is Winnie Christopher, and she was just like a sister to me. She knew her own father but never was around him much. He married again and raised a new family. He died a few years ago. I asked Winnie if she went to her daddy's funeral, and she said, "I went to my daddy's funeral in '41." That was when my daddy died.

After Winnie married she was always taking in children. We'd go over, and my mama would say, "Who's that?" Winnie would say, "Oh, that's so and so; her parents are separated." Mama said one time, "Well, you already have lots of children." It was during the Depression. It cost a lot to keep them. Winnie told her, "You took me home with you, didn't you?"

Mama never said anything else about Winnie's children.

We had food in the thirties, but I ate enough chicken to last me a lifetime. I can remember when you couldn't have found $50 in the whole Pleasant Valley Township.

The bank at Wakonda went broke, and that was what ruined my dad. His place was almost paid for, and he had $12,000 in the bank— enough to pay off the mortgage. But when the bank closed, he lost that money. Some people said the banker absconded with the money, that he'd taken it out in a suitcase in the night.

If my father had lived two more years, he could have been solvent again, but he died before he paid off that land.

July / August 1989

DEATH IN WINTER

Delphine Red Shirt

I REMEMBER THE winters in South Dakota through the 1960s, when people lived in canvas tents. Some of them were my relatives. I remember visiting a distant cousin who lived with her husband and six children in a canvas tent along Porcupine Creek. Her tent looked dark from the rubber tires they burned to keep warm. Their floor was the frozen earth and a thin canvas covering. They had a small wood-burning stove, which they used for cooking and heat. Her children developed tuberculosis, and they were moved into a house that the government brought from a closed military base. That was the year they brought many of the houses we called "igloo" houses because it was said they were brought from Alaska. They brought them and plunked them here and there on tribal land, and people moved into them.

I became fully aware of my world those first winters in South Dakota, when the wind chill drops below zero and the car battery dies. The times when Momma's laundry did not dry and she brought it into the house all frozen and left it steaming by the wood stove.

The nights pass slowly there in the winter. In the morning you find the sun shining weakly, far out on the eastern horizon, back over the ridge where it competes with the clouds all winter. The role the sun plays in the winter is neutral; all power belongs to winter. The cold is everything. It can overpower you if you are not careful. We lost many relatives and friends, young and old, to the cold sub-zero winters. They died, like many others, when their secondhand cars, "Indian cars," we call them, stalled along the roadside, and no one came by all night. They fell asleep in their cold cars, never to awaken. Sometimes alcohol was blamed, but those of us who had lived there through many winters know that it can happen to anyone. "Tasaki pi," my mother would say. They froze to death, just like the people who were wounded at Cakpe Opi, or Wounded Knee. They were left to freeze in the snow.

Nov / Dec 1999

LONG HOLLOW IN WINTER

Bernie Hunhoff

BAD WEATHER IS no stranger to northeast South Dakotans. The deadly trinity of cold, snow and wind is as common there as anywhere in the continental United States. But a particular place, Long Hollow, has gained special notoriety.

Sisseton is 1,203 feet above sea level, but by the time you climb to the top of Long Hollow, only four miles to the west, the elevation nearly doubles. "In the summer it can be ten degrees cooler than down below in town with a nice breeze," said Joe Schuch, a retired county extension agent who has observed Long Hollow's weather phenomena for many years. "The problem is that in the winter it is that much colder, and you aren't quite as happy about the breeze."

Even on nice winter days, area residents try to avoid the hollow. Clayton Week, a retired farmer, is a walking reminder of why that is a good idea. He and a cousin, Charlie Almos, nearly died atop the hollow in 1937. "Our families lived about 10 miles west of Sisseton, and because it was so far to town Charlie and I batched it," he said. "We lived upstairs on our own in a house in town for two years so we could attend high school."

Snow had drifted over Highway 10 so badly that car and truck travel was nearly impossible. Consequently, the boys hadn't seen their families for several weeks. When school recessed on a sunny Friday afternoon, they decided to walk home. When they started to climb Long Hollow, they noticed that only a few feet of the telephone poles were still showing above the snow. But they kept moving west. "When we got to the top of the hill, it started to get dark. That's when the wind hit. It was terrible."

Week remembers that they couldn't see, could hardly walk, and were freezing in a hurry. He vividly remembers some of their conversation. "Let's sit down and rest," he told Almos.

"No," his cousin replied. "We're not sitting down."

They prodded each other along the hollow, refusing to allow the other to stop. "You get to the point where you lose your common sense and you don't really know right from wrong," he said. "If either of us would have been alone he would have probably laid down and rested and that would have been the end."

The homesick cousins trudged onward, snow stinging their faces. Their fingers and toes were numbed and heavy. The cold wind sucked the oxygen from their lungs. They wondered silently whether they would escape the hollow alive. They couldn't see the road or any other landmarks except for the tops of telephone poles. Finally they saw the Tobias Herigstad farm yard and stumbled to the front door. Tobias and his wife, Bertha, rushed the boys indoors and fed them a warm meal.

The cousins were not the first or last to dare death on Long Hollow, but they may be among the luckiest. Awful stories have been recorded through the years; other incidents have probably been lost to history. One of the saddest episodes happened Jan. 6, 1903. Knut Throndson and his daughters, Theoline, 13, and Menne, 15, took a horse and sleigh across the hollow to visit the Herigstads. The weather was bright and warm.

Upon their return through the hollow in late afternoon, however, the sky darkened and the wind began to blow. Suddenly they were in a full-fledged prairie blizzard. In white blackness, they veered from their accustomed path. The sled hit a boulder and broke a runner. Throndson, a tough man who had emmigrated from Norway just 11 years earlier, unhitched his team and told each of his girls to hold onto a horse's tail. Then he took the reins and led the horses and his daughters toward their farmhouse.

When he arrived home, he found that both of his daughters were missing. He retraced his path to the Herigstads without seeing them; then he and Tobias searched all night in the storm. The grief-stricken father and his friend called the girls' names but their shouts were swallowed by the roaring storm. At sunrise they found the girls' frozen bodies near the Herigstad farm. Through the years, the Herigstads had rescued many travelers. Still, they were devastated that the two teenage neighbors died less than 400 yards from their door.

Roberts and Marshall counties are home to the Sisseton Wahpeton Sioux Tribe, and Native Americans have lived in the wooded coteau for many generations. They understand the dangers of the hollow in winter, and are cautious in their winter excursions. Still, two Indians, Clarence and Joseph Grey, became lost in a November storm in 1958. They were both in their late 30s, strong and wise in the ways of the outdoors. Joseph was a World War II veteran who had received a Purple Heart for battle injuries. They had grown up along nearby Grey Lake and were considered expert hunters, trappers and fishermen. Search parties found no sign of them, so friends and family had hope, until the brothers' bodies were found the following spring under snowdrifts in the evergreen trees that grow on the hollow.

Jan/Feb 2002

GRAVE IN THE HIDEWOOD

Bernie Hunhoff

JUST WEST OF Interstate 29 as it cuts through the Hidewood Hills of Deuel County, two nearly forgotten graves lie high on a pasture hill. Floyd Haug discovered the graves when he rented the land 45 years ago. He was fixing fence in early May when he saw two perfect rectangles of blue flag flowers. He suspected that the flowers were planted to mark a gravesite, and when he visited the landowner, Ed Koppman, his hunch was confirmed.

The land was homesteaded by a Norwegian settler, Per Gustav Erikson, and his wife, Ida Mary. Henry Wells, a local historian, figures the Eriksons came by train to Gary, and probably used their savings to buy a horse and wagon to drive to their new home in Hidewood Township. In the early 1880s they had a baby daughter, but during the harsh winter of 1885-86, a diphtheria outbreak struck the territory. Ida Mary and her daughter died. Because the snow was so deep and the ground so frozen, their bodies were placed in two wooden boxes built by a neighbor. The grieving young settler kept the coffins in a shed until spring, when he dug two graves and buried them above the valley. He probably had no money for a permanent marker, so he planted blue flag flowers, cousins to the iris, in the overturned soil. Then he sold his claim for $300 to Peter Dahl. Nothing else is known of Per Gustav.

Well over a century later, the blue flag flowers still mark the simple gravesite. They have outlasted many pioneer grave markers.

Sept / Oct 1999

"WE PAY ATTENTION TO STORMS NOW"

Janice Holler, victim of a tornado near Bristol in 1996

DOUG WAS STUNNED when he crawled out. Everything he'd spent 30 years building up was gone. It kind of puts you in shock. Even the shelter belt was ripped out. That's the first time I was homeless. It took as long to rebuild the house as it took to build it, eight months. The tornado kind of wiped everything away. It not only took the roof, it blew out the west wall, even ripped up the kitchen floor. It tossed steel bins around like tin cans. It was dreadful, something you don't ever really get over. It sticks with a person. We pay attention to storms now.

May / June 2001

One Case, One Epidemic

John Maciejewski

MY FIRST SYMPTOMS were anything but subtle, a jolting onset. The heavy, throbbing headache that began in school grew worse during the afternoon softball game in neighboring Harrold. Next morning, the headache was still there, but now accompanied by a stiffness down my neck and back. My parents decided an immediate trip to St. Mary's Hospital in Pierre was in order.

Dr. Jahraus wasted no time. He ordered my immediate transfer to a treatment center at Hot Springs. Within an hour, I was on my way to the Pierre Airport by hearse. A small, yellow plane stood ready, piloted by Cecil Ice. My first experience in the air might have been scary, but the pounding headache kept my mind off any fears. We landed on a primitive grass strip outside of town. An official transport vehicle was waiting — not a hearse this time — and soon I was in the West River Crippled Children's Hospital. During that epidemic year, 1952, the hospital housed and cared for 180 victims of polio.

Jan/Feb 2001

Starting Over as an Ex-Con

Ray Peterson

THE BIGGEST PRISON break in South Dakota history occurred on August 17, 1922 in Sioux Falls. Deputy Warden Arthur Muchow entered the tailor shop to quell a disturbance, and four men jumped him. Somebody stabbed him in the stomach with a homemade knife. His scream brought Warden Jameson on the run. When the warden entered the shop, somebody knocked him down and took his keys. Outside the wall, the four commandeered a tourist's car and headed west.

They robbed a hardware store in Lake Andes, taking two revolvers, a shotgun, a rifle, ammunition, clothing and cash. Two airplanes and a pack of bloodhounds joined the search. Ten days after escaping, they were cornered in Cheyenne River country near Creighton. One of the prisoners was shot in the head, another in the foot. The three survivors were convicted of assault with intent to kill and sentenced to life in prison. They were released on a writ of habeas corpus in 1944.

Joe Forman, one of the three, came home to Yankton and got a job as a bartender at Walt Hannon's Nugget Bar on Third Street. When I met him in 1947, he was driving a cab for Richard Merrigan. But that didn't last long. Merrigan lost business because his competitor passed the word at Mount Marty and Yankton colleges that he had an ex-con driving for him: "You don't want the college girls riding with him."

Forman was a big man. He must have weighed at least 250 pounds, but he wasn't fat. He walked with a limp from the bullet in the foot. He was quiet. He never said much, but you didn't want to mess with him. When cab driving didn't work out, Merrigan put Forman to work building his new salvage yard on the east edge of town. In 1949, Forman helped build Oahe Dam north of Pierre. By 1952 he was in Eagle Butte, tending bar at the municipal liquor store. Before Forman came to town, the cowboys routinely threw the bartender out and served themselves. Forman was hired to straighten the place out, which he did. The first guys who messed with him, he started throwing them around like coveralls.

I was still a kid, 15 years old. I'd left my boyhood home in Yankton, and was bumming around, looking for a ranch job or something to do. I went into the bar and I recognized Joe Forman. He told me that once he cleaned the place up, the city fathers wanted to get rid of him. Joe was a big guy with a tough-looking face, not too pretty.

Later that summer an Indian kid and I went into the bar. Forman took one look at us and asked if we'd been eating. We said yes, but he said, "I don't think so." He gave us a note and sent us to the restaurant to get a meal.

Jan / Feb 2001

AN INNOCENT MAN HUNG

John Egan, great-grandson of the executed

HOODED WITH ankles bound together, Thomas Egan dropped heavily when the trap was sprung. A shudder swept the crowd when the rope snapped. Egan thudded to the ground, alive. Lift him up and do it again? Or would that be a mystic form of double jeopardy? Up he went. The second drop was botched when the trap was released before the noose was properly in place. The third try was successful.

If the hanging was bizarre, it paled in comparison to a development years afterward, in Seattle, Wash. On her deathbed, Thomas Egan's stepdaughter, Catherine, called Dr. W.C. Woodward and others to her side. "I killed my mother," she confessed. "We quarreled. I hit her over the head … no one ever suspected me. My stepfather was hung for the crime."

July / August 1994

FIGHTING FOR THE ISLAND

Billie James & Scott Stoel

AFTER THE FLOODWATERS of 1881 receded and the land dried, the view from the bluffs by Vermillion was transformed. Instead of looking down the hill and seeing the wide Missouri flowing by, the Vermillion River, puny in comparison, meandered through the vacated riverbed. Where Kidder Island once stood in the middle of the river, it was now connected to a large slice of Nebraska cut off by the flood. The new river channel lay miles off beyond the cottonwoods of the former peninsula.

Although the piece of land was firmly connected to South Dakota, the area became known as The Island. It was disputed territory. Residents did not know if they were Nebraskans or South Dakotans. And it wasn't long before people took advantage of this confusion. Some families farming The Island refused to pay taxes to Nebraska. Squatters took over parts of the old riverbed and planted crops. The Island became a haven for gambling, bootlegging and prostitution. Most of the saloons were shoddy shanties built on a sandbar covered with willows that stood in the widest part of the old river channel.

The Island was also well known for a huge whirlpool nearby. During a flood, it was said buildings, boats and even boxcars would disappear down into the watery vortex. One story claims a church was sucked into the whirlpool, its bell still ringing. Howard Morse remembered when the whirlpool went dry, leaving it full of carp. "We took them out to where the airport is now and we buried a carp in each melon hill for fertilizer. After about three days, those carp began to get slippery and stinky."

In 1939, clothing store-owner A.O. Kirby made a sort of land grab on The Island. He paid nominal fees for quit-claim deeds to property owners. The matter ended up in court and Kirby lost. He did not take the ruling well. He set out on a rampage of revenge, intending to kill everyone involved. He walked down main street with a 20 gauge shotgun toward the law offices of Payne and Olson. Kirby walked up the stairs to the firm and shot and killed Peter Olson at his desk. Olson's law partner, Jason Payne, entered the room and Kirby leveled the shotgun at him. Phillip Crew, an associate at the law firm, attempted to wrest the gun from Kirby and the pair fell down the stairs and onto the sidewalk. Police arrived and arrested Kirby. He was tried, found guilty and served seven years of a 10-year sentence.

Sept/Oct 1994

WAGES OF A HARD DAY'S WORK

Jerry Wilson

ED TUBBS WORKED at the Susquehanna Mill near Edgemont. In the early days he considered his job a good one. "When the mill opened in 1956, John McKnight and John Curl and I were among the first hired," he said. "The Fourth of July was the first paid holiday I ever had."

Tubbs isn't so fond of the uranium mill any longer. Now he has trouble breathing, his kidneys and bladder are damaged, he fights skin cancer and melanoma, and his legs are weak, recently requiring an artificial hip. "That's from the stairs," he said. "We literally had to run up and down six flights of stairs to keep the lines open. Sometimes we slid down the banisters to get to a clog faster. I did that for 16 years. The roaster ran up to 2,000 degrees. Another thing is hearing loss. The noise was terrific. You had to holler to make yourself heard to a guy standing next to you. Between the heat and the noise you could hardly stand to be in there. It was so noisy you had to go outside just to change your mind."

Jan/Feb 2001

PACKING HOUSE BLUES

Mark Anderson, Morrell worker and union spokesman

I GUESS THE BEST way to describe our wages at the packing house is that we went from being the highest paying manufacturing jobs in the country to the lowest in about 10 years. In July of 1982 a worker at Morrell's in Sioux Falls started at $11.27 an hour. When you go to work today, 12 years of inflation later, you start at $8 an hour.

Jan/Feb 1995

LOSING A MOTHER

Lakota elder Steve Charging Eagle of the Cheyenne River Reservation

WHEN I WAS TWO and a half, my mother died and my father and uncle raised me. On Mother's Day, even today, I remember her and wonder what she looked like and what kind of woman she was. The love and care of a mother I missed in my life. It is a sorrow I still feel in my heart. That is one of the reasons I keep going to church. I hope to see her someday.

Nov/Dec 1995

SPENCER: A TOWN BLOWN ON THE MAP

Bernie Hunhoff

SOMETIMES, YOU'RE not appreciated until you're gone. Ask the people of Spencer. The quiet town of 320 seldom got any attention from the world-at-large over the last century. Like a hundred other seemingly forgotten farm towns in East River, most folks figured it would eventually dry up and blow away and never be missed.

Well, it did blow away. Spencer was destroyed by a tornado on the evening of May 30, 1998. But much to everybody's surprise — maybe because of the suddenness of its leaving — people actually cared. Everybody wanted to help. A KELO-TV telethon raised $638,000 overnight. Eight thousand people from five states answered Governor Bill Janklow's call for help. Vice President Al Gore came to see what was left of the town and pledged emergency aid. Stores and clubs and churches collected offerings. People cared about the town after all.

Thanks to all that assistance, there will be a Spencer in the years ahead. What it will look like is uncertain, a reality it shares with about 200 other lesser-known towns in South Dakota.

July/August 1998

A LESSON FROM PRISON

Kendall Hottmann

MY BROTHER, MERLYN, was in first grade and I was in third grade on Sept. 3, 1930, when our father, John C. Hottmann, came to school to take us to our grandfather's farm between Hoven and Tolstoy where three suspects had taken refuge from a Hoven bank robbery. I will never forget the sight of the slain robber lying on the ground covered with a blanket. One robber was injured and the third was tied up.

The president of the bank was later convicted of conspiracy in the robbery and was sent to the South Dakota Penitentiary along with the two robbers who survived. Our father took us to the prison to see the former banker and to teach us what happens when you disobey the law. The clang of those metal doors closing behind us left a very lasting impression.

July/August 1998

Traditional Ways Versus Bingo

Joe Flying Bear, Dakota medicine man from Eagle Butte

I STAND FOR traditional ways. I have two sons but they're away from me. They walked in white man's ways. I don't know if my medicine will be carried on by one of my sons. I don't think so. Too much thinking about your way of life. Money-making is what they have to do now. Now the people drive cars. There's no tipis and they wear shoes. We can talk our own language, but the younger generation knows nothing. It's hard to go back to the way we used to live. It's good to live in those days, but we're away from them now. I'm the only one that's left behind.

We're losing our language now. My grandfather said, "Indians are suffering the four directions today." They want money. They want a car. They want something. Many people in the community, when the sun is dawning, they rest in bingo. Where are they getting their money? They sell their furniture and valuable things and go to bingo.

Jan/Feb 1999

From Vietnam to Pine Ridge

Chuck Richards, decorated combat veteran

IT'S LAKOTA TO go into war, to test ourselves like our ancestors did. I volunteered for the special forces to face my fears, to see if I had the courage to go out in the Vietnam jungles in a five-man recon team.

Killing another human being doesn't feel very good. In war, when you made a kill, the soldiers look up to you as a hero. At the time you kill or you die. You get an adrenaline rush. All senses, all thought completely leave you. You go insane, turn into a machine. When it's over, if you're still alive, you have a comedown period of bad shakes, coughing, sick to your stomach. You remember when your position was overrun by the enemy, and they came right in on top of you. You fought with your bare hands, your knife, a shovel. The dead are everywhere.

One day you're in battle, the next you're home. Then the war really starts. The nightmares come, the flashbacks, the sounds, the smells. It never leaves. It just gets stronger and stronger.

Jan/Feb 1999

The Lesser of Two Evils

"EVERYBODY WAS coming out here in box cars because they were going to get rich," said Opal Kozel, who homesteaded near Blunt in 1908. "Nobody got rich. But we found a good place to live." She remembered her dad kept a big old bull snake under the farmhouse porch to keep the rattlers away.

March/April 1997

Myself and I

Badger Clark

Faces, but all of them tired and old,
Music, but all too loud,
For I and myself have lost our hold,
Swirled in the shifting crowd,
Under the spread of a smokeless sky
We must find each other, myself and I.

An Unlikely Home

By Roger Holtzmann

CAROLYN AND I were looking to buy our first house. One prospect was an old brick home at 3rd & Pearl in Yankton — not "brick" in the sense of grandeur and permanence but "brick" in a way that suggested the whole thing could tumble if even one brick was disturbed. So much for curb appeal.

"It's got wood floors," said the real estate agent. Even that attempt to put the building's best foot forward took all of her training. The floors were indeed tight-grained fir. We could see the wood because there was a large, square hole in the living room where a floor furnace had been hung. The whole house sagged toward that point — if nature were allowed to run its course everything would sooner or later end up there.

We didn't know it then, but the sad house was a piece of Dakota history. It had been built in 1875 by Governor John L. Pennington, a carpetbagger appointed to his post in Dakota Territory though he'd never been west of Alabama. Yankton was a mostly clapboard town in those days, so Pennington's two-story brick home must have been a grand sight indeed. It was built of soft brick manufactured locally, and of timbers from riverboats that were being dismantled two blocks to the south. During the course of his four-year term, Gov. Pennington met many notables of Dakota Territory within its walls. Riverboat captains, military officers, missionaries and Indian chiefs had trod the same boards we did. Only we looked down as we walked, afraid we might fall in a hole. "We'll have to talk it over," we said, edging toward the door.

"Of course." The agent flashed her professional smile and pretended we hadn't been a complete waste of time.

We kept looking, and eventually found a place without a hole in the floor. Time passed, the world turned, empires fell, and one fine day I answered a help-wanted ad. The address I was given for my rendezvous with destiny didn't ring any bells, but I remembered the building, and was amazed at the transformation. The brick walls that were ready to suffer the fate of those at Jericho had been jacked back to straight and neatly tuck-pointed. It was no longer "that old brick building at Third & Pearl, just past Steiner's Meat Market." It was "The Pennington House," with a sign out front and everything.

My interview was with Bernie Hunhoff, publisher of *South Dakota Magazine*. I had never worked for a newspaper or magazine. I didn't have a degree in journalism. To top it all, I had no experience with Macintosh computers, which the ad specifically required. I was quite sure I'd have the job sewed up by lunch.

Ignorance is bliss, as they say. Had I known more about the man across the desk, I would have been too much awed by him to be so breezily confident. There's a truly remarkable story behind Bernie's rise to the top of the publishing world. He was born in a log cabin ... oh, wait. Wrong legend. The real story is that he was raised on a small Yankton County farm, the fourth of eight sons born to Bernard and Margaret Hunhoff. After high school he attended Mount Marty College, graduating in 1974, and landed a job on U.S. Rep. Frank Denholm's staff. That ended abruptly when Larry Pressler's election that same year put all of Denholm's people in the unemployment line. Most of them stayed in Washington. Bernie came home to South Dakota. After stints on newspapers in Watertown and Madison, he took a public relations job at the USD School of Medicine. While working there and living in Gayville, a small town halfway between Yankton and Vermillion, he started his own newspaper, the weekly *Observer*, in 1978; it quickly grew and earned a reputation for excellence, but Bernie wasn't out of ideas just yet. In true entrepreneurial style, he sold what he'd created in order to pursue another dream: *South Dakota Magazine.*

Bernie hit the road with cardboard page mock-ups, talking to potential readers and advertisers across the state, explaining over and over and over what he had in mind. South Dakotans were intrigued, but cautious. We don't just hand $9 over to some guy who walks in off the street hawking subscriptions to a magazine that doesn't exist. Some insisted on six-month trial subscriptions instead of the usual one-year variety. Others showed little appreciation for the breadth and diversity of where they lived. They wondered what he would write about after featuring the Corn Palace and Mount Rushmore. If such skepticism had ruled the day there would be no story to tell, and no magazine, no book of stories, and the Pennington House would probably have been bulldozed by now. Thankfully, the skeptics were few. Enough people took a chance for Bernie and his wife, Myrna, to begin putting the first issue together on the tops of Myrna's washer and dryer in Gayville.

Looking back isn't always pleasant. Things that seemed wonderful when you did them can be embarrassing in retrospect. Ask anybody who has a picture of themselves in striped bell-bottom pants, or with a bouffant hairdo and cat-eye glasses. That's how it is for Bernie, I think, when he looks back on the first issue of *South Dakota Magazine.* Shortly after I started working here we discovered a bundle of that first issue while cleaning out a storeroom. With characteristic Dakota frugality we ran an advertisement in the next magazine offering them for sale. In essence the ad, which Bernie wrote himself, said: First issue of *South Dakota Magazine* for sale, though we haven't any idea why you'd want one. The cover is ugly, it wasn't supposed to be green, the whole thing is really crude, printed on cheap paper, etc.

"Gee," I said to no one in particular, "these ought to go pretty fast."

The premiere issue of *South Dakota Magazine,* which rolled off the press in May of 1985, was all that and more. Aside from the pea-green cover and a splash of yellow on the back, there wasn't a bit of color. To be blunt, even the black and white photographs weren't wonderful. And yet ... people liked what they saw. The second issue carried letters of congratulation from Senator James Abdnor and future-

Governor George Mickelson. Maybe they were just being nice — politicians are like that sometimes — but "regular" people were equally encouraging. That is best measured by the growth in circulation. Almost without exception, the magazine has grown by a thousand or more subscribers every year. Sometimes Bernie and other staffers knocked on doors to sell subscriptions. Other years we relied mostly on paid advertising flyers in newspapers. Some years we had neither the time or money for either. But the magazine kept growing and growing.

The success or failure of an enterprise often seems inevitable when viewed in hindsight. With a circulation of 38,000 and an enviable statewide reputation, *South Dakota Magazine* today would have to be judged an unqualified publishing success. In 1985, however, that result must have seemed anything but assured to Bernie and Myrna, and their first employee, Alma Korslund (who incidentally, is still recording new subscriptions as I write this a room away, just down from where the hole was in the floor).

In the 1980s, new subscriptions trickled in while bills arrived in a flood — a situation almost any small business owner relates to. Typesetting machines, designed by the devil and sold by a company chronically short of spare parts, inevitably broke down on deadline day. Photo opportunities were missed when old cameras mysteriously malfunctioned. Bernie may give the impression that he waltzes about the state, camera and notepad in hand, always looking for another good story. He does that, now and then. But he and the rest of us have also dealt with printer errors, tax audits, leaky roofs, postage increases, proofreading gremlins, and all the other joys of publishing.

Even if dollars were short, we always felt rewarded by the appreciation shown by the ever-growing family of readers. Many sent notes with their renewal checks. For a long time, Bernie tried to respond to every handwritten comment.

Readers would occasionally raise complaints. A few were disgusted by our story and picture about a huge rattlesnake hunt at Mobridge. Even more were mad about our story titled "Here Piggy Piggy," a little piece about hog butchering that sought to find humor, or at least irony, in the odd predicament of a young man who shot a pig in the head, only to have it run back in the middle of the herd. He then walked through the pigs, looking for his victim, and calling, "Here, Piggy Piggy..."

We still make mistakes. In September of 2002, we featured a John Green painting of a rattlesnake on the cover. We thought it was a cute snake, and the artist added an olive branch in its fangs to soften the look. But we might as well have reprinted "Here Piggy Piggy..." Thousands of South Dakotans hate snakes. Hundreds of readers complained and a few dozen even cancelled their subscriptions. To a magazine staff that once walked the streets and knocked on doors for subscriptions, that hurts. Bernie immediately apologized in print, and said that he now understood why the big city magazines always put pretty girls on the cover rather than snakes. The November issue featured a young lady in a Santa hat. We have hundreds of the infamous "snake issue" lying about the office, and someday we'll probably run an ad and try to sell them, ugly or not.

So it hasn't been politics and religion that gets us in hot water, it's animals. But such lapses in editorial judgment have been rare. Publishing *South Dakota Magazine* is an enjoyable experience and our relationship with readers is the best part.

An aura of romance for South Dakota now pervades the Pennington House. The old governor (who was a publisher himself, by the way) probably wishes he were here today. So might the chiefs and generals who sat in the parlors with him. A dozen people now work here. We get many visitors, including regular readers and a few Dakota notables, but very few generals or chiefs.

It's a great place to be if you love South Dakota. I found a home in The Pennington House after all. And so have thousands and thousands of people who have joined as members of our reading family.

Roger Holtzmann joined the magazine editorial staff in 1990.

To the Editor

Many people have written about their experiences with A.M. Jackley, so when I ordered a subscription, I wrote of going on a snake hunt with A.M., my cousin by marriage.

A man in St. Paul, Jerry Hall, also has a subscription and called me, wanting to know how I knew Jackley.

When I told him Jackley had been married to my mother's cousin, Rosa, Jerry paused a minute, then said Rosa Jackley was his father's cousin.

Anyway, due to the subscription, I got in touch with a cousin that I hadn't seen since I was a kid. *South Dakota Magazine* has many benefits!

Cora McQuisten
Renner

INDEX

CONTRIBUTORS